Financing State and Local Governments

Studies of Government Finance: Second Series

TITLES PUBLISHED

Who Pays the Property Tax? A New View, by Henry J. Aaron
Federal Tax Reform: The Impossible Dream? by George F. Break and Joseph A. Pechman
The Individual Income Tax (rev. ed.), by Richard Goode
Inflation and the Income Tax, Henry J. Aaron, Editor
Federal Tax Policy (3d ed.), by Joseph A. Pechman
Financing State and Local Governments (3d ed.), by James A. Maxwell and J. Richard Aronson
Federal Budget Policy (3d ed.), by David J. Ott and Attiat F. Ott
Comprehensive Income Taxation, Joseph A. Pechman, Editor
A Voluntary Tax? New Perspectives on Sophisticated Estate Tax Avoidance, by George Cooper
Must Corporate Income Be Taxed Twice? by Charles E. McLure, Jr.
What Should Be Taxed: Income or Expenditure? Joseph A. Pechman, Editor
Financing Government in a Federal System, by George F. Break
The Economics of Taxation, Henry J. Aaron and Michael J. Boskin, Editors
How Taxes Affect Economic Behavior, Henry J. Aaron and Joseph A. Pechman, Editors
The Value-Added Tax: Lessons from Europe, Henry J. Aaron, Editor
Economic Effects of Social Security, by Henry J. Aaron
The Peculiar Problem of Taxing Life Insurance Companies, by Henry J. Aaron
Federal Tax Policy (4th ed.), by Joseph A. Pechman
Who Paid the Taxes, 1966–85? by Joseph A. Pechman
Assessing Tax Reform, by Henry J. Aaron and Harvey Galper
Taxes, Loans, and Inflation: How the Nation's Wealth Becomes Misallocated, by C. Eugene Steuerle
Financing State and Local Governments (4th ed.), by J. Richard Aronson and John L. Hilley

Financing State and Local Governments

Fourth Edition

J. RICHARD ARONSON
JOHN L. HILLEY

Studies of Government Finance
THE BROOKINGS INSTITUTION
WASHINGTON, D.C.

First and second editions, 1965 and 1969, by James A. Maxwell
Third edition, 1977, by James A. Maxwell and J. Richard Aronson

Library of Congress Cataloging in Publication data:

Aronson, J. Richard (Jay Richard), 1937–
Financing state and local governments.
(Studies of government finance. Second series)
Third ed. by James A. Maxwell and J. Richard Aronson.
Bibliography: p.
Includes index.
1. Finance, Public—United States—States.
2. Local finance—United States 3. Intergovernmental fiscal relations—United States. I. Hilley, John L.
II. Maxwell, James Ackley, 1897–1975. Financing state and local governments. III. Title. IV. Series.
HJ275.A83 1986 336.73 85-48207
ISBN 0-8157-5518-X
ISBN 0-8157-5517-1(pbk.)

9 8 7 6 5 4 3 2 1

THE BROOKINGS INSTITUTION is an independent organization devoted to nonpartisan research, education, and publication in economics, government, foreign policy, and the social sciences generally. Its principal purposes are to aid in the development of sound public policies and to promote public understanding of issues of national importance.

The Institution was founded on December 8, 1927, to merge the activities of the Institute for Government Research, founded in 1916, the Institute of Economics, founded in 1922, and the Robert Brookings Graduate School of Economics and Government, founded in 1924.

The Board of Trustees is responsible for the general administration of the Institution, while the immediate direction of the policies, program, and staff is vested in the President, assisted by an advisory committee of the officers and staff. The by-laws of the Institution state: "It is the function of the Trustees to make possible the conduct of scientific research, and publication, under the most favorable conditions, and to safeguard the independence of the research staff in the pursuit of their studies and in the publication of the results of such studies. It is not a part of their function to determine, control, or influence the conduct of particular investigations or the conclusions reached."

The President bears final responsibility for the decision to publish a manuscript as a Brookings book. In reaching his judgment on the competence, accuracy, and objectivity of each study, the President is advised by the director of the appropriate research program and weighs the views of a panel of expert outside readers who report to him in confidence on the quality of the work. Publication of a work signifies that it is deemed a competent treatment worthy of public consideration but does not imply endorsement of conclusions or recommendations.

The Institution maintains its position of neutrality on issues of public policy in order to safeguard the intellectual freedom of the staff. Hence interpretations or conclusions in Brookings publications should be understood to be solely those of the authors and should not be attributed to the Institution, to its trustees, officers, or other staff members, or to the organizations that support its research.

To Judith Libby Aronson

J.R.A.

In honor of my mother, Dorothy Myers Hilley,
and in memory of my father, William Allen Hilley

J.H.

Foreword

STATE AND LOCAL finances have expanded remarkably over the last forty years. The expenditures of state and local governments have increased at a higher average annual rate than either the gross national product or the expenditures of the federal government. The corresponding and necessary increases in state and local revenues have been made possible by higher property and sales taxes, greater reliance on income taxes, sharply increased debt, and federal grants-in-aid. Perhaps the most dramatic changes have occurred in the fiscal relations among the three levels of government.

This edition of *Financing State and Local Governments,* like its predecessors, examines the incidence of the major state and local taxes and assesses the capacity of state and local governments to carry their debt burdens. It documents recent trends and forces that have been influencing state and local governments. Expenditure growth of state and local governments has slowed; the federal government has cut back on the level of its grant-in-aid programs; and the tax limitation movement has nudged the local revenue structure toward increased reliance on fees and user charges. This edition also includes a new chapter on financing education and expanded analyses of debt finance, the financing of state and local pension plans, and the state corporate income tax.

The author of the first edition of *Financing State and Local Governments,* published in 1965, was James A. Maxwell of Clark University. Professor Maxwell revised the book in 1969 and, before he died in 1975, he and J. Richard Aronson of Lehigh University revised it again for an edition published in 1977. This fourth edition still bears the mark of Maxwell's remarkable understanding of government finance. Yet much has changed since 1975, and this revision contains a significant amount of new material.

This volume is the twenty-second in the Brookings Studies in Goverment Finance second series, which is devoted to examining issues in taxation and public expenditure policy. Work on the project as part of the

Brookings Economic Studies program was initiated under the guidance of Joseph A. Pechman and completed under Alice M. Rivlin. J. Richard Aronson is William L. Clayton Professor of Economics and director of the Fairchild-Martindale Center for the Study of Private Enterprise at Lehigh University, in Bethlehem, Pennsylvania. John Hilley is senior economist for fiscal and monetary affairs of the U.S. Senate Committee on the Budget.

The authors wish to thank several people who helped produce this volume. The editor was Alice M. Carroll, who also edited the second and third editions. Her understanding of the style and substance of the volume was a great help in preserving its original intent—to present a broad, factual overview of state and local finance. Asuman Baskan of Lehigh University provided excellent research assistance, and Carolyn A. Rutsch of Brookings checked the accuracy of the data. The manuscript was typed by Diane Steele at Lehigh University and by Anne Willis and Michelle Adams in Washington.

The views expressed here are the authors' alone and should not be ascribed to the persons whose assistance is acknowledged, to Lehigh University, to the Senate Budget Committee, or to the trustees, officers, or staff members of the Brookings Institution.

BRUCE K. MAC LAURY
President

April 1986
Washington, D.C.

Contents

Introduction 1
Interstate Comparisons *2*
Grants-in-Aid *3*
State Taxes *4*
Local Taxes *5*
Nontax Revenue *6*
Borrowing *7*
Budgeting *7*
Education Finance *8*
Whither State and Local Finance? *9*

1. Development of the Federal System 10
The Historical Balance of Federal, State, and Local Power *11*
Functional Distribution of Expenditures *21*
Apologia for Federalism *24*

2. Fiscal Performance and Capacity 31
Patterns of Aggregate Expenditure *32*
Measures of Relative Fiscal Capacity and Tax Effort *37*
Patterns of Tax Preference and Utilization *40*
Conclusion *46*

3. Federal Intergovernmental Transfers 48
Trends in Federal Transfers *48*
The Need for Federal Grants *50*
Grant Forms *53*
Grant Features *58*
Problems Raised by Grants *60*
Functions Aided by Grants *62*
Continuing Issues in Grant Design *71*

4. State Intergovernmental Transfers 75
Structure of Local Governments *75*
Transfers to Local Governments *78*
Conclusion *85*

5. State Taxes on Individual Income and Sales 86

Taxes on Individual Incomes *86*
Taxes on Sales *90*
Sales Tax or Income Tax? *100*

6. Other State Taxes 103

Corporation Income Tax *103*
Death and Gift Taxes *115*

7. The Property Tax 120

Significance to State and Local Governments *120*
Incidence and Economic Effects *123*
The Base of Property Taxation *126*
Assessment *128*
The Role of the States in Reform *134*
Erosion of the Tax Base *135*
State Assessment of Property *140*
Conclusion *141*

8. Nonproperty Taxes and Nontax Revenue 142

Local Nonproperty Taxes *142*
Nontax Revenue *151*
Conclusion *159*

9. State and Local Debt 160

Types of Debt *167*
Tax Exemption *170*
Debt Limitations *175*
The Nonguaranteed Bond *177*
Bonds for Industrial Development and Other Nontraditional Purposes *179*
Reform of Borrowing Limitations *181*

10. Earmarked Revenues, Retirement Systems, and Capital Budgets 183

The Budgetary Process *183*
Earmarked Revenues *188*
State and Local Retirement Systems *194*
Capital Budgets *203*

11. Education Finance 208

Trends in Enrollments and Expenditures *210*
The Federal Role in Financing Education *212*
Equity in Education *214*
Expanding Parental Choice in Education *218*

12. Whither State and Local Finance? 222
Revenue and Expenditure Limitations *223*
Deductibility of State and Local Taxes from Federal Income Taxes *229*
Conclusion *232*

Appendix: Statistical Tables 235

Bibliography 255

Index 259

Text Tables

1–1. Trends in State-Local Expenditures and Federal Grants-in-Aid, 1954 and 1975–84 21
1–2. Percent of Direct General Expenditure for Civil Functions by the Federal Government, 1958, 1968, 1978, and 1984 24
1–3. Percent of General Expenditure for Civil Functions by All Levels of Government, 1958, 1968, 1978, and 1984 25
1–4. Federal Intergovernmental Payments for Selected State-Local Civil Functions, 1958, 1968, 1978, and 1984 27
2–1. States Accounting for Highest and Lowest Proportions of State-Local Direct General Expenditure, 1984 32
2–2. States with Highest and Lowest Per Capita General Expenditure, Excluding Federal Grants, 1984 34
2–3. Per Capita Direct General Expenditure and Distribution of Total General Expenditure of State-Local Governments, by Function, 1984 37
2–4. Variation in Per Capita Expenditure of States by Percent of State-Local Direct General Expenditure, by Function, 1984 38
2–5. Tax Base and Tax Rate Data for Three Hypothetical States, Each Having Three Residents 39
2–6. Relative Fiscal Capacity and Tax Effort under a Representative Tax System (RTS), by State, 1982 41
2–7. Relative Fiscal Capacity and Tax Effort Based on Per Capita Personal Income, by State, 1981 42
2–8. Distribution of States by Percent of Total Revenue Collected from Property Taxes, 1984 43
2–9. Distribution and Rank of Major Sources of State Tax Collections, 1922, 1938, 1948, 1968, and 1984 44
2–10. Distribution of States by Percent of Total State Tax Revenue Collected from Selected State Taxes, 1984 46
3–1. Historical Trend of Federal Grant-in-Aid Outlays, Selected Years, 1950–84 49
3–2. Federal Grant-in-Aid Expenditures, by Function, 1972, 1976, 1980, and 1984 51
3–3. Federal Expenditures for General-Purpose, Broad-Based, and Specific-Purpose Grants, 1972, 1976, 1980, and 1984 52

3–4. Federal Tax Expenditures Aiding State and Local Governments, 1984 59

3–5. Federal Intergovernmental Transfers to Local Governments, 1984 73

4–1. Number and Type of Governmental Units in the United States, 1957, 1967, 1977, and 1982 76

4–2. Tax Collections and Direct General Expenditure of State and Local Governments, Selected Years, 1948–84 81

4–3. State Intergovernmental Payments, by Purpose, 1984 82

4–4. State Intergovernmental Expenditure, State Direct General Expenditure, and Local General Revenue, Selected Years, 1902–84 82

5–1. State Individual Income Tax Collections, Highest and Lowest States, 1984 88

5–2. State Revenue from Selective Sales Taxes, 1984 91

5–3. Distribution of States by General Sales Tax and Individual Income Tax Collections Per Capita, 1984 95

5–4. Distribution of States by General Sales Tax Rate, as of December 1984 97

5–5. Incidence of Federal and State-Local Taxes under Most Progressive and Least Progressive Assumptions about Tax Burdens, by Income Class, 1980 100

6–1. Distribution of States by Collections Per Capita from State Corporation Income Taxes, 1984 104

6–2. State Corporation Income Tax Revenue, Selected Years, 1948–84 105

7–1. Property Tax Collections and Total Federal, State, and Local Tax Collections, Selected Years, 1902–84 121

7–2. General Revenue of Local Governments, 1927 and 1984 122

7–3. Local Government Property Tax, Tax Revenue, and General Revenue, by Type of Governmental Unit, 1984 123

7–4. Estimated Effective Property Tax Rates under Two Sets of Incidence Assumptions, by Income Class, 1980 125

7–5. Distribution of States by Ratios of Assessed Value to Sales Price of Real Property, 1956, 1966, 1971, and 1981 129

7–6. Illustrative Calculation of a Coefficient of Dispersion for Nine Properties 130

7–7. Coefficients of Intra-area Dispersion for Principal Median Assessment Ratios for Nonfarm Houses, Selected Local Areas, 1956, 1966, 1971, and 1981 131

7–8. Distribution of Selected Local Areas by Coefficient of Intra-area Dispersion for Assessment Ratios of Nonfarm Houses, 1956, 1966, 1971, and 1981 133

7–9. Distribution of States by Coefficient of Intra-area Dispersion for Nonfarm Houses, 1956, 1966, 1971, and 1981 134

7–10. Homestead Exemptions in Twenty States and the District of Columbia, 1981 137

8–1. Percent of Local Tax Revenue Collected from Various Sources, Selected Years, 1948–84 144

8–2. Local Nonproperty Tax Revenue, by Type of Tax, 1973 and 1984 144
8–3. Local Nonproperty Taxes as a Share of Total Local Tax Collections, Selected Cities, 1973 and 1984 145
8–4. Local General Sales Taxing Units and Their Rates, by State, 1984 146
8–5. Local Income Taxing Units and Their Rates, by State, 1984 150
8–6. Reliance on Local Income or Wage Taxes, by Selected Large Cities, 1972 and 1984 151
8–7. Local Government User Charges, 1957, 1977, and 1983 157
8–8. State Government User Charges, 1973 and 1984 158
9–1. State and Local Debt Outstanding, Selected Years, 1902–84 162
9–2. Interest Expenditure of State and Local Governments per $1,000 of Personal Income, Selected Years, 1902–84 163
9–3. Indexes of State and Local Debt, Selected Years, 1938–84 164
9–4. Change in Per Capita Total Debt of State Governments and Forty-eight Largest Cities, 1966–84 165
9–5. Debt Service Estimates of State and Local Governments, 1966, 1973, and 1984 166
9–6. State Long-Term Debt, by Function, 1941, 1973, and 1984 167
9–7. Long-Term Debt of Forty-three Largest Cities, by Function, 1941, 1973, and 1984 168
9–8. Outstanding Long-Term and Short-Term State and Local Debt, 1966, 1973, and 1984 170
9–9. Yields on High-grade Long-term Municipal and Corporate Bonds, Selected Years, 1928–84 173
9–10. Estimated Holdings of State and Local Securities, by Type of Owner, 1966, 1973, and 1984 174
9–11. New Long-Term, Tax-Exempt Bonds by Traditional and Nontraditional Purposes, Selected Years, 1970–82 180
10–1. Governmental Insurance Trust Revenue, by Purpose and by Level of Government, 1984 189
10–2. Number of Beneficiaries and Ratio of Beneficiaries to Membership in State and Local Retirement Systems, 1957, 1962, 1967, 1972, and 1982 198
10–3. Assets of State and Local Retirement Systems, 1957, 1962, 1967, 1972, and 1982 199
10–4. Receipts and Payments of State and Local Retirement Systems, 1957, 1962, 1967, 1972, and 1982 200
10–5. Pension Fund Estimates and Annual Benefit Levels under Various Assumptions Concerning Wage Growth and Interest Rates 201
10–6. Illustrative Effect of Capital Budgeting on Total Annual Spending and Taxing 205
11–1. Expenditure for Education, Selected Years, 1930–84 209
11–2. Expenditures of Educational Institutions, by Source of Funds, 1970, 1976, and 1982 209
11–3. School Enrollment, 1900, 1940, 1960, 1970, and 1984 210

11–4. Support for Public Elementary and Secondary Education, Selected Years, 1920–84 211
11–5. Highest and Lowest Expenditures for Public Elementary and Secondary Schools, by State, 1984 212
12–1. Measures Limiting State Expenditures or Collection of Revenue, 1976–82 224

Appendix Tables

A–1. General Expenditure for Civil Functions, by Classification of Intergovernmental Payments and Level of Government, Selected Years, 1902–84 237
A–2. Tax Collections, by Type of Tax and Level of Government, Selected Years, 1902–84 238
A–3. Direct General Expenditure for Civil Functions by All Levels of Government, Selected Years, 1902–84 239
A–4. General Expenditure for Civil Functions as a Percent of Gross National Product, by Level of Government, Selected Years, 1902–84 239
A–5. Annual Rates of Increase in State and Local Expenditures, by Function, 1958–73 and 1973–84 240
A–6. General Expenditure for Civil Functions by State and Local Governments, Selected Years, 1902–84 240
A–7. State and Local Expenditures as a Percent of Total Direct General Expenditure for Civil Functions, Selected Years, 1902–84 241
A–8. State-Local Per Capita General Expenditure Including and Excluding Federal Grants, by State, 1984 242
A–9. States' Ranks in Per Capita Income and Per Capita General Expenditure, Excluding Federal Grants, 1984 243
A–10. Percent of State Tax Revenue Collected from Selected Taxes, by State, 1984 244
A–11. Relative Per Capita Redistribution of Federal Income Attributed to Grant and Equalization Measures, by State, 1982 245
A–12. State Intergovernmental Expenditure, by Function, Selected Years, 1902–84 246
A–13. State Intergovernmental Expenditure as a Percent of Local General Expenditure, by Function, Selected Years, 1902–84 246
A–14. State Individual Income Tax and General Sales Tax Collections Per Capita, Ranked by State, 1984 247
A–15. Operating Revenue and Expenditure of Local Utilities, 1953, 1963, 1973, and 1984 248
A–16. State Government User Charges, by Major Categories of Governmental Service, 1953, 1963, 1973, and 1984 249
A–17. Per Capita Personal Income and Per Capita Long-Term State and Local Debt Outstanding, by State, 1984 250
A–18. Long-Term Debt of State and Local Governments Outstanding at End of Fiscal Year, 1949, 1957, 1968, 1978, and 1984 251

A–19. Distribution of States by Percent of State Government Net Long-Term Debt in Full Faith and Credit Form, 1941, 1949, 1966, 1973, and 1984 252
A–20. Net Long-Term Nonguaranteed State Government Debt, Per Capita, of States without Full Faith and Credit Debt, 1941, 1966, 1973, and 1984 252
A–21. State Expenditures and Revenues for Public Elementary and Secondary Schools, Ranked by Total Expenditure, 1984 253

Figures

1–1. Percent of General Expenditure for Civil Functions by Federal and State-Local Governments, Selected Years, 1902–84 15
1–2. Relative Use of Various Taxes by Federal, State, and Local Governments, Selected Years, 1902–84 16
1–3. Percent of General Expenditure for Selected Civil Functions Contributed by Federal and State-Local Governments, 1958, 1968, 1978, and 1984 26
2–1. States Ranked by Per Capita Income and Per Capita General Expenditure, Excluding Federal Grants, 1984 35
2–2. Major Sources of State Tax Collections, 1984 45
4–1. Tax Collections and General Expenditure of State and Local Governments, 1948–84 80
4–2. Distribution of State Intergovernmental Expenditure, by Function, Selected Years, 1902–84 83
4–3. State Intergovernmental Expenditure as a Percent of Local Expenditure, by Function, Selected Years, 1902–84 84
5–1. Distribution of States by General Sales Tax and Individual Income Tax Collections Per Capita, 1984 96
9–1. Percent of State and Local Debt in Full Faith and Credit and Nonguaranteed Form, 1949, 1957, 1968, 1978, and 1984 178
10–1. Illustrative Effect of Capital Budgeting on Total Annual Spending and Taxing 206

Financing State and Local Governments

Introduction

WHICH LEVEL of government, the federal or the state and local, bears major responsibility for providing civilian (nondefense) services in the United States? The answer is state and local, and by a considerable margin. In fact, when it comes to civilian services, state and local governments together spend more than two and one-half times as much as the federal government. Education, roads, welfare, public health, hospitals, police, sanitation are primarily state and local responsibilities, and their cost falls mainly on state and local sources of revenue.

A great surge of state and local activity began after World War II. Spending on their functions had been reduced or postponed during the war and the Great Depression that preceded it. With the end of war, both the need and the desire grew to expand and improve the nation's capital and social infrastructure. For many years the increase in state and local spending was unambiguous. Whether spending was measured in nominal terms or on an inflation-adjusted basis, in per capita terms or in relation to gross national product, the rising trend was clear. But between 1978 and 1982 per capita state-local spending in constant-dollar terms actually declined and, in 1984, real per capita expenditure had almost reached the level of 1978. Will state and local expenditures resume their upward trend or have new public priorities been established? This is one of the main concerns of this book.

What governmental functions are mainly state and local? Education is the single most important responsibility of state and local governments, but in recent years spending growth has slowed and education expenditure now claims a smaller share of the gross national product than in the 1970s. On the other hand, government spending on public welfare and health has exploded, growing more rapidly than either total state and local expenditures or the GNP. Also, the aged have become a larger proportion of the population and continuing advances in medicine have lengthened lives and enlarged the range of treatments. This has resulted in relatively large increases in expenditures on health and hospitals.

Roads are another traditional function of state and local governments. The interstate highway system has largely been completed but repair and maintenance of all roads and bridges will be extremely costly. Policy decisions will have to be made concerning the federal and state-local roles in numerous infrastructure programs.

What governmental duties, and what means of finance, belong at the state and local, rather than the federal, level? Broad lines of division are constitutionally provided, but history has blurred them. Moreover, the boundaries of localities and of states are porous, and the effects of state and local financial decisions are not tightly circumscribed within a geographic area. When are these spillovers of national concern? Do states have too many functions? Have they the sources of revenue appropriate to their functions? Perhaps no neat division of functions is possible or desirable because some government functions should be handled by joint action, through federal-state cooperation. Such intergovernmental cooperation, discussed in chapter 1, provides structural flexibility in a federal system.

Interstate Comparisons

Chapter 2 provides quantitative background for interstate fiscal comparisons. The essential feature that emerges is diversity, both in overall expenditures and expenditures on particular functions.

Comparisons of state government expenditures are treacherous. One state government may perform functions that in another state are left to localities. Accordingly, a better basis for interstate comparison is the per capita amount spent (and raised) by both state and local governments. Such state expenditure figures diverge greatly; the highest per capita expenditures are more than two and one-half times as large as the lowest (excluding atypical Alaska).

What are the reasons? Most obviously, a rich state (in which residents, on the average, have large incomes) will spend more than a poor state, although some states spend considerably more and some considerably less per capita than might be expected. Density of population, urbanization, and so on, have less discernible effects on expenditures. Much of the divergence in per capita expenditure, state by state, can be explained by historical and political differences. When relative expenditure on particular functions is examined, once again diversity rather than uniformity is the rule.

There are alternative techniques for measuring the fiscal capacity of states. One measure, the yield of the representative tax system, calculates the amount of revenue a state would raise if it taxed all its bases at national average rates. The other measure is simply the per capita income of the governmental entity. Relative fiscal effort is measured by comparing the amount of revenue actually raised by a state to its fiscal capacity. The variety of patterns of taxes levied by state governments is as notable as the lack of variety in those levied by local governments. Even when a similar tax is imposed in many states, it is not necessarily utilized in the same way.

Grants-in-Aid

For decades neither state nor local governments have depended wholly on their own sources of revenue. Chapters 3 and 4 examine the grants (intergovernmental transfers) made by the federal government to state and local governments, and those made by state governments to local governments.

Federal grants to state and local governments increased rapidly during the 1970s, nearly quadrupling in nominal terms and growing by 80 percent on a constant-dollar basis. But in the early 1980s the Reagan administration was able to reverse that trend. Between 1980 and 1984, federal grants measured in constant dollars declined by 14 percent. The amount of federal grants also declined as a percent of both federal and state-local expenditures.

At the same time there was a shift in the relative use of different forms of grants. The greatest number continued to be specific categorical grants for particular and limited purposes; their main aim is to raise the level of provision of programs in which a strong federal interest exists. With the pronounced multiplication of grants in the 1960s and the early 1970s, a reaction developed that led to experiments with block grants covering broadly defined functions within which each state allocates its expenditure among programs. The Omnibus Budget Reconciliation Act of 1981 revitalized the consolidation effort, and broad-based grants, which represented about 9 percent of the total value of federal grants in the late 1970s, grew to approximately 13 percent in 1984.

The federal government also introduced a revenue-sharing program in the 1970s that provided funds to be used for whatever purposes state and local governments chose. The Reagan administration advocated elimination of general revenue sharing as a means of reducing the federal budget deficit. Termination, however, would seem to run counter to the goals of simplifying the system of federal grants-in-aid and of providing state and local governments with broad-based rather than categorical grants.

Federal grants redistribute income among the states. Money is raised through a progressive tax system that brings in more from rich than from poor states. In turn, many grants allocated by formula provide more for poor than for rich states. For what grants is such distribution appropriate? What is the desirable amount of redistribution? These questions are addressed in chapter 3.

State grants and shared taxes provided approximately 36 percent of local general revenue in 1984. Education received the bulk (62 percent) of such aid, with public welfare second (13 percent) and highways third (5 percent). General support aid amounted to 10 percent. Beyond doubt most states have permitted, and even facilitated, the proliferation of local units (over 82,000 existed in 1982); grants have sometimes encouraged them to perpetuate the existence of inefficient units. The grants themselves have been fragmented in amounts, purposes, and formulas. In many states consolidation would bring clear gains. Moreover, grants could be used as an instrument to speed reorganization of local units.

State Taxes

Chapters 5 and 6 examine the taxes used by state governments. The states pioneered in the use of income taxation in the United States, but two world wars and the depression of the 1930s have led the federal government to become the prime user of this source of revenue. In recent years, however, state governments have been increasing their use of income taxes. In 1948, income taxes accounted for only 16 percent of total tax revenues but in 1984 they provided over 38 percent. Yet there is significant variation among the states in the features of the income taxes that they have enacted. The value of exemptions and deductions varies a great deal as do the level and progressivity of rate structures.

In the last several years, the differences among states' corporate income taxes have become pronounced. Numerous states "decoupled" from the federal definition of taxable corporate income to avoid revenue losses from the depreciation allowances embodied in the Economic Recovery Tax Act of 1981. Other aspects of state taxation of business income have also caused problems. State formulas for apportioning the taxable share of the net income of multistate and multinational businesses have created a storm of controversy. Much can be gained if greater uniformity can be introduced in state practices.

Congressional rejection of the general sales tax as a federal revenue source during the 1930s and World War II encouraged state entry, just as strong federal use of income taxation slackened its adoption by the states. Twenty-one states adopted a retail sales tax during the years 1933–38, and eight more during 1947–51. State legislatures were irresistibly attracted by the revenue productivity of the sales tax and the gradual, somewhat concealed method of payment. The defect of regressivity was sometimes alleviated through exemption from the tax base of purchases of food, clothing, and medicine, and through a sales tax credit against income tax liability. Now forty-five states employ the sales tax and it remains the primary revenue-producer for states, even though state revenues from income taxation in 1975–84 increased at a faster annual rate than revenues from sales taxation.

Death taxes—mostly inheritance taxes—were levied by states long before the federal government, in 1916, enacted an estate tax (on the entire net estate left by a decedent). In the 1920s, mostly to checkmate efforts in Florida and Nevada to repeal inheritance taxes, Congress provided an 80 percent credit against the federal tax liability for death taxes paid to the states. Since then, increases in the federal tax, with no enlargement of the credit, have reduced the importance of the credit and thereby created a strong incentive for states to compete for wealthy individuals by lowering death tax rates. The result has been decreased reliance on state death taxes. Since the late 1970s, many states have eliminated their death taxes, replacing them with a pick-up provision that passes through to the state the amount of tax allowable as a federal tax credit.

Local Taxes

The general property tax, once a major source of state revenue, has become primarily a local tax. In 1984 it produced 75 percent of local tax revenue.

As indicated in chapter 7, the most serious fault of the property tax is inaccurate assessment. The inequity of unequal valuations to taxpayers residing in the same area is obvious. But unequal aggregate assessed valuations from locality to locality also have serious faults; state governments have used these valuations to set ceilings on local debt and property tax rates, and to determine local shares of state grants and county taxes.

State governments appear to be the prime movers in rehabilitating the property tax. Perhaps the most dramatic change since the Advisory Commission on Intergovernmental Relations published its recommendations for property tax reform in 1963 has been development of the circuit breaker. This is a technique that provides property tax relief without eroding a local government's tax base. The lack of movement toward uniformity of assessment within property tax jurisdictions, however, indicates that property tax reform is not yet complete.

Fiscal conservatives have wanted to limit the revenue productivity of the property tax. Their main goal, of course, is to limit the size of the public sector, and to achieve this purpose, limits have been imposed on property taxes. What may have been achieved, however, is not a reduction in the size of government but rather a shift to other financing techniques such as fees and user charges.

In the 1930s, driven by desperate financial needs, a few large cities enacted nonproperty taxes—New York a retail sales tax, Philadelphia an earnings tax. These examples, which have been imitated by other cities in a limited number of states, are examined in chapter 8. While such taxes have many faults, the persuasive argument in their favor is that no alternatives of greater merit are visible.

Nontax Revenue

State and local governments raise nontax revenue from public service enterprises (such as water, electric power, gas, and public transit companies), and from user charges for noncommercial services. The former, except for public transit, are usually self-supporting, although much debate goes on concerning what sums in lieu of taxes a public enterprise should include as costs. Public transit systems incur substantial deficits; users are subsidized in kind by taxpayers.

The services that hospitals, housing, education, sanitation, and so on, provide are regarded as partly collective or welfare in content, although measurable benefits accrue to individual consumers. Pursuit of welfare objectives through low user charges, however, may be excessive; state and local governments might secure needed revenue from higher charges.

Direct cash payments to the poor in lieu of low user fees would appear superior on both efficiency and equity grounds.

Since the late 1970s, local user charges have been the fastest growing component of local government revenues. The charge that has been growing most rapidly is the special assessment. This is a mandatory fee levied on property to pay for specific investments in sidewalks, street paving, and other municipal services. The expanded role for user charges results both from their acceptance by the public and the need of localities to replace those sources that were curbed as a result of the tax and expenditure limitation movement.

Borrowing

Chapter 9 demonstrates that state and local governments continue to borrow heavily to finance capital expenditures for highways, sewerage, and so on. An important and distinctive characteristic of state and local debt is that its interest is exempt from the federal income tax.

In most states either statutory or constitutional limitations are placed on the state's power, and the power of its local governments, to issue general obligation bonds. It is clear, however, that these limits have been breached by a mushroom-like development of ingenious devices. The most important one has been nonguaranteed bonds, which generally carry higher yields than full faith and credit bonds; they now make up about 65 percent of state and more than half of local long-term debt.

Have state and local governments issued too much debt? Although debt per capita more than doubled between 1973 and 1984, debt service payments in relation to general revenues have declined. The overall picture appears to be satisfactory. However, the financial difficulties encountered in New York City and other metropolitan areas in the mid-1970s are constant reminders that the quality of debt is not uniform among state and local units and that the possibility of financial crisis is real.

Budgeting

As explained in chapter 10, the job of budgeting at the state and local levels is one of efficient allocation of limited resources to meet public needs. In most states and a growing number of cities, preparation of the budget falls on the executive, although this desirable practice is often frustrated by the exemption of important agencies from executive control. The next step, examination and appraisal of the budget, falls on the legislative branch. Implementation of the budget follows, with the executive responsible for seeing that funds flow to the designated purposes, in the correct amounts, and at the proper time.

The comprehensiveness of state and local budgets is often impaired by earmarking of revenue from particular sources to particular programs by statutory or constitutional provision. Removing programs from the budgetary process may be justifiable for government enterprises, and also when the benefits secured by particular users of services are linked with the payments collected from them. But in most state budgets, earmarking goes beyond these guidelines.

Some kinds of state and local expenditures raise special difficulties in budgeting, notably those that are large and irregular and that yield services stretching into the future. Simply as a matter of procedure, these should be bundled together into a capital budget (which will be a section of the total budget). Should the items in a capital budget be financed by borrowing? Should the rule be pay as you use or pay as you go? A practicable and effective compromise would be for state and local governments to appraise with severity the capital items for which borrowing is approved, and to vary the volume of borrowing for capital improvements, raising it in years of recession and lowering it in boom years. Such a policy would serve to assure some degree of equity between generations of taxpayers and would also help in countering cyclical fluctuations in government income.

The retirement systems of state and local governments are large and potentially volatile fiscal arrangements. In recent years the financial condition of most plans has improved, as rates of yield on pension fund assets have risen faster than rates of increase in wages, the base for calculating fixed retirement benefits. But the situation could deteriorate quickly. Inflation or the liberalization of pension provisions can be expected to have a dramatic effect on the estimated value of the unfunded liabilities of these plans.

Education Finance

Education is the largest function supported by state and local governments. During the 1960s and 1970s federal involvement increased as attention was focused on educational opportunity among racial and income groups. In the 1970s the states emerged as the dominant force in moving toward the reform of school finance systems. Landmark constitutional decisions indicated that in order to pass constitutional muster, states' systems of education finance would have to treat poor school districts fairly in relation to wealthier districts.

In the 1980s two strong forces, discussed in chapter 11, have been at work. One is a diminished federal role in financing education as growth in federal spending for education has been curbed. The second is the demand by the electorate that public schools improve the quality of education. The "excellence initiatives" that have been launched in several states, along with the continued pursuit of equity, are likely to result in an even greater role for state governments.

Whither State and Local Finance?

Chapter 12 looks to the future of the federal system of government finance. State and local governments are at a financial crossroads. A diminishing federal role in financing civilian functions is now apparent. At the same time, state and local governments are being called on to provide an expanded and improved range of services. Although the fiscal position of these governments has recently improved, there is apprehension about the long-term availability of revenue to support programs. The spirit of the tax expenditure limitation movement that dominated the 1970s is still present. In addition, President Reagan's call for a New Federalism raises questions about the assignment of government responsibilities in the federal system as well as the means of financing them. And the president's call for the repeal of the deductibility from federal income taxes of state and local taxes if heeded could have a significant effect on the ability and willingness of state and local governments to supply public services at current or increased levels.

CHAPTER ONE

Development of the Federal System

Many considerations . . . seem to place it beyond doubt that the first and most natural attachment of the people will be to the governments of their respective States.

James Madison, *The Federalist*

What's past is prologue.

The Tempest

THE UNITED STATES is a federal union, governed by a Constitution that splits the functions of government between a sovereign central government and sovereign states. The powers of the national government are enumerated in article 1, section 8 of the Constitution; the Tenth Amendment reserves to the states all powers neither delegated to the national government nor prohibited to the states. Nowhere mentioned in the Constitution are many of the vital citizen needs that today dominate the domestic scene: education, relief, public health, highways, and so forth. These functions are neither granted to the national government nor specifically prohibited to the states.

In addition to the national government and the state governments, a great number (82,290 in 1982) and variety of local governments exist in the United States. Unlike the federal-state relationship, the state-local relationship is not one between sovereign governments. The states are by law the masters of these local governments; that is, the relationship is unitary. This concept is known as Dillon's rule, after Justice John F. Dillon of the Supreme Court of Iowa who declared:

> Municipal corporations owe their origin to, and derive their powers and rights wholly from, the [state] legislature. It breathes into them the breath of life, without which they cannot exist. As it creates, so it may destroy. If it may destroy, it may abridge and control.[1]

1. *City of Clinton* v. *Cedar Rapids and Missouri River RR. Co.*, 24 Iowa 475 (1868).

The federal-state and state-local relations that now prevail, however, do not always conform with this strong legal statement. The practical power of states to alter and control local governments is limited, and the federal government spends money on functions that might seem to belong to the states.

The Historical Balance of Federal, State, and Local Power

Since the nation was formed, nation-state and state-local relations have not remained static. The power of the states vis-à-vis the federal government has waxed and waned as the federal structure adjusted to changes in social philosophy and environment. In this century, and particularly in the 1930s, major shifts in both absolute and relative terms have occurred in the functions, expenditures, and revenues of all levels of government. In the 1930s, many observers predicted the obsolescence of federalism; since World War II, however, a new intergovernmental equilibrium has emerged in which state and local vitality is manifest.

These developments are reviewed in the following section, which focuses on the relative contributions during this century of federal and state-local governments to overall expenditures for civil purposes and relates these to periods of significant change in the evolution of American federalism.

The First Century of Federalism

In the years of the Confederation, 1781–88, the states were so strong that they threatened the survival of a national government. Congress had no real power to administer, and especially to finance, its limited functions. Expenses of the national government were allocated to the states, and each state was expected to raise its allotment through its own officers. The results were nearly disastrous, and yet attempts to strengthen the financial powers of Congress failed because amending the Articles of Confederation required state unanimity. The feeling grew that the Articles provided the wrong kind of government. A strong nation would emerge only with a government that could levy taxes for its own use through its own officers.

Federal powers were greatly increased in the new Constitution—written in 1787, ratified by the necessary number of states in 1788, and effective March 4, 1789. Congress received the power "to lay and collect taxes, duties, imposts and excises, to pay the debts and provide for the common defense and general welfare of the United States."[2] This meant that, in addition to exclusive control over customs, it was to have concurrent jurisdiction with the states in practically all fields of taxation. In the first decade of its existence, the national government exercised—and even extended—its financial powers. The debts both of the Confederation and of the states were successfully refunded, customs duties were assessed by national officers, a system of federal excises was established, and a Bank of the United States was created.

Despite these vigorous steps, the divisive forces latent in the new federalism revived. During the next sixty years the state governments gained such strength that, once again, they threatened the existence of the national government. Geographic expansion brought into the Union new states with diverse sectional interests and, in addition, the old cleavage between North and South was deepened by the spread of cotton and slavery. Most statesmen, obsessed with the perplexities of federalism, came to believe the national functions should be held to a minimum in order to preserve the Union.[3]

The deference paid to the states did not succeed. Instead, the sectional rift deepened until the nation drifted into the Civil War, which settled the issue of national supremacy by force. The Union was not a compact among the states; the national government was entitled to enforce its constitutional decisions in the face of state objections.

The effect of the Civil War and of events subsequent to it—such as carpetbag government in the South—was to diminish the prestige of the states. When, in the last two decades of the nineteenth century, many southern states remade their constitutions, extensive and crippling restrictions on legislatures and executives were imposed. Scholars, observing these trends, had forebodings about the future of the states. They foresaw a continuing gravitation of power toward the national government.[4]

2. Subject to the qualification that "all duties, imposts and excises shall be uniform throughout the United States."

3. These developments are examined in James A. Maxwell, *The Fiscal Impact of Federalism in the United States* (Harvard University Press, 1946), chap. 1.

4. John W. Burgess, professor of political science at Columbia University, observed in 1886 that legislative and judicial powers were "gravitating towards the national government," and that police powers were "passing over to the municipalities." This was not, in his opinion, a "pendulum-swing"; rather did he forecast that "in the twentieth century, the

What was the federal performance at this time? James Bryce, although aware of many defects, was favorably impressed, and certainly this judgment is correct if comparison is made with performance before the Civil War. But the scope and range of federal activity were very modest, as the next section indicates.

Revival of the States

Around the turn of the new century, the state governments began to stir. A look at overall governmental expenditures in 1902 provides a base from which change may be judged. Expenditure for civil functions then totaled $1,243 million, compared to $695,046 million in 1984. In 1902, federal spending amounted to about one-fifth of the total. The relative importance of local governments is perhaps the striking feature of governmental expenditure early in the century:[5]

Level of government	*Expenditure (millions of dollars)*	
	1902	*1984*
Federal	230	191,762
State	134	201,310
Local	879	301,974

commonwealth will occupy a much lower place in our political system, the Nation a much higher, and the municipalities a much more distinct and independent sphere." "The American Commonwealth: Changes in its Relation to the Nation," *Political Science Quarterly,* vol. 1 (June 1886), pp. 32–34. In 1890 Simon N. Patten, professor of political economy at the University of Pennsylvania, found an economic explanation for the decline of the states. This was the absoluteness of the boundary lines—"the unchangeableness of the territorial extent of our states." The remedy would be to create "natural boundaries for each state" and thereby restore vitality. "The Decay of State and Local Governments," *Annals of the American Academy of Political and Social Science,* vol. 1 (July 1890–June 1891), pp. 39–40. In the opinion of other contemporary observers, the inert performance of the state governments was not compensated for by vigor at the local level. James Bryce, in 1888, critical as he was of the states, declared that "the government of cities is the one conspicuous failure of the United States." *The American Commonwealth,* vol. 2 (London: Macmillan, 1889), p. 281.

5. U.S. Census Bureau, *Historical Statistics of the United States: Colonial Times to 1957* (U.S. Government Printing Office, 1960), pp. 722–30; Census Bureau, *Governmental Finances in 1983–84* (GPO, 1985), table 11. Expenditures on defense, international affairs, veterans' services, and interest on the debt are excluded, since in this book the intergovernmental balance of power is a major issue. A decision to spend more or less for defense is, beyond dispute, a federal function; no question is raised of encroachment on, or withdrawal from, the state-local sphere. Attention is therefore focused on spending for civil purposes.

Local governments accounted for 70.7 percent of total general expenditures for civil functions in 1902. By 1984 the situation was quite different. Federal spending accounted for 27.6 percent of the total and the share of state spending had increased more than two and one-half times, to 29.0 percent. Local governments' total spending had declined to a 43.4 percent share in 1984.

These figures hide a decision concerning the classification of intergovernmental payments—that is, payments by the federal government in the form of grants and shared taxes to state and local governments (and similar payments by the states to local governments). Against which level of government should these sums be charged? A choice must be made in order to avoid double counting. When the federal government raises $1 million that it gives to state governments to spend for, say, highways (instead of spending $1 million directly for its own purposes), the $1 million can be charged either to the state government, the government that makes the final disbursement, or to the federal government, the originating level of government. If the state government is chosen for the charge, the total expenditure of the final disbursing level of government (the level that receives the grant) is larger, while that of the originating level of government (the level that pays the grant) is smaller, than when the opposite alternative is chosen. Because federal intergovernmental payments were not important in 1902, distribution of the $1,243 million in spending for civil purposes is almost identical when grants are charged to the disbursing level of government and when they are charged to the originating level:[6]

Level of government	*1902 expenditure (millions of dollars)*	
	Disbursing level	*Originating level*
Federal	230	237
State-local	1,013	1,006

But in 1984 the growth of federal intergovernmental expenditures to $99,015 million caused a spread in the two methods of distributing the $695,046 million total:[7]

Level of government	*1984 expenditure (millions of dollars)*	
	Disbursing level	*Originating level*
Federal	191,762	290,777
State-local	503,284	404,269

6. Census Bureau, *Historical Statistics*, pp. 725, 727.
7. Census Bureau, *Governmental Finances in 1983–84,* tables 10, 11.

When the reckoning of civil expenditures is made by assigning intergovernmental expenditures to the final disbursing level, relative federal expenditures have risen from 18.5 percent of the total in 1902 to 27.6 percent in 1984. When the comparison is made by assigning intergovernmental expenditures to the originating level, relative federal expenditures have risen sharply from 19.1 percent to 41.8 percent. The key is federal intergovernmental payments.

The Quarter Century 1902–27

What happened in the years between 1902 and 1927? In that period the absolute amount of spending for civil purposes rose rapidly, but again the relative shares changed little (see figure 1-1). In the 1920s the federal share declined slightly because concern over the large hangover of expen-

Figure 1-1. *Percent of General Expenditure for Civil Functions by Federal and State-Local Governments, Selected Years, 1902–84*

Intergovernmental payments charged to the level of government making the final disbursement

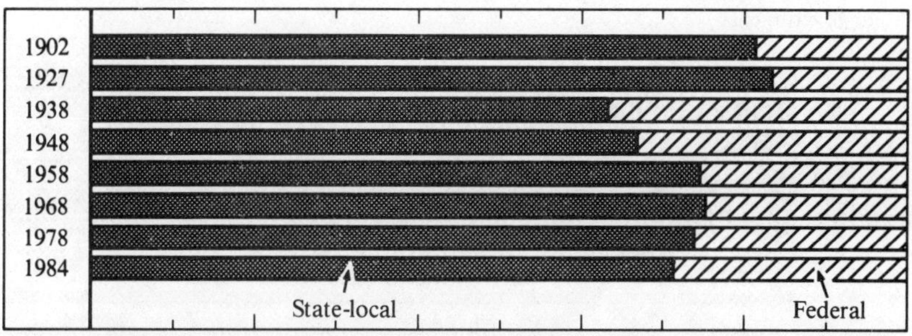

Intergovernmental payments charged to the originating level of government

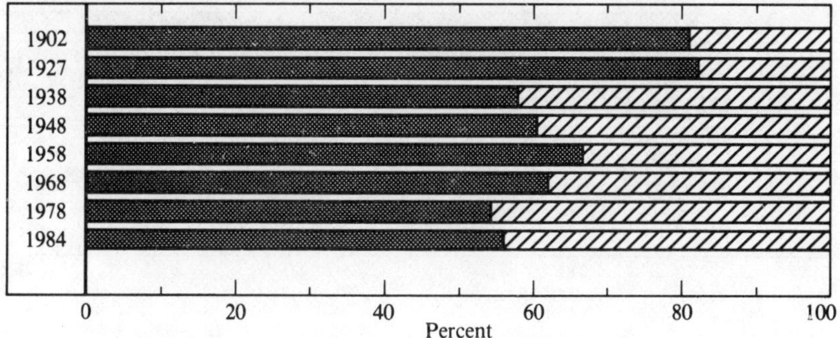

Source: Appendix table A-1.

Figure 1-2. *Relative Use of Various Taxes by Federal, State, and Local Governments, Selected Years, 1902–84*

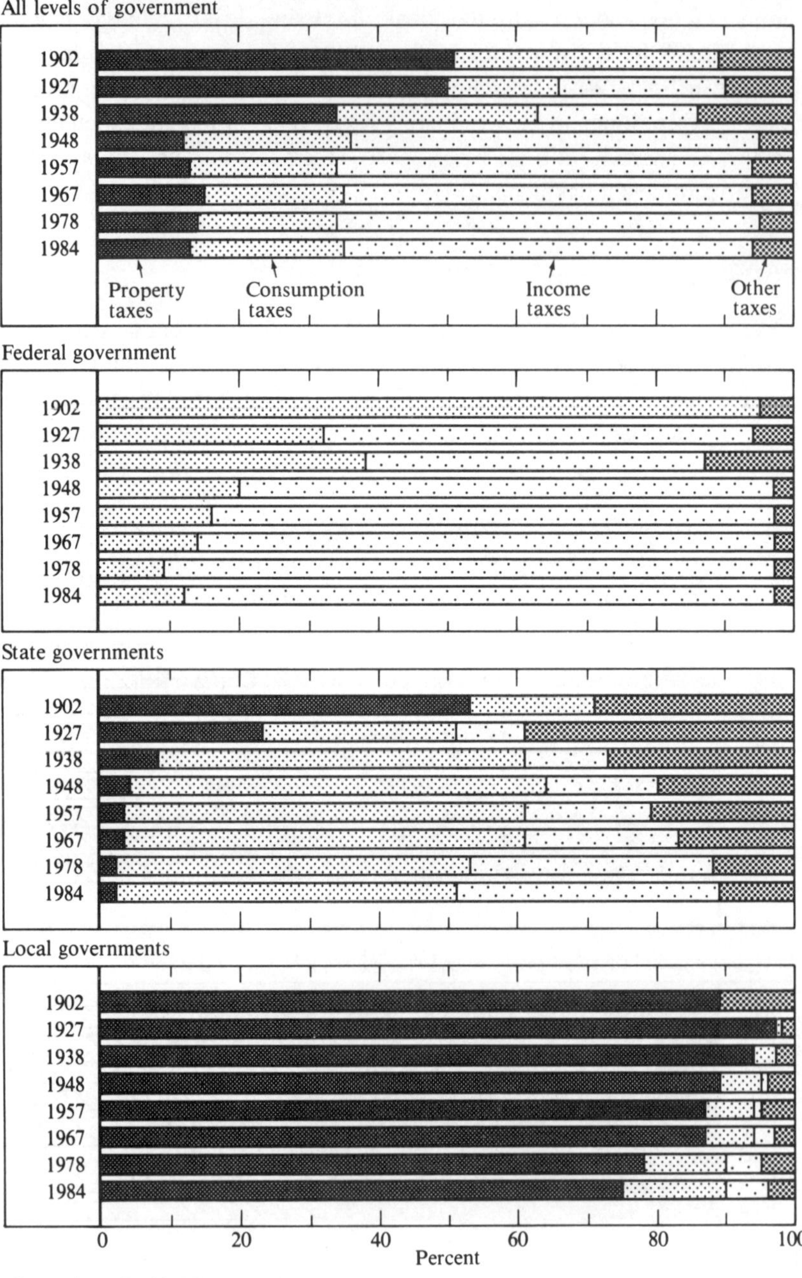

Source: Appendix table A-2.

ditures from World War I stimulated the feeling that citizen demands for new and better public services should be directed to state and local governments. Federal intergovernmental payments were unimportant and whether they are charged to the disbursing or originating level of government, the federal share of civil expenditure for 1927 in figure 1-1 is around 17 percent.

In the years from 1902 to 1927 there was little change in the proportion of total taxes collected by each level of government. The state share did increase somewhat (see appendix table A-2). Major alterations did take place, however, in the structure and composition of taxes (see figure 1-2). In 1902 income taxation was so small that it was not recorded separately; by 1927 it accounted for 64 percent of federal and 10 percent of state tax revenues. In 1902 taxes on consumption were dominant at the federal level (95 percent of the total) and significant at the state level (18 percent); in 1927 their importance at the federal level was declining and at the state level was increasing. Only at the local level was there little change in tax composition. Both in 1902 and in 1927 the property tax provided almost all of local tax revenues.

Before the Great Depression of the 1930s, one main feature of government finances with respect to expenditure for civil functions was the small role the federal government played vis-à-vis state and local governments, a role that seemed unlikely to grow soon. With respect to taxation, however, the federal government had been pushed by World War I to move strongly into taxes on income, both individual and corporate. In the 1920s the rates of these taxes were sharply reduced, but there was no repeal; the framework was retained. Nonetheless, state governments had reason to be content with their prospects. They were assuming new functions and extending their control over old ones. New and productive revenues in the form of taxation of motor fuel had been discovered and developed; joint occupancy of income and death taxation with the federal government seemed practicable since federal rates were low.

The Depression of the 1930s

The decade of the 1930s brought more drastic change to the intergovernmental financial structure in the United States than had the preceding one hundred and forty years. The force behind the change was a depression without precedent in its intensity and duration. A powerful shift in social philosophy developed when it became clear that state and local governments could not cope with obvious relief and welfare needs. Local governments simply ran out of money as property tax collections declined and tax delinquencies rose, and as they found themselves unable to borrow. State governments came to the rescue, but their efforts were both laggard and inadequate. After 1933, the federal government intervened, at first mostly by mounting emergency programs of public works, work relief, and direct relief. Then in 1935 the Social Security Act provided a federal program of old-age insurance, a federal-state system of unemployment insurance, and an extensive system of grants for public assistance which pushed state and local governments into these programs and reimbursed them for about half of their costs. Other governmental programs proliferated. Sometimes the new expenditure was wholly federal; quite often joint federal-state financing was provided.

Thus the 1930s brought a major intergovernmental redistribution of expenditure for civil purposes (see figure 1-1). The most remarkable change was the increase in the federal contribution in the form of intergovernmental grants, the bulk of which were emergency grants for the Federal Civil Works Administration, the Public Works Administration, and the Federal Emergency Relief Administration, although after passage of the Social Security Act in 1935 expenditure on regular grants grew steadily. Direct federal spending also grew.

In the 1930s, judicial doctrine showed a centralizing bias. For half a century after 1880 the Supreme Court had marked out a fairly clear boundary between federal and state activities; it stood as referee to solve jurisdictional disputes. Whether in response to shifts in social philosophy or as a reaction to contradictory precedents, a new judicial interpretation emerged in the 1930s that "accepted a reading of the general welfare clause that places no discernible judicial limits on the amounts or purposes of Federal spending."[8] The Supreme Court became unwilling also to place restraints on government regulation of economic affairs.

In the 1930s a critical chorus arose, repeating much more vehemently than in the 1880s that the states were obsolete and should be scrapped. Simeon E. Leland, a well-known professor of public finance, believed that the states should become "administrative areas" of the national government. It was, he avowed, anomalous to have forty-eight states fumble ineffectively with similar problems. An eminent political scientist, Luther

8. U.S. Commission on Intergovernmental Relations, *A Report to the President* (The Commission, 1955), p. 29. This report, prepared under the chairmanship of Meyer Kestnbaum, is known as the Kestnbaum Report.

Gulick, was equally specific. The states were no longer vital organizational units; "dual federalism" was an artificial concept since state governments could not deal "even inefficiently with the imperative, the life and death tasks of the new national economy." What had they done, what could they do, about regulation of utilities, about protecting bank deposits, about social insurance? These programs were "mostly national in scope. It is extremely wasteful, and in most cases impossible, to solve them state by state."[9] No one spelled out the timing of the dissolution of the states; fulfillment could presumably await the millennium.

Half a century later, the entire analysis and indictment seem unrealistic. The economic disaster that struck the United States in the 1930s required a reallocation and also an enlargement of governmental functions. Realization of this necessity did not come easily. A period of fumbling, of debate over governmental responsibilities, and of improvisation was inevitable. Only gradually could a new alignment of functions, and especially of governmental finance, evolve. When this came, the federal structure was found to be intact, and the states, as units of government, had gained in strength.

Postwar Resurgence of State and Local Spending

Before this revitalization occurred, World War II intervened. Even more than in World War I, state and local finances were put on a standby basis. As federal spending in the years from 1940 to 1944 expanded tenfold (from $10.1 billion to $100.5 billion), state and local spending declined (from $11.2 billion to $10.5 billion).

But when the war ended, the federal government rapidly dismantled its military establishment and prepared to reestablish its prewar pattern of activities.[10] State and local governments prepared to catch up on deficiencies in public construction resulting from depression and war. On the surface their finances seemed strong; revenues were abundant, and never had interest rates on state and local securities been so low. However, the cold war, followed by actual war in Korea, soon clouded the optimistic outlook because it brought to a halt, and then reversed, the drop in federal

9. These and similar references are given in W. Brooke Graves, *American State Government* (Heath, 1936), pp. 746–53.

10. Through the Employment Act of 1946, the federal government assumed the new function of promoting economic stabilization. This did not, however, require provision of new federal programs.

tax rates. State and local governments, instead of occupying sources of revenue vacated by the federal government, found that they would have to compete with the federal government for the taxpayer's dollar.

State and local expenditures have shown a remarkable growth since the end of World War II. They represented 6.8 percent of gross national product in 1948 and 13.4 percent in 1984 (see appendix table A-4). Higher standards of demand for education, welfare, public health, highways, housing, and so forth, required state and local action. Even when intergovernmental payments are attributed to the originating level, the distribution of spending for civil purposes in 1948 and 1984 shows that state and local governments held their position (see figure 1-1).

Between the years 1948 and 1984 the federal share of tax collections decreased from 74.0 percent to 56.4 percent, while the state and local shares grew. A surprising feature was the recovery of the property tax, which had lost ground during the 1930s. After the war it revived and displayed considerable strength; by 1984, however, its proportional share of total taxes had declined to 13 percent (see figure 1-2). State governments have discovered that income taxation can be a useful source of revenue; it contributed 16 percent of their revenue in 1948 and 38 percent in 1984.

The End of the Trend

Spectacular increases in state and local spending and in federal grants-in-aid to state and local governments occurred after World War II. The trends began to weaken, however, in the 1970s. Table 1-1 provides expenditure data in both nominal and inflation-corrected terms. Between 1954 and 1975 the annual rate of increase in state and local expenditures was 10.1 percent before correcting for inflation and 6.2 percent when the value of these expenditures is adjusted with the GNP deflator. The nominal rate of increase was 9.1 percent between 1975 and 1984. But when these expenditures are calculated in real terms, the rate of increase falls to 1.9 percent.

The new trend in spending patterns is more obvious for federal grants-in-aid. The nominal annual rate of increase dropped from 14.3 percent for the period 1954–75 to 8.0 percent for the years 1975–84. In inflation-corrected terms, the annual rate of increase fell from 10.3 percent per year for the 1954–75 period to 1.3 percent per year for the 1975–84 period.

Table 1-1. *Trends in State-Local Expenditures and Federal Grants-in-Aid, 1954 and 1975–84*

Year	GNP deflator (1954 = 100)	Direct general state-local expenditures: Current dollars	Direct general state-local expenditures: Constant dollars	Intergovernmental grants: Current dollars	Intergovernmental grants: Constant dollars
			Billions of dollars		
1954	100	30.7	30.7	3.0	3.0
1975	211	229.5	108.8	49.6	23.5
1976	222	255.6	115.1	69.1	31.1
1977	235	273.0	116.2	73.0	31.1
1978	253	295.5	116.8	79.2	31.3
1979	274	326.0	119.0	85.2	31.1
1980	300	367.3	122.4	90.8	30.3
1981	328	405.6	123.7	94.6	28.8
1982	348	433.5	124.6	86.0	24.7
1983	362	464.7	128.4	88.5	24.4
1984	375	503.3	134.2	99.0	26.4
			Annual rate of increase (percent)		
1954–75	...	10.1	6.2	14.3	10.3
1975–84	...	9.1	1.9	8.0	1.3

Sources: U.S. Census Bureau, *Historical Statistics of the United States: Colonial Times to 1970*, pt. 2 (U.S. Government Printing Office, 1975), pp. 1126–27; Census Bureau, *Governmental Finances in 1983–84* (GPO, 1985), table 10, and earlier issues; Council of Economic Advisers, *Economic Indicators*, various issues. In all tables years are fiscal unless otherwise noted and figures are rounded.

Functional Distribution of Expenditures

This brief historical review of governmental finances indicates that while the nation has been buffeted by strong economic forces, federalism in the United States has been flexible. The division of aggregate governmental expenditure for civil purposes—federal versus state and local—changed in the 1930s with growth in the federal share and decline in the state-local share. The shift is more emphatic when federal grants are reckoned as federal rather than state-local expenditure.

What rationale can be offered concerning the division of functions between the federal government on the one hand, and state-local governments on the other? The framers of the Constitution had a rationale; they drew lines that set limits to the powers of the national government. The lines were not clear-cut in 1788, and they are not clear-cut today. The scope of government has grown, and the economy of the nation is much more integrated. As a result, the concept of the separation of governmental functions, federal versus state-local, has been replaced by another concept of federal-state relations, cooperative federalism. A presidential commission described it this way in 1955:

> Under current judicial doctrine, there are still limits on the coercive powers at both levels [National or State], but the National powers are broad and the possibilities by means of spending are still broader. The crucial questions now are questions of policy: which level ought to move? Or should both? Or neither? What are the prudent and proper divisions of labor and responsibility between them? These are questions mainly for legislative judgment, and the criteria are chiefly political, economic, and administrative, rather than legal. The emphasis is on mutual and complementary undertakings in furtherance of common aims.[11]

The case for decentralized decision and administration is strong, but federal participation in finance, coupled with modest federal coordination and guidance, is consistent with and necessary for the performance of governmental tasks at the state-local level.

A modern rationale for cooperative federalism can be developed through analysis of the benefits derived by people from governmental services. Some of these services are collective and national in nature. The clearest instance is national defense where government considers the need of citizens in the aggregate. As a logical consequence, government raises the revenue for this expenditure by general taxes which are assessed on individuals according to standards of equity. The collective nature of the benefits dictates that this substantial expenditure must be allocated among taxpayers according to whatever standards the legislature deems appropriate. At the other end of the spectrum, government renders services that are semicommercial in nature; certain individuals are the direct beneficiaries, the government charges them for the service, and individuals may choose to consume whatever amount they wish. A modest collective interest is perceived to be present (else provision would be left in private hands), but it is veiled. Examples are toll highways and water supply.

Between these extremes all other governmental services may be ranked according to the relative importance of their collective, compared with their individual, interest. Thus, educational services are rendered to individuals who thereby receive direct benefits; but these services are also beneficial to the whole society. This spillover of benefits creates such a strong collective interest that the cost of primary and secondary education is defrayed by general taxes, not by charges to the recipients. Many important features of public health services also have a spillover of benefit

11. Kestnbaum Report, p. 33.

to the whole society. Welfare services form another distinguishable group of the large in-between category. Here also the benefits accrue directly to recipients, but society is collectively benefited because provision of these services satisfies deeply ingrained humanitarian feelings. Moreover, linking individual benefit with individual payment would be absurd since the recipients are, by definition, without means. In short, finance by general taxation is inevitable and appropriate; government provides the services as a collective duty.

How can these generalizations be applied in deciding between federal or state-local provision of a particular government service? One that is rendered to the nation as a whole (collectively)—defense—is clearly federal. The outlook of each state and local government is, on the other hand, circumscribed; the services each provides are for individuals in a limited geographic area. Some variation of type and level of provision is acceptable, and even desirable. Sometimes, however, the benefits from a state or local service spill over and have an impact outside the government's boundaries. Primary and secondary education is an obvious example. Although the benefit of an educated citizenry undoubtedly reaches beyond the boundaries of the locality where the students are educated, this national interest was not until the 1960s recognized by Congress through federal grants-in-aid. Provision is left mainly to local and state governments because direct benefits accrue to individuals in a locality and because local (and state) governments are strongly responsive and sensitive to the demands of citizens concerning details. The cost is provided through taxes levied at the local and, to a smaller extent, the state level.

Public welfare services are another bundle of functions administered mainly at the state-local level of government. The benefits accrue directly to individuals; responsiveness of government to the variety of individual needs is vital; detailed administration is inevitable. The services are rendered mainly to needy persons. During the depression of the 1930s, the opinion emerged strongly that some minimum level of provision should be achieved over the nation. Since this would not result if the states were left to their own devices, federal assistance by grants was enacted. By 1984 these grants supported over 70 percent of expenditures for public welfare (table 1-2). As a result, state and local governments have been stimulated to offer welfare services, though not at a uniform level; but even in poor states a minimum level for recipients has been feasible.

In the years since World War II the most important civil functions provided by government, measured by relative expenditure, have been

Table 1-2. *Percent of Direct General Expenditure for Civil Functions by the Federal Government, 1958, 1968, 1978, and 1984*

	Intergovernmental payments excluded				*Intergovernmental payments included*			
Function	*1958*	*1968*	*1978*	*1984*	*1958*	*1968*	*1978*	*1984*
Education	5.4	5.6	6.7	6.6	9.3	16.5	16.5	13.8
Public welfare	1.3	12.3	30.5	26.8	48.9	60.4	67.5	72.1
Highways	1.6	1.2	1.1	2.0	18.5	30.5	26.0	27.3
Health and hospitals	23.7	28.7	24.6	21.8	26.0	35.4	32.0	28.7

Source: Appendix table A-3; Census Bureau, *Governmental Finances in 1983–84*, tables 9, 10.

education, public welfare, highways, and health and hospitals. Together, as table 1-3 shows, they have accounted for more than half of the total expenditures for civil functions. Education has always been the single function far in the lead. Expenditure for public welfare rose sharply in the 1930s and is now in second place.

What shifts have occurred in the relative expenditures of the different levels of government? When the figures used are those of direct general expenditures—when intergovernmental transfers are regarded as spent by the level making the final disbursement—the shifts in federal versus state-local levels between 1958 and 1984 appear, with the exception of the public welfare category, to be modest (see payments excluded columns of table 1-2). But the federal government, in addition to its direct general expenditure, made growing intergovernmental expenditures (see table 1-4), and if these are credited to it (and thus included in federal spending), the federal share rises significantly (see table 1-2). The two sets of graphs in figure 1-3 show that the federal share of the expenditure for education in 1984 can be figured at 6.6 percent or 13.8 percent; for public welfare at 26.8 percent or 72.1 percent; for highways at 2.0 percent or 27.3 percent.

In short, the overlapping of governmental activities, federal and state-local, increased significantly in the quarter century. Although certain services are still performed at the state-local level, the federal government has greatly enlarged its provision of grants. By specifying conditions for receipt of the grants, it indicates the existence of some national interest in performance of the services.

Apologia for Federalism

The direct expansion of federal power, so forceful a trend in the 1930s, has not continued, but the indirect expansion, through grants, persisted

Table 1-3. *Percent of General Expenditure for Civil Functions by All Levels of Government, 1958, 1968, 1978, and 1984*

Function	*1958*	*1968*	*1978*	*1984*
Education	28.1	32.0	29.7	27.1
Highways	14.5	10.8	6.2	5.8
Public welfare	6.3	8.3	13.6	12.7
Health and hospitals	7.8	7.8	8.3	4.9
Other	43.4	41.2	42.2	49.5

Source: Appendix table A-3.

until the 1980s. The states are, so it seems, geographic units that can handle many functions more flexibly, and therefore more in accord with heterogeneous citizen demands, than the national government. State boundaries must be accepted as immutable, and therefore so must the states' diversity in population, resources, and area. It is through this diversity, like that of sovereign nations, that the states have acquired loyalties and affection over the decades that lubricate the machinery of government.

More philosophical reasons may be advanced for a belief that, if the states did not exist, there would be need to invent them. One reason, put cogently, is that the states are laboratories in which limited experiments in government or administrative techniques can be made. Such experiments, even when they fail, may have more than mere negative value. They may indicate why and what kind of federal action is needed. Oklahoma's experiment in guaranteeing bank deposits failed, but it and similar attempts by other states disclosed defects that could be, and were, remedied by a national scheme in 1933 that created a federal corporation to insure bank deposits. In the early years of the twentieth century, state and local governments experimented with techniques of government budgeting and accounting. To these experiments the federal Budget and Accounting Act of 1921 owed a great deal. The Wisconsin income tax of 1911 preceded the federal income tax of 1913. The federal Social Security Act of 1935 grew out of much state investigation and some experimentation with old-age insurance, unemployment insurance, and public assistance. Marked progress here had to wait for federal intervention; yet with respect to unemployment insurance and public assistance, Congress chose to act through the techniques of cooperative federalism. The state governments were pioneers in the use of measures of fiscal capacity in grant programs, and the Highway Safety Act of 1966 was built wholly on state experience over many years. An awareness and appreciation of federalism might not only enable Congress to decide what cooperative programs are appropriate, but conversely to reject programs that are inappropriate.

Figure 1-3. *Percent of General Expenditure for Selected Civil Functions Contributed by Federal and State-Local Governments, 1958, 1968, 1978, and 1984*

Intergovernmental payments charged to the level of government making the final disbursement

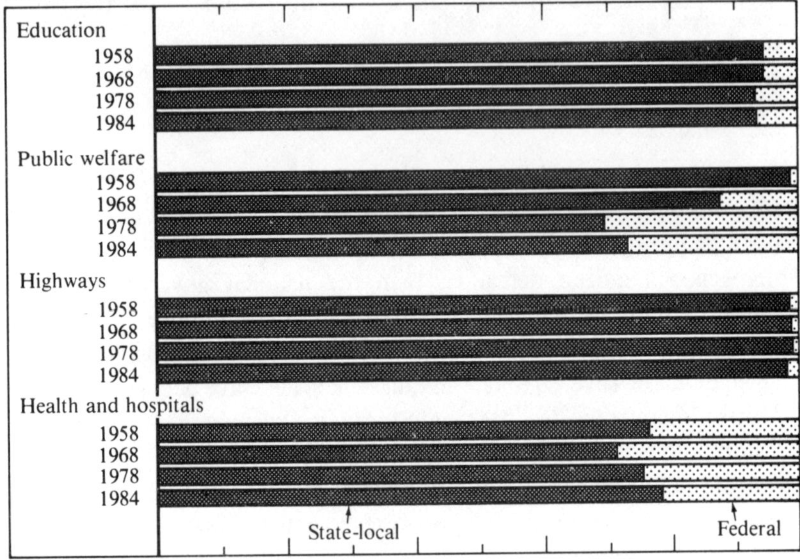

Intergovernmental payments charged to the originating level of government

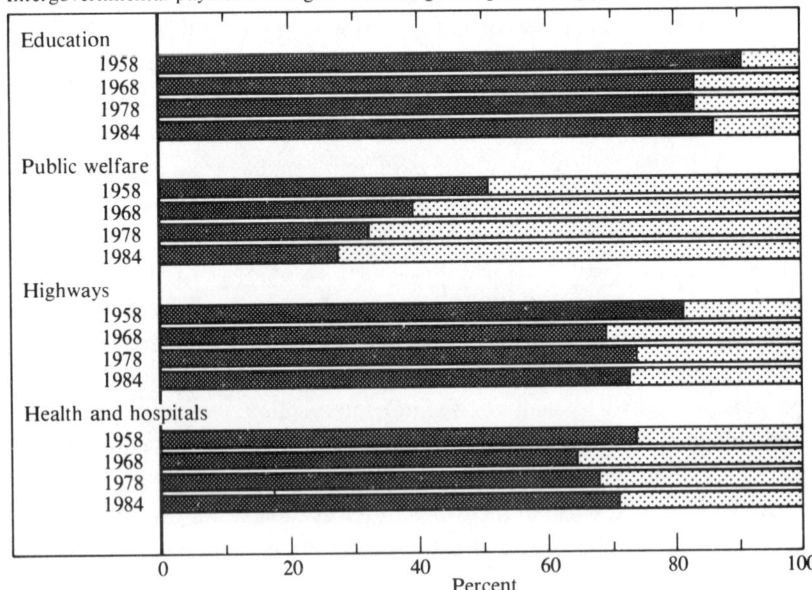

Source: Table 1-2.

Table 1-4. *Federal Intergovernmental Payments for Selected State-Local Civil Functions, 1958, 1968, 1978, and 1984*

Millions of dollars

Function	*1958*	*1968*	*1978*	*1984*
Education	653	4,727	11,602	13,608
Public welfare	1,799	5,407	20,051	40,054
Highways	1,478	4,291	6,197	10,204
Health and hospitals	110	718	2,464	4,070
Other	795	2,910	38,858	31,079
Total	4,835	18,053	79,172	99,015

Source: Census Bureau, *Governmental Finances in 1983–84*, table 10, and earlier issues.

A century ago, Woodrow Wilson noted the value of the states as training grounds in the practice of government: "The governorship of a State is very like a smaller Presidency; or, rather, the Presidency is very like a big governorship. Training in the duties of the one fits for the duties of the other."[12] The case for federalism, in the minds of many men, rests on a still more exalted and abstract merit: that state and local governments are bulwarks of democracy. Only where the people of a nation have adequate powers of decision can they develop a public spirit, and the specific knowledge and techniques that give life to free institutions.[13]

The structure of state government has been an object of continuous concern. In 1953 a Commission on Intergovernmental Relations was set up to reappraise federalism, and to "study the means of achieving a sounder relationship between Federal, state, and local governments."[14] It reported, in 1955, a "real and pressing need for the States to improve their constitutions," many of which restricted "the scope, effectiveness, and adaptability of State and local action."[15] State legislatures, it suggested, should provide a more equitable system of representation.[16] The power of

12. *Congressional Government* (Houghton Mifflin, 1885), p. 253.

13. George C. S. Benson, "Values of Decentralized Governments—1961," in George C. S. Benson and others, *Essays in Federalism* (Claremont Men's College, Institute for Studies in Federalism, 1961), pp. 5–16, makes an eloquent case for federalism. See also Terry Sanford, *Storm Over the States* (McGraw-Hill, 1967), especially chap. 12, which includes examples of state leadership.

14. *Public Papers of the Presidents: Dwight D. Eisenhower, 1953* (Government Printing Office, 1953), p. 140. Fifteen of the commission's members were appointed by the president, five by the president of the Senate, and five by the Speaker of the House.

15. Kestnbaum Report, pp. 37–38. See also Committee for Economic Development, *Modernizing State Government* (New York: CED, 1967); CED, *Modernizing Local Government to Secure a Balanced Federalism* (New York: CED, 1966).

16. In 1964 the Supreme Court held that the equal protection clause of the Fourteenth Amendment requires each state to have a legislature so chosen that, in both houses, each member represents substantially the same number of people. *Reynolds* v. *Sims*, 377 U.S. 533 (1964).

governors was unreasonably limited by the establishment of independent agencies and boards, by the election of numerous state administrative officers, and by the lack of control over budgeting. State legislatures fettered their own power, and that of the localities, to tax and borrow; they earmarked too much revenue; they created, and should mitigate, tax conflicts.[17]

The response to the Kestnbaum Report was unprecedented. Two decades later the states had reordered their constitutions, their executive structures, and their legislatures. The Advisory Commission on Intergovernmental Relations—a permanent agency established in 1959 that was successor to the presidential commission—reported in 1981 that the states could no longer be described as "weak sisters" or "antiquated." In fact, "the transformation of the states, occurring in a relatively short period of time, has no parallel in American history."[18] The ACIR warned that not all states had made equal progress and that all could benefit from additional improvement. Yet, through constitutional reform, and new amendment and revision procedures, great strides had been made in improving the efficiency of all three branches of state government—executive, legislative, and judicial.[19]

Another problem that has raised doubts about the resiliency of federalism appears to be abating. The growth of metropolitan areas and the fiscal disparities between central cities and their suburbs, most acute in the East and Midwest, was a major dilemma of the 1960s and 1970s. The metropolitan area is not a single governmental unit governed by one legislative body. Rather it encompasses a large number of independent jurisdictions, each responsible in some degree for supplying services such as education, water, sewage disposal, and law enforcement. When these fragmented jurisdictions debate their respective fiscal responsibilities, economic decisions are often obstructed or postponed. And when a metropolitan area spreads across state borders, solution of these problems requires negotiation and agreement among sovereign units.

Central cities attract high-cost citizens, whose welfare needs must be met either through high local taxes or through assistance from state or federal governments. Traditionally, per capita tax collections have been higher in central cities than in their suburban areas—29 percent higher in

17. Kestnbaum Report, especially pp. 38–47, 93–99.

18. ACIR, *State and Local Roles in the Federal System* (Washington: ACIR, 1982), p. 3.

19. Ibid., pp. 3–10.

1981. Such large differentials in tax demands create an incentive for taxpayers to move to areas of low fiscal pressure.[20]

The higher revenue collections per capita of the central cities have been outpaced by their expenditures. In 1977, per capita expenditures in central cities were 43 percent higher than those in their suburbs. By 1981, the discrepancy had narrowed to 39 percent.[21]

What has caused the lessening, at least in percentage terms, of the disparities between central city and suburb? It is in part due to the fact that suburbs are now under more financial pressure. But the narrowing is also due to the fact that some central cities were able to use annexation and consolidation to widen their resource base and that they received relatively more state and federal aid than did the suburbs. "The bleak picture of the beleagured, poverty-stricken central city surrounded by rich white suburbs," the ACIR noted in 1981, did not "describe reality in most Southern and Western metropolitan areas and even some Midwestern ones."[22] Cities do appear to be viable units and although there remain very serious problems in some cities in the East and Midwest, the record seems to indicate that the flexibility of cooperative federalism can offer solutions to urban problems.

Recently, many thoughtful analysts have expressed concern that cooperative federalism has been a license for uncontrolled federal expenditures, the result being public sector growth without purpose. The "national interest," they claim, is a shallow concept on which to justify federal involvement in functions otherwise the responsibility of state and local governments.[23] The need to simplify and rationalize the very complicated federal grant-in-aid system is clear and a realignment of federal versus state and local responsibilities may be in order.[24]

20. For an analysis of how fiscal factors can affect intra-area population shifts, see J. Richard Aronson, *Public Finance* (McGraw-Hill, 1985), pp. 288–94. Also see ACIR, *Regional Growth: Interstate Tax Competition,* A-76 (Washington: ACIR, 1981), pp. 4–8.

21. ACIR, *Fiscal Disparities: Central Cities and Suburbs, 1981* (Washington: ACIR, 1984), p. 12. The data in these calculations are for the nation's 37 largest standard metropol itan statistical areas.

22. Ibid., p. 4.

23. See ACIR, *The Federal Role in the Federal System: The Dynamics of Growth—The Condition of Contemporary Federalism: Conflicting Theories and Collapsing Constraints,* A-78 (Washington: ACIR, 1981), pp. 1–25.

24. A popular reform would shift responsibility for welfare and health programs mainly to the federal government and put more responsibility for programs in education, transportation, law enforcement, health and hospitals, environmental protection, natural resources, and economic development on the states. For a summary of the reform proposals of the

Recent administrations have tried to control the size of the federal government, and President Reagan made a formal proposal for intergovernmental reform that he called the New Federalism. The key elements were a sharp reduction in the aggregate level of funding for grants-in-aid; consolidation of many categorical grants into block grants; an intergovernmental swap of programs, with the federal government assuming responsibility for medicaid and the states taking full control of food stamps and aid for families with dependent children; and a return to the states of many federal programs in education, transportation, community development, and social services.[25]

The concept, which was presented with great fanfare by the president in his 1982 budget message, proved to be controversial. Those who favored the idea stressed the advantages to be gained by simplifying the grant system, improving management of and compliance with federal regulations, and increasing allocative efficiency so that state and local governments could have more authority in determining the set of services they would provide.

Many persons, however, opposed the idea, fearing the effects of massive fiscal change. They warned that the impact of significant reductions in federal funding would be fiscal strain on state and local governments. They also pointed out that rich states would be better able than poor states to adjust to federal fund reductions and that the disparity among the states in the level of social services provided would widen.

The Reagan administration has had some success in stopping the growth of intergovernmental transfers and in consolidating fragmented programs. But it is far from clear that the pressing and complex needs of state and local governments can be met if federal financial support is reduced. Cooperative federalism, although a fuzzy concept, provides a framework within which the public sector can face the problems of a changing society.

ACIR, the National Governors Association, and others, see Claude E. Barfield, *Rethinking Federalism—Block Grants in Federal, State, and Local Responsibilities* (Washington: American Enterprise Institute, 1981), pp. 59–80.

25. See John L. Palmer and Isabel V. Sawhill, eds., *The Reagan Experiment* (Washington: Urban Institute, 1982), pp. 157–217; Joseph A. Pechman, ed., *Setting National Priorities: The 1983 Budget* (Brookings, 1982), pp. 151–86; *Special Analyses, Budget of the United States Government, Fiscal Year 1983,* special analysis H.

CHAPTER TWO

Fiscal Performance and Capacity

There is a great deal of difference between Peter and Peter.

Don Quixote

THE DIVISION of governmental functions between a state government and the local governments that are its creatures varies widely among the fifty states. The quantitative evidence in the form of expenditures is, however, hard to interpret, most obviously because of state intergovernmental transfers. Some state governments take over and perform functions that others leave in local hands and assist by grants-in-aid. In the former case, performance of functions may, with some qualifications, be regarded as centralized; that is, the state governments make a relatively large part of direct general expenditure. In the latter case, performance is decentralized. Table 2-1 shows the ten state governments that in 1984 spent the highest and the ten that spent the lowest proportions of total state-local direct expenditures. Two states with a high percentage, Hawaii and Alaska, are the youngest in the nation, and local units of government may not have had time to become entrenched there. But no such simple explanation will serve for the other high states, or for the states with low percentages where relative decentralization seems to prevail.

The fact is that interstate comparisons of state government finances (or of local government finances) are treacherous and may be quite misleading about the relative levels of services provided by the states. More revealing comparisons can be made, state by state, of aggregates or subaggregates of state plus local expenditure and revenue. Such figures, when expressed per capita or per $1,000 of personal income, provide a more useful measure of state-by-state differences in governmental provision of services and collection of revenues.

A per capita measure of expenditure has limitations chiefly because population (the denominator) is by itself an inadequate proxy for expenditure needs. Some groups in the population—for example, dependent children and the aged—require extra public expenditure. States differ in meeting their responsibilities, and refined measurement should allow for

Table 2-1. *States Accounting for Highest and Lowest Proportions of State-Local Direct General Expenditure, 1984*[a]

Highest states	*Percent of state-local expenditure*	*Lowest states*	*Percent of state-local expenditure*
Hawaii	79.8	New Jersey	37.8
Vermont	61.6	Kansas	37.5
Rhode Island	59.9	Wyoming	37.1
Delaware	59.7	Colorado	35.2
Kentucky	56.7	Texas	35.1
Alaska	56.1	Arizona	34.3
North Dakota	55.3	California	33.5
Maine	53.4	New York	32.9
West Virginia	52.7	Nevada	32.4
South Dakota	52.3	Florida	30.9

Source: U.S. Census Bureau, *Governmental Finances in 1983–84* (U.S. Government Printing Office, 1985), table 26. In all tables years are fiscal unless otherwise noted and figures are rounded.

a. General expenditure is that for all purposes other than specifically defined utility, liquor store, and insurance trust operations. Direct general expenditure excludes intergovernmental expenditure.

variations among states. Per capita expenditure is a rough measure also because it makes no allowance for price or quality differences, state by state, of public goods. Educational services may be cheaper in Mississippi than in Massachusetts, or it may be that, if account is taken of quality, the reverse is true. A similar uncertainty exists with respect to the pricing of other governmental services. Moreover, state variation in expenditure is not explicable wholly by objective needs and financial capacity; noneconomic and intangible factors, which stem from different historical backgrounds, are important.

This brief enumeration of some of the factors that might affect the levels of state and local expenditure has two purposes. First, it warns that the measure of differences used below—per capita direct expenditure—is imperfect; second, it indicates that a more refined measure would be difficult to construct. (For reasons mentioned later, figures of state and local revenue when expressed per $1,000 of personal income are not unambiguous measures of revenue effort.)

Patterns of Aggregate Expenditure

For the fiscal year 1984, state and local direct expenditures for the nation averaged $2,131 per capita. All direct expenditures made by state and local governments are included in this figure, whether the funds were provided from their own sources or by federal grants.[1]

Some idea of the spread among states in per capita state and local expenditures in 1984 is given in the following list:[2]

Per capita expenditure (dollars)	*Number of states*
Under 1,600	3
1,600–1,799	8
1,800–1,999	10
2,000–2,199	7 ($2,131 U.S. average)
2,200–2,399	14
2,400–2,599	4
Over 2,600	4

These figures include funds from the federal government; in order to secure figures of per capita expenditure by states from their own sources, federal grants must be deducted. For 1984 the average per capita state and local expenditure, less federal grants, was $1,720. The six states with the highest and the six with the lowest per capita expenditure on this basis are shown in table 2-2. New York, one of the highest states, spent $2,420 per capita in 1984. Arkansas, the lowest state, spent $1,104. The figures of per capita state-local expenditures can be made more readily comparable by assigning the value of 100 to the national average ($1,720) and computing relative numbers that express how much each state spends in relation to this national average. Table 2-2 shows that New York has an expenditure relative of 141 and thus spent from its own sources 41 percent more than the national average; Arkansas, with an expenditure relative of 64, spent 36 percent less than the average. Twenty-five states spent less than the average and twenty-five states more.

Efforts have been made to discover and measure the significant variables (other than population) that explain the diversity among the states. The most important other variable or "cause" is income. In general, more will be spent by state and local governments in a "rich" state—one with a high per capita income—than in a "poor" state. The state-by-state relationship between per capita income and per capita state-local government expenditure, excluding federal grants, is presented in figure 2-1. The

1. The amount that state and local governments spend on their citizens is the sum of direct state expenditures plus direct local expenditures. State intergovernmental expenditures (going to local governments) must be excluded to avoid double counting.

2. See appendix table A-8.

Table 2-2. *States with Highest and Lowest Per Capita General Expenditure, Excluding Federal Grants, 1984*

Highest states	*Per capita expenditure (dollars)*	*Expenditure index*[a]	*Lowest states*	*Per capita expenditure (dollars)*	*Expenditure index*[a]
Alaska	7,743.49	450	Missouri	1,296.27	75
Wyoming	2,984.60	174	Mississippi	1,278.64	74
New York	2,420.28	141	North Carolina	1,256.80	73
Minnesota	2,147.66	125	South Carolina	1,232.98	72
Nevada	2,066.71	120	Tennessee	1,199.68	70
New Mexico	2,006.20	117	Arkansas	1,104.49	64

Source: Appendix table A-8.
a. U.S. average = 100. Index computed by dividing a state's per capita state-local expenditure by the national average, $1,720. The New York expenditure index, for example, is ($2,420 ÷ $1,720) × 100 = 141.

general pattern shows that income and government expenditure tend to rise together, with expenditure rising somewhat less sharply than income. For every 10 percent increase in a state's per capita income, state-local expenditure increases, on the average, by approximately 7 percent. This average relationship, however, has many exceptions. Quite often states that rank low in per capita income have a higher rank in per capita expenditure; conversely, states that rank high in income quite often have a lower rank in per capita expenditure. And some states spend much more, and some much less, than one would expect in terms of their per capita income. For example, Connecticut and New Jersey, which in 1984 ranked second and third in per capita income, ranked twenty-second and tenth in terms of per capita expenditure (see appendix table A-9). Utah and New Mexico which ranked forty-eighth and forty-first in per capita income ranked thirty-first and sixth in per capita expenditure.

The influence of other quantifiable variables has also been explored, notably population density (population per square mile) and urbanization (percentage of population living in urban places). As population density increases, per capita state-local expenditure tends to decrease, but not uniformly and not for all functions. Per capita expenditure for police and fire protection tends to rise with population density. Increase in urbanization has a modest tendency to increase per capita expenditure, but not that for highways. Moreover, the population density and urbanization variables are themselves highly correlated.

Except for the distinct relationship between per capita income and per capita expenditure, statistical analysis of factors that affect state expenditures indicates considerable diversity among the states.[3]

3. Examples of pioneering statistical work aimed at understanding per capita public expenditures are Glenn W. Fisher, "Determinants of State and Local Government Expendi-

Figure 2-1. *States Ranked by Per Capita Income and Per Capita General Expenditure, Excluding Federal Grants, 1984*

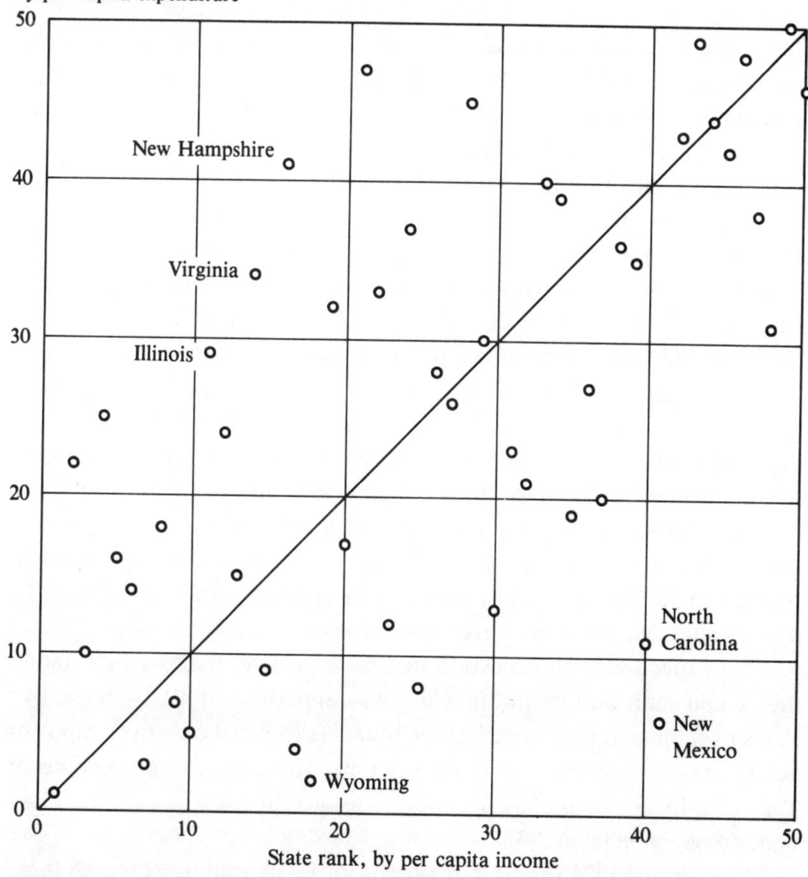

Source: Appendix table A-9.

tures: A Preliminary Analysis," *National Tax Journal*, vol. 14 (December 1961), pp. 349–55; Glenn W. Fisher, "Interstate Variation in State and Local Expenditure," *National Tax Journal*, vol. 17 (March 1964), pp. 54–74; Roy Bahl, "Studies on Determinants of Public Expenditures: A Review," in Selma J. Mushkin and John F. Cotton, eds., *Sharing Federal Funds for State and Local Needs: Grants-in-Aid and PPB Systems* (Praeger, 1969), pp. 184–207. For a more recent analysis see Dennis Zimmerman, "On The Relationship Between Public Goods Theory and Expenditure Determinant Studies," *National Tax Journal*, vol. 28 (June 1975), pp. 227–39.

Before statistical analyses of state expenditure levels were undertaken, the diversity among the states was attributed solely to differences in historical background or political philosophy. Studies completed during the 1960s and 1970s demonstrated that socioeconomic variables are important determinants of state and local spending. But the pattern of relative importance among variables and the amount of variation in expenditure levels explained by these variables differed across these studies. A more recent method of analysis known as *public choice* includes explicit consideration of how variations in political institutions across states affect state and local fiscal patterns. Using models of public decisionmaking, public choice analysts attempt to see how various political rules affect outcomes. The voting rules specified by state constitutions and the degree of control enjoyed by bureaucrats in developing referenda proposals, for example, have been shown to be important determinants of spending levels.[4]

In 1984, as table 2-3 shows, education was by far the most important type of spending of state and local governments. It absorbed $746 per capita of total general state-local expenditure. That represented 35 percent of expenditures for all of the functions shown in table 2-3.

What state-by-state variation in per capita functional expenditures is found? This is examined by first calculating the expenditure in each state for each major function as a percent of total state and local expenditure. If, for example, Maine—a poor state—spent approximately the same share of its total expenditure on education in 1984 as Connecticut—a rich state—this would indicate that the function was appraised similarly in the two states even though their actual expenditures (expressed either per capita or per $1,000 of income) were quite different. These relative proportions of total state-local expenditure spent by the states in 1984 on selected functions are given in table 2-4.

The extent of state variation in proportionate expenditure on each function can be measured first by calculating the standard deviation of that function, and then calculating the coefficient of variation—a measure that expresses the degree to which the states vary in their proportionate spending on the particular function. The lower the value of the coefficient, the more similar the proportionate amounts spent by the states; the higher the value, the greater the variability.

4. See William A. McEachern, "Collective Decision Rules and Local Debt Choice: A Test of the Median-Voter Hypothesis," *National Tax Journal*, vol. 31 (June 1978), pp. 129–36; Thomas Romer and Howard Rosenthal, "Political Resource Allocation, Controlled Agendas and the Status Quo," *Public Choice*, vol. 33 (1978), p. 33.

Table 2-3. *Per Capita Direct General Expenditure and Distribution of Total General Expenditure of State-Local Governments, by Function, 1984*

Function	*Per capita expenditure (dollars)*	*Percent of total spending*
Education	745.72	35.0
Highways	167.33	7.9
Health and hospitals	196.56	9.2
Public welfare	274.01	12.9
Interest	121.51	5.7
General control	55.02	2.6
Fire protection	34.73	1.6
Other	536.25	25.1
Total	2,131.13	100.0

Source: Census Bureau, *Governmental Finances in 1983–84,* table 24.

The coefficients of variation in table 2-4 indicate that variation in state-local spending for education is modest. This expenditure falls into two parts, one for elementary and secondary schools and another for higher education. The low variation is explicable by the relative similarity of expenditure on elementary and secondary schools. Variation in expenditures for the other functions is much greater than that for education. Apparently, expenditure preferences of state and local governments for most functions are quite diverse from state to state.

Measures of Relative Fiscal Capacity and Tax Effort

Comparisons of state expenditures gain in cogency if they can be based on a measure of tax effort in which the revenues available to state and local governments are related to a relevant, uniform base. Finding a uniform base—that is, measuring a governmental unit's fiscal capacity—is not a simple matter, however. There is more than one way to measure the fiscal capacity of a state or local government.

The simplest and most often used measure of relative fiscal capacity is a state's per capita personal income. An alternative measure, devised by the Advisory Commission on Intergovernmental Relations (ACIR), is called the "yield of the representative tax system." The hypothetical tax data in table 2-5 are used to describe these two measures.

For ease of calculation, each of the hypothetical states in table 2-5 is assumed to have three residents. The most straightforward method of measuring fiscal capacity is to calculate state relative per capita income. This would make state C the richest ($60,000 per resident) and state A the

Table 2-4. *Variation in Per Capita Expenditure of States by Percent of State-Local Direct General Expenditure, by Function, 1984*

Function	*Mean*	*Standard deviation*	*Coefficient of variation*[a]
Education	35.46	3.98	11.22
General control	2.54	0.39	15.35
Financial administration	1.89	0.32	16.93
Highways	8.00	2.24	28.00
Interest on general debt	5.55	1.57	28.29
Fire protection	1.60	0.44	27.50
Public welfare	12.50	3.71	29.68

Source: Census Bureau, *Government Finances in 1983–84*, tables 24, 27. Numbers are rounded.

a. Computed by dividing the standard deviation by the mean, and then multiplying this by 100. The coefficient of variation for expenditure on education, for example, is (3.98 ÷ 35.46) × 100 = 11.22.

poorest ($20,000 per resident). It is also common to express relative fiscal capacity in terms of index numbers with the value of the state with median per capita income set equal to 100. State ranking according to relative personal income would appear as follows:

State	*Per capita personal income (dollars)*	*Relative fiscal capacity (median state = 100)*
C	60,000	150
B	40,000	100
A	20,000	50

Per capita personal income is easy to calculate but it is not necessarily the best measure of fiscal capacity. The yield of the representative tax system (RTS) can be used to calculate how much revenue a governmental unit could raise if it applied average tax rates to the tax bases under its jurisdiction. Each state in table 2-5 can be assumed to tap each of the three tax bases—personal income, value of retail sales, and value of property—for its revenue. The average tax rate for each base is derived by calculating the total revenues from that base and dividing by the total value of the base. Thus the national average tax rate to be applied to personal income is $18,000 ÷ $360,000 = 0.05 = 5 percent; for retail sales the rate is $7,500 ÷ $150,000 = 0.05 = 5 percent; and for property is $17,500 ÷ $350,000 = 0.05 = 5 percent.

When the average rate is applied to the value of each base, the following yields can be expected:

	Revenue (dollars)		
Tax base	*State A*	*State B*	*State C*
Income	3,000	6,000	9,000
Sales	2,500	2,500	2,500
Property	10,000	5,000	2,500
Total	15,500	13,500	14,000

Table 2-5. *Tax Base and Tax Rate Data for Three Hypothetical States, Each Having Three Residents*

	State A			State B			State C		
Item	Tax base (dollars)	Tax rate (percent)	Tax revenue (dollars)	Tax base (dollars)	Tax rate (percent)	Tax revenue (dollars)	Tax base (dollars)	Tax rate (percent)	Tax revenue (dollars)
Personal income	60,000	0.100	6,000	120,000	0.050	6,000	180,000	0.033	6,000
Value of retail sales	50,000	...	0	50,000	0.070	3,500	50,000	0.080	4,000
Value of property	200,000	0.040	8,000	100,000	0.055	5,500	50,000	0.080	4,000
Total revenue	...	...	14,000	...	...	15,000	...	...	14,000
Per capita revenue	...	...	4,667	...	...	5,000	...	...	4,667

Source: J. Richard Aronson, *Public Finance* (McGraw-Hill, 1985), p. 344.

These figures show how much each state would raise if it taxed each of its bases at a rate of 5 percent. When this yield of the representative tax system is used as a measure, instead of state A having the lowest fiscal capacity, it has the highest. The states' rankings using an RTS base would be as follows:

State	*Per capita yield (dollars)*	*Relative fiscal capacity*
A	5,167	111
C	4,667	100
B	4,500	96

A state or local government's tax effort is found by relating the amount of revenue it raises to its fiscal capacity. The two measures of fiscal capacity thus provide two measures of relative effort. When the per capita revenue collections in table 2-5 are applied to the per capita personal income of the states, the ranking by relative tax effort is as follows:

	Personal income ratio		
State	*Dollars*	*Percent*	*Relative tax effort*
A	4,667/20,000	0.233	186
B	5,000/40,000	0.125	100
C	4,667/60,000	0.078	62

On the other hand, when tax collections are related to the yield of the RTS, the tax effort rankings are as follows:

	RTS yield ratio		
State	*Dollars*	*Percent*	*Relative tax effort*
B	5,000/4,500	1.110	111
C	4,667/4,667	1.000	100
A	4,667/5,167	0.903	90

One must be extremely careful in using and interpreting relative fiscal capacity and tax effort data. First of all, which measure of relative capacity is more appropriate? The answer rests in the use to which the data will be put. Per capita personal income is probably the better measure of residents' ability to pay taxes. On the other hand, the RTS yield is perhaps the better measure of the ability of a governmental unit to raise revenue. One should keep in mind that for any one state or local government the ability of residents to pay taxes and the ability of governments to raise revenue are not the same thing.[5]

Also, two governmental units may differ in their tax effort ratio not because they wish to provide different levels of public services but because they use different amounts of debt or nontax revenues. Finally, a high relative effort ratio may either indicate the desire for a large public sector or just reflect a sudden drop in fiscal capacity. Tables 2-6 and 2-7 show recent estimates of capacity and effort for state and local governments using both personal income and the RTS yield. Notice the inverse relation between capacity and effort. It is quite common for rich states to have a lower index of effort and poor states to have a higher relative effort index than capacity index.[6]

Patterns of Tax Preference and Utilization

In examining the use of taxes, a major difference between state and local governments should be borne in mind. Local governments throughout the nation show little variety in the type of tax they utilize. In 1984, 75 percent of their tax revenue was from the property tax,[7] and in thirteen states this figure topped 95 percent, as table 2-8 shows.

State governments, however, show great variety in the use and the weight of their taxes. Sixty years ago states relied heavily on the property

5. For the national government the ability of citizens to pay taxes and the ability of the government to raise taxes are the same. However, for state and local governments this is not true. People live and work in different jurisdictions and this may allow people to escape taxes. Moreover, under certain conditions state and local governments may be able to export taxes to those living in other states or cities.

6. Advisory Commission on Intergovernmental Relations, *Measures of State and Local Fiscal Capacity and Tax Effort* (Washington: ACIR, 1962). ACIR, *Measuring the Fiscal Capacity and Effort of State and Local Areas* (Washington: ACIR, 1971). ACIR, *1981 Tax Capacity of the Fifty States* (U.S. Government Printing Office, 1983), and *1982 Tax Capacity.*

7. See appendix table A-2.

Table 2-6. *Relative Fiscal Capacity and Tax Effort under a Representative Tax System (RTS), by State, 1982*

State	*Fiscal capacity index*	*Tax effort index*
Alaska	312	180
Wyoming	201	105
Nevada	151	63
Texas	130	66
Oklahoma	126	78
Colorado	121	81
Connecticut	117	99
Hawaii	117	105
California	116	99
Delaware	115	84
New Mexico	115	83
North Dakota	115	83
Louisiana	113	82
Montana	110	97
Kansas	106	88
New Jersey	106	113
Florida	104	72
Washington	102	93
Massachusetts	101	119
Maryland	100	106
New Hampshire	100	75
Minnesota	99	111
Oregon	99	95
Illinois	98	107
Nebraska	97	94
Arizona	96	92
Iowa	96	105
Virginia	94	90
Michigan	93	120
New York	92	170
Ohio	92	94
West Virginia	92	86
Missouri	91	82
Indiana	89	88
Pennsylvania	89	106
Vermont	89	103
South Dakota	87	91
Wisconsin	87	128
Idaho	86	85
Utah	86	97
Georgia	84	96
Maine	84	107
Kentucky	82	89
North Carolina	82	94
Rhode Island	81	133
Arkansas	79	81
Tennessee	77	86
Alabama	74	87
South Carolina	74	96
Mississippi	71	92

Source: Advisory Commission on Intergovernmental Relations (ACIR), *1982 Tax Capacity of the Fifty States,* M-142 (GPO, 1985), p. 16.

Table 2-7. *Relative Fiscal Capacity and Tax Effort Based on Per Capita Personal Income, by State, 1981*

State	*Fiscal capacity index*	*Tax effort index*
Alaska	131	455
Connecticut	122	92
New Jersey	116	101
California	114	102
Wyoming	111	141
Illinois	110	99
Nevada	110	83
Maryland	109	96
New York	109	139
Washington	108	85
Colorado	107	88
Delaware	106	91
Massachusetts	106	121
Hawaii	105	125
Kansas	103	92
Michigan	103	109
Minnesota	103	106
Texas	102	83
Iowa	100	101
Nebraska	99	93
Pennsylvania	99	96
Virginia	99	85
Ohio	98	85
Oklahoma	98	95
Florida	97	76
North Dakota	97	94
Rhode Island	97	108
Wisconsin	96	114
New Hampshire	95	74
Oregon	95	105
Arizona	93	101
Indiana	93	86
Missouri	92	81
Louisiana	91	99
Montana	90	117
Georgia	85	93
Idaho	85	88
South Dakota	84	95
Vermont	83	106
North Carolina	82	92
Maine	81	110
New Mexico	81	125
Tennessee	81	81
Kentucky	80	90
West Virginia	80	94
Utah	79	106
Alabama	78	86
Arkansas	77	84
South Carolina	77	93
Mississippi	71	96

Source: ACIR, *1981 Tax Capacity of the Fifty States*, table 4.

Table 2-8. *Distribution of States by Percent of Total Revenue Collected from Property Taxes, 1984*

Percent of revenue	*Number of states*[a]	*Percent of revenue*	*Number of states*[a]
25–30	1	65–70	4
30–35	0	70–75	3
35–40	0	75–80	3
40–45	2	80–85	7
45–50	0	85–90	3
50–55	0	90–95	6
55–60	4	95–100	13
60–65	5		

Source: Census Bureau, *Governmental Finances in 1983–84*, pp. 6–14
a. Includes the District of Columbia (27.7 percent).

tax, which provided more than one-third of their tax revenue. Licenses for motor vehicles and operators were a poor second in importance, death and gift taxes third, and corporation income tax fourth (see table 2-9). In 1984 the first three were not very important. The individual income tax, however, had become a very significant source of revenue. But the most important source of revenue to emerge over the period was taxes on sales and gross receipts, especially at the retail level. Currently, the two main targets of state taxes are consumption and income. The pattern of major state tax revenue sources in 1984 is shown in figure 2-2.

This pattern took shape in the 1930s. In 1927, for example, taxes on sales of specific items brought in 28 percent of state tax collections (of which 58 percent was from taxes on motor fuel); none of the revenue, however, was from general sales taxes. Property tax was losing favor as a source of state revenue, and the expectation was widespread that diminished federal reliance on income tax would bring increasing use by the states. As indicated in chapter 1, this expectation was not fulfilled. With the Great Depression, states did turn to taxation of individual income—six states enacted such a tax in 1933. In those dreary years the falling yield of income tax was distressing to state governments. The unfamiliar and unpopular retail sales tax, however, did bring in the revenue, and thus a trend started.

While the number of state governments utilizing particular types of taxes does not indicate the weight of the taxes, it does reveal a rough pattern of state preferences. In 1984 only two states (New Hampshire and Alaska) failed to utilize either a general sales tax or an individual income tax, a sharp decline since World War II, as the following numbers of states using these taxes show:[8]

8. ACIR, *State and Local Taxes, Significant Features, 1968* (GPO, 1968), pp. 12–13; U.S. Census Bureau, *State Government Finances in 1973* (GPO, 1973), pp. 19, 21; ACIR,

Table 2-9. *Distribution and Rank of Major Sources of State Tax Collections, 1922, 1938, 1948, 1968, and 1984*

Type of tax	*1922*	*1938*	*1948*	*1968*	*1984*
	Percent of total state tax revenue				
Sales and gross receipts	14.1	53.4	59.9	57.6	48.7
General	...	14.3	21.9	28.7	31.8
Selective	14.1	39.2	38.0	28.9	16.9
Motor fuel	1.4	24.8	18.7	14.2	6.3
Alcoholic beverage	...	5.6	6.3	3.1	1.5
Tobacco product	...	1.8	5.0	5.2	2.1
Other	12.8	7.0	8.0	6.4	7.1
Income	10.7	12.2	16.1	24.0	37.8
Individual	4.5	7.0	7.4	17.1	29.9
Corporate	6.1	5.3	8.7	6.9	7.9
License	31.5	16.0	14.5	10.6	6.1
Motor vehicle and operators'	16.1	11.5	8.8	6.8	3.5
Miscellaneous	15.4	4.5	5.7	3.8	2.5
Other	43.7	18.4	9.6	7.7	7.5
Property	36.7	7.8	4.1	2.5	2.0
Death and gift	7.0	4.5	2.7	2.4	1.1
Miscellaneous	...	6.1	2.8	2.8	4.4
	Rank in importance as source of state tax revenue				
Property	1	4	8	8	7
Motor vehicle and operators' license	2	3	3	5	5
Death and gift	3	8	9	9	9
Corporate income	4	7	4	4	3
Individual income	5	5	5	2	2
Motor fuel	6	1	2	3	4
General sales	...	2	1	1	1
Alcoholic beverage	...	6	6	7	8
Tobacco product	...	9	7	6	6

Sources: Census Bureau, *Historical Statistics of the United States: Colonial Times to 1957* (GPO, 1960), pp. 727–28; Census Bureau, *State Government Finances in 1984* (GPO, 1985), table 6, and earlier issues.

Type of tax	*1928*	*1941*	*1951*	*1973*	*1984*
General sales only	0	8	13	9	8
Individual income only	12	14	12	4	3
Both	0	16	19	36	37
Neither	38	12	6	1	2

In 1984 thirty-seven states utilized both taxes; over time the number in this group has grown and may grow somewhat more in the future.

In 1984 twenty-seven states secured half or more of their tax revenues

Significant Features of Fiscal Federalism, 1984 Edition (Washington: ACIR, 1985), tables 53, 60. Hawaii and Alaska are included in all years. Connecticut, Massachusetts, New Hampshire, and Tennessee levied taxes on nonwage income only and therefore are not included in the number of states using both taxes.

Figure 2-2. *Major Sources of State Tax Collections, 1984*

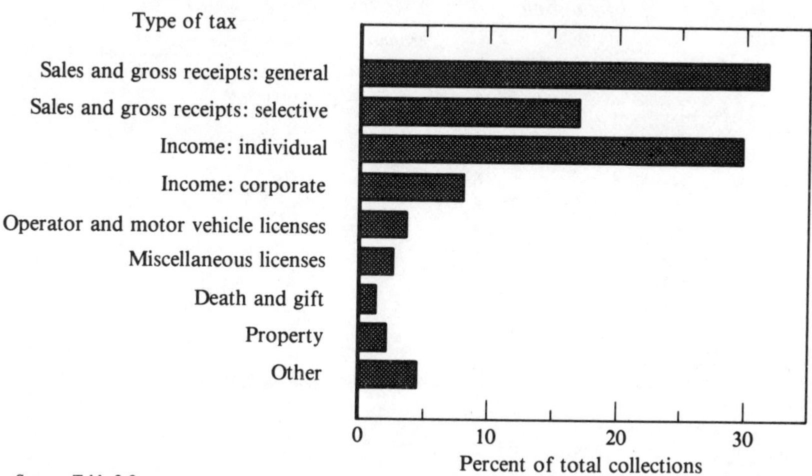

Source: Table 2-9.

from taxes on all sales and gross receipts (see table 2-10). If a comparison is made of percentage tax receipts from individual income tax and general sales tax in the thirty-seven states that in 1984 levied both, it appears that the yield of the sales tax was larger in twenty-one states.[9]

Interstate Tax Competition

In an environment in which both people and capital are highly mobile, the issue of interstate tax competition is important. A difference of opinion exists on whether that competition seriously damages the federal system. As suggested by the ACIR, there would be reason for worry if there were evidence that some states were losing jobs and capital investment to other states because their tax rates were too high or that they were unable to stem the outflow because the tax cuts would curtail spending on public services and cause severe hardship.[10]

But clear evidence on the impact of interstate competition does not exist. Although it is often claimed that differences in state tax rates alone are important elements in the location decisions of people and businesses, there are several reasons to believe that that notion is based on incomplete

9. See appendix table A-10.

10. ACIR, *Regional Growth: Interstate Tax Competition*, A-76 (Washington: ACIR, 1981), p. 4.

Table 2-10. *Distribution of States by Percent of Total State Tax Revenue Collected from Selected State Taxes, 1984*

	Number of states taxing		
Percent of total state revenue	*Total sales and gross receipts*	*General sales and gross receipts*	*Individual income*[a]
80–90	2	0	0
70–80	3	0	0
60–70	6	0	1
50–60	16	4	0
40–50	14	10	7
30–40	4	13	16
20–30	2	16	12
10–20	2	2	3
Less than 10	1	0	1

Source: Appendix table A-10.

a. Alaska, Connecticut, Florida, Nevada, New Hampshire, South Dakota, Tennessee, Texas, Washington, and Wyoming excluded.

analysis. First, interstate differences in levels of taxation are softened by the deductibility of state and local income, sales, and property taxes from the federal income tax base. Further, it is unreasonable to believe that location decisions are made on the basis of tax differences alone. Surely, individuals and businesses are as much interested in the services provided by government.

The ACIR has concluded that "state-local tax differentials, as they influence interregional development, do not currently constitute a problem for our federal system."[11] The evidence simply does not support the idea that tax differences determine location decisions. Certainly they enter into the decision calculus, but the most important factors in determining the sites that business and industry choose have been economic forces such as costs of construction, energy, and labor.[12]

Conclusion

This brief survey indicates that levels of state-local expenditure per capita vary greatly from state to state. Even when the force of differences in the level of state income is excluded, the functional patterns remain diverse, except for expenditure on local schools and housekeeping functions.

11. Ibid.
12. Ibid., pp. 32–34.

Is a "satisfactory" level of governmental services being provided in "poor" states, and if not, how can it be provided? One may believe that a poor state should make an above-average fiscal effort to achieve a satisfactory level. But if, despite such an effort, the level of state-local services remains unsatisfactory, should financial aid be provided by the federal government? If so, in what form? And how should one measure the fiscal capacity and relative tax effort of states? The alternative measures based on personal income per capita and the yield of the representative tax system do not necessarily produce similar results.

With respect to revenues, the plight of many local governments is well known. Despite strong incentives and vigorous efforts, they have been unable to diversify. State governments have more revenue flexibility. Most of them have found taxation of consumption both suitable and responsive to their needs, but forty-three tax individual income and forty-six tax corporate income, and all but one levy death and gift taxes. Several minor taxes are limited to a few states. Severance taxes, now important only for Texas, Alaska, Oklahoma, and Louisiana, can be utilized only by states where mining is significant. Document and stock transfer taxes can raise important revenue only for states like New York and Florida that have a heavy volume of transfers of intangible property.

The major sources of revenue, state and local, are examined in detail in the chapters that follow. The fact that all or most state governments utilize a tax does not mean that they do so in the same fashion. Diversity of practices is the rule.

For many decades neither the state nor local governments have depended wholly on revenue derived from their own sources. Annual intergovernmental transfers have been made, principally through grants-in-aid. The grants, discussed in detail in chapter 3, have served a multitude of purposes, not all of them harmonious.

CHAPTER THREE

Federal Intergovernmental Transfers

A VERY IMPORTANT development during the past fifty years has been the proliferation of intergovernmental grants and shared taxes. These transfers of funds originate either with the federal government, flowing to the states and in a smaller volume to local governments, or with state governments, flowing to local governments. In 1984, federal payments totaled $100 billion and state payments amounted to $108 billion. Although the total amount and scope of these transfers is likely to remain large, their importance in relation to other sources of revenue and to the gross national product is likely to fall in years to come.

Trends in Federal Transfers

The history of federal aid for certain functions, notably road construction and education, is quite old. In 1802, when Ohio was admitted as a state, Congress declared that 5 percent of the proceeds from the sale of public lands in the state should be applied to the construction of roads, and this precedent was followed for other western states.

In 1818 Congress provided that states be given 5 percent of the net proceeds of land sales within their boundaries, with the stipulation that 3 percent be used "for the encouragement of learning, of which one-sixth part shall be exclusively bestowed on a college or university."[1] Thereafter, Congress ceded millions of acres as an endowment for public schools, and, by the Morrill Acts, gave both land and money to establish colleges in every state. These early grants were outright donations with no matching requirement and no federal supervision. Not until 1887, when the Hatch Act made grants to each state to establish agricultural experiment stations, did Congress impose the modest condition that a financial report be submitted annually. And not until 1911, by the Weeks Act, which

1. 3 Stat. 430.

Table 3-1. *Historical Trend of Federal Grant-in-Aid Outlays, Selected Years, 1950–84*

Year	Total grants-in-aid (millions of dollars)[a]	Federal grants as a percent of: Budget outlays — Total	Budget outlays — Domestic[b]	State and local expenditures[c]	Gross national product
1950	2,253	5.3	9.3	10.4	0.8
1955	3,207	4.7	13.7	10.1	0.8
1960	7,019	7.6	17.1	14.7	1.4
1965	10,910	9.2	17.5	15.3	1.7
1970	24,065	12.3	22.0	19.2	2.5
1975	49,791	15.0	20.9	23.0	3.4
1976	59,094	15.9	21.4	24.2	3.6
1977	68,415	16.7	22.4	25.9	3.7
1978	77,889	17.0	22.5	26.8	3.7
1979	82,858	16.5	21.8	26.3	3.5
1980	91,451	15.5	20.6	26.3	3.6
1981	94,762	14.0	18.7	25.2	3.3
1982	88,195	11.8	16.1	21.9	2.9
1983	92,496	11.4	15.8	21.6	2.9
1984	97,577	11.5	16.0	21.2	2.7

Source: *Special Analysis, Budget of the United States Government, Fiscal Year 1986*, p. H-19. The grant-in-aid series in the budget includes aid to the governments of Puerto Rico and U.S. territories; certain payments in kind (primarily commodities donated to school lunch and other nutrition programs); and payments to private, nonprofit entities operating under state auspices or within a state plan. It excludes payments for research conducted by public universities. In all tables years are fiscal unless otherwise noted and figures are rounded.

a. From 1975 forward, includes grants that are not included in budget outlays.

b. Excludes outlays for national defense and international affairs.

c. As defined in the national income and product accounts.

offered grants for forest fire protection, did Congress impose advance federal approval of state plans and federal supervision of performance. Several other federal grants—including highways (1916) and vocational education (1917)—were provided in the next two decades.

A great upsurge in federal grants began in the 1930s. After a temporary subsidence during World War II, growth continued, at first slowly and then explosively, in the 1960s and 1970s. The number of grants rose from 181 in 1963 to 534 by 1981.[2] And, as can be seen in table 3-1, federal expenditures for grants increased continuously throughout the 1960s and 1970s. Not only did the absolute level rise, but grant expenditures came to represent a significantly larger proportion of federal budget outlays—from 9 percent of the budget in 1965 to a high of 17 percent in 1978. From the viewpoint of state and local governments, federal grants evolved into an

2. Advisory Commission on Intergovernmental Relations, *Categorical Grants: Their Role and Design*, A-52 (U.S. Government Printing Office, 1978), p. 25. See also, ACIR, *A Catalogue of Federal Grant-in-Aid Programs* (GPO, 1984), p. 2.

increasingly important source of revenue. In 1965, federal grants were equal to 15 percent of state and local expenditures, but they had risen to over 26 percent by the end of the 1970s—even as state and local revenues from own sources rose at double-digit annual rates.

In the early 1980s, however, both the number of grant programs and the level of federal funding for nonentitlement programs declined as the Reagan administration was able to consolidate many specific or categorical grants into broad-based block grants while simultaneously reducing the level of federal expenditures for these programs. Although federal intergovernmental transfers continued to grow in nominal terms—because of the continued growth of entitlement expenditures—the proportionate share of federal grants in state and local expenditures declined.

These broad trends in the level of aggregate grant expenditures conceal numerous changes in the composition of grant outlays. The dominant categories of the 1950s and 1960s were public assistance and welfare, but late in the 1960s the fastest growing grants were for education and public health. In the 1970s, there were rapid increases in grants for environmental and energy programs as the nation responded to the problems of pollution and to the difficulties created by the oil shocks. In addition, with the implementation of general revenue sharing in 1973, general fiscal assistance increased sharply in relative importance but then declined as nominal expenditures for the program were virtually frozen over the remainder of the decade and into the 1980s. Table 3-2 makes clear that the dominant and growing grant categories for the 1980s were to be income security, health, entitlement programs, and commerce and transportation.

Table 3-3 shows the changing forms of grant assistance. While the consolidation of categorical programs into broad-based grants has reduced the number of grants, specific-purpose grants are still dominant, accounting for around 80 percent of grant outlays. Broad-based grants have gained in importance, accounting for approximately 13 percent of grant expenditures in the 1984 budget. The form of assistance that has shown the most significant relative decline is general revenue sharing.

The Need for Federal Grants

The number and variety of federal grants is extremely large. The basic principles on which this very complex system rests recognize the need to improve allocation of resources, achieve vertical fiscal balance and hori-

Table 3-2. *Federal Grant-in-Aid Expenditures, by Function, 1972, 1976, 1980, and 1984*

Millions of dollars

Function	*1972*	*1976*	*1980*	*1984*
National defense[a]	50	89	93	95
Energy, natural resources, environment	788	3,083	5,862	4,313
Agriculture	496	425	569	1,832
Commerce, transportation	5,065	7,984	13,091	15,015
Community and regional development	2,523	3,445	6,486	5,157
Education, training, employment, social services	9,478	14,141	21,862	16,669
Health	6,010	10,914	15,758	21,837
Income security	9,040	10,948	18,495	25,678
Veterans' benefits	19	52	90	66
Administration of justice	322	795	529	69
General government	66	117	138	171
General fiscal assistance	518	7,102	8,478	6,677
Total	34,375	59,094	91,451	97,577

Sources: *Historical Tables, Budget of the United States Government, Fiscal Year 1986*, table 12.2; *Special Analysis, Fiscal 1986*, table H-16.

a. Includes international affairs.

zontal equity across states, alter the distribution of government responsibility within the federal system, and promote fiscal innovation and experimentation within the federal system.

Allocation of Resources

Intergovernmental transfers can correct inefficiencies that arise when either the benefits or costs of an activity spread beyond the jurisdiction undertaking the activity. For example, there may be geographic spillovers in the benefits associated with a state's spending for education as individuals relocate and apply the skills they have learned in one jurisdiction to jobs in others. In fact, one might say that the entire nation benefits from an educated citizenry. However, if the national benefits of education exceed those accruing to the state or local area, and spending decisions are based on local benefits, a potential inefficiency arises. Thus federal grants that induce greater expenditure on education would be in order. Other notable areas where local benefits and costs may diverge from those of the state or nation include public health, the environment, and transportation.

VERTICAL FISCAL IMBALANCE. The federal government's major sources of revenue are individual and corporate income taxes, both of which are responsive to economic growth and inflation. State and local governments,

Table 3-3. *Federal Expenditures for General-Purpose, Broad-Based, and Specific-Purpose Grants, 1972, 1976, 1980, and 1984*

Type of Grant	*1972*	*1976*	*1980*	*1984*
		Millions of dollars		
General purpose	516	7,150	8,594	6,848
General revenue sharing	...	6,243	6,829	4,567
Other[a]	516	907	1,765	2,281
Broad based	2,855	6,172	10,332	12,961
Community development	...	983	3,902	3,819
Health block grants	90	128	83	1,308
State education block grants	...	...	...	489
Employment and training	...	1,698	2,144	1,545
Social services block grant	1,930	2,251	2,763	2,788
Low-income home energy assistance	...	...	...	2,024
Other	835	1,112	1,440	988
Specific purpose	31,004	52,015	79,354	77,768
Total	34,375	65,337	98,280	97,577
		Percent of total		
General purpose	1.5	10.9	8.7	7.0
Broad based	8.3	9.4	10.5	13.3
Specific purpose	90.2	79.6	80.7	79.7

Source: *Special Analysis, Fiscal 1986*, p. H-22.
a. Includes shared revenues from the Tennessee Valley Authority.

however, rely mainly on property and sales taxes. The revenue elasticities of these levies are significantly lower than that of the income tax.[3] Responsibility for providing the bulk of nondefense public goods and services lies with state and local governments, and demand for these services since the end of World War II has grown more than proportionately to the population. The result has often been a vertical imbalance, with state and local obligations growing more quickly than the ability to finance them. The gap has been closed, at least in part, by federal grants.

The use of grants to offset vertical fiscal imbalance became controversial when the federal budget went into deep deficit in the 1980s and state and local budgets were in surplus. The reduction in federal tax rates mandated by the Economic Recovery Tax Act of 1981 can perhaps be thought of as providing state and local governments with the ability to raise their own tax rates so as to become less dependent on intergovernmental grants. And while direct federal grants have diminished, state and local governments continue to benefit from federal tax expenditures—primarily the deductibility of state and local taxes from income and the exclusion of interest income on state and local bonds.

3. ACIR, "Wage and Income Taxation" (Washington: ACIR, 1985).

HORIZONTAL EQUITY. Yet another rationale for federal fiscal transfers stems from concern for achieving equity among citizens of different states. Because governmental units differ in their fiscal capacities, citizens in a poor area will have to bear a heavier tax burden to provide the same level of public services available to those in a richer area. Federal transfers that vary inversely with a jurisdiction's fiscal capacity—called equalizing grants—can help remove this source of inequity.

Distribution of Power in a Federal System

Grants-in-aid affect the distribution of political and economic power among governmental units. Some observers have viewed with alarm the expanding role of the federal government and are suspicious of the centralization of power that this implies. While accepting the need for federal financial assistance, they are wary of the loss of autonomy that may accompany such aid. From this viewpoint, federal grants offer a middle ground through which financial resources are acquired but direct federal control is avoided. The impact that a grant has on governmental authority depends, however, on the form and conditions of the grant.

Experimentation and Innovation

Grants encourage experimentation and innovation. They offer a way of testing the desirability and feasibility of new programs. The experience and results of these undertakings provide important information to be used in the design of other state or federal programs aimed at similar goals.

Grant Forms

The funds that the federal government offers to state and local governments to achieve specific federal goals are provided through categorical and block grant programs. Undesignated fiscal help is provided through general revenue sharing. In addition to these transfer programs, the federal government provides substantial aid through the transfer of funds implicit in federal tax allowances for state and local taxes and debt.

Categorical Grants

The most common form of federal grant is the categorical grant, designed to achieve well-defined goals of the national government. In practice, categorical grants have found their greatest use in the social services area, with funding for activities ranging from community development to health research to beautification and recreation. The two basic categorical types are project grants, in which federal administrators play a crucial role in choosing recipients, and formula grants, in which recipients meeting the qualifying criteria are entitled to funds based on a legislated formula.

Project grants carry no automatic entitlement to funds, even when statutory criteria are met. Rather, distribution of funds is determined by a federal administrator, based on an application and review process. Funds for formula grants, on the other hand, are made available to all recipients who meet the criteria. Typically, the recipient government is required to match a portion of the federal formula grant and may play a role in determining eligibility criteria.

Block Grants

The block grant, a form of grant that has grown in importance in recent years, gives recipient governments substantial discretion in the use of funds. The Advisory Commission on Intergovernmental Relations (ACIR) defines block grants as those that go "chiefly to general purpose governmental units in accordance with a statutory formula for use in a variety of activities within a broad functional area largely at the recipient's discretion."[4]

The first block grants were offered under the Partnership for Health Act of 1966. It consolidated sixteen categorical grants in the health area and lessened federal requirements for oversight and paperwork. Within a decade, however, numerous categorical programs had been passed in virtually identical areas, leading to an absolute and proportionate decline in the funding of the block grant. A second block grant program, the Omnibus Crime Control and Safe Streets Act of 1968, was also overwhelmed as Congress set more and more requirements on allocations for its various functions and increased reporting and review requirements under the program.

In 1971 President Nixon proposed the consolidation of 129 categorical grant programs into 6 block grant programs in the areas of education, law

4. ACIR, *The Intergovernmental Grant System: An Assessment and Proposed Policies, Summary and Concluding Observations* (GPO, 1978), p. 3.

enforcement, community development, urban development, manpower training, and transportation. This proposal was a response to the many criticisms of categorical grants that had surfaced over the years and an effort to strengthen the role of state and local units in carrying forward social programs. In line with the latter objective, the block grants gave discretion to local officials in the use of the funds in order to strengthen their position relative to federal administrators. The grant programs also reduced compliance costs and lowered or eliminated matching requirements as a way of strengthening the fiscal position of state and local governments.

One of two major block grant programs that came out of the Nixon proposals was Title I of the Comprehensive Employment and Training Act of 1973 (CETA). It provided formula funding (based on unemployment and poverty rates in the applying jurisdiction) to cities and counties to be used in programs providing work experience, job training, placement, and counseling. While giving greater discretion than existed under the previous categorical grants in this area, the federal government maintained substantial influence through requirements that targeted funds to areas in greatest need. Yet CETA went the way of earlier block grant programs as federal officials, fearing that funds were not being properly allocated to meet national priorities, applied more and more restrictions, which led local officials to claim that the program was, in effect, categorical.

The second block grant program created during the Nixon administration, the Housing and Community Development Act of 1974, consolidated seven categorical programs into one block grant. Funds were allocated on a formula rather than a competitive basis. But to qualify for funds, the recipient government had to establish that its program would meet federal requirements. Again, federal review and oversight grew over time as concern mounted that the funds were not being allocated in line with congressional priorities. In addition, the question arose whether localities possessed the administrative structure that would enable them to implement programs effectively without federal oversight and assistance. The evolution of these early block grant initiatives illustrates vividly the fundamental tension underlying the block grant approach—how to give wide discretion to local authorities in the use of the funds but also insure that national intentions are met.

New life was breathed into the block grant approach to intergovernmental funding by the Reagan administration. The Omnibus Budget Reconciliation Act of 1981 consolidated numerous categorical programs into block grant programs and handed primary responsibility for the allocation of funds and administration of the programs to the states. As a result, broad-based block grants grew from 9 percent of federal intergovernmental transfers in the late 1970s to approximately 13 percent in 1984.

Six of the block grants were created by combining existing categorical programs, while three were modifications of existing block grants. The grants provided funding for health services, social services, community development, education, and energy. States were given freedom to allocate funds among programs within each block grant and some leeway in shifting funds between block grant categories.

General Revenue Sharing

Revenue sharing is an approximate synonym for an unconditional or general-purpose grant. By such a grant the donor government does not manifest an interest in specific functions of the recipient government; rather it provides funds that recipients may use as they choose. One rationale offered in support of these general-purpose grants is that the federal government's revenue base is more responsive than other governments' to economic growth, and that a redistribution of funds might help state and local governments accommodate public service demands without major increases in tax rates. Also, by drawing on funds raised through the progressive federal tax system, states would have less need to employ taxes that are widely regarded as regressive.

Revenue sharing is also seen as a force for reducing differences in levels of public service arising from differences in jurisdictions' fiscal capacities. And it is viewed as a way of strengthening the role of states and localities in the federal system by allowing them to set their own spending priorities and develop the administrative ability to carry forward their programs. Grants that permit programs to be tailored to local needs could enhance the effectiveness of government and might encourage greater citizen participation in the local decisionmaking process.

In the fall of 1964 a Task Force on Intergovernmental Fiscal Cooperation, created by President Johnson, recommended federal provision of unconditional grants to state governments.[5] President Johnson did not accept the plan, but in August 1969 President Nixon made a formal pro-

5. This step was inspired by Walter W. Heller, chairman of the Council of Economic Advisers. The task force was headed by Joseph A. Pechman. The proposal came to be known as the Heller-Pechman plan.

posal of revenue sharing to the Congress. That proposal, markedly altered first by the House Ways and Means Committee, then by the Senate Finance Committee, became law in 1972 as the State and Local Fiscal Assistance Act. The act provided general-purpose grants of $30.2 billion for five years, one-third going to the state governments and two-thirds to general-purpose local governments (numbering 38,552 at the beginning of 1972). Each state would be assigned its entitlement under whichever of two allocation formulas gave it the larger amount. Under one formula, adopted from the House bill, allocation was determined by population, per capita income (inversely), urbanized population, tax effort, and revenue collections from personal income taxation. Under the other, adopted from the Senate bill, the determinants were population, per capita income (inversely), and tax effort. The House formula was favorable to highly populated and rich states, the Senate one to rural and poor states.

Because the two formulas would raise the total allotment above the grant total, each state's allotment would be cut by the percentage that all allotments exceeded the grant total. Within each state the formula for allocating funds to general-purpose local governments was, in general, based on three factors: population, per capita income (inversely), and tax effort.[6]

After the initial five-year funding, revenue sharing was extended for four years at close to the same level of funding. In 1980, however, when the program again came up for extension, the relatively healthy condition of state treasuries, combined with the prospect of growing federal deficits, led Congress to exclude the states from revenue sharing. County, city, and township governments would receive $4.6 billion annually through 1986.

Over time, the value of revenue sharing grants has declined, both as a result of appropriations failing to keep pace with inflation and the reduction of nominal funding levels beginning in 1981. In the first full year of the program (1973), revenue sharing accounted for 3.3 percent of spending by local governments but the portion had fallen to 1.5 percent by 1982.[7]

How successful has the program been in promoting its intended goals of

6. Tax effort for a state area is calculated as the ratio of total state and local tax revenue to personal income of the residents of the state. For local governments, tax revenues are adjusted to exclude revenue used to finance education (to get around the awkward fact that, while some general-purpose local governments have the responsibility for financing education, independent school districts sometimes have the responsibility).

7. Census Bureau, *Governmental Finances in 1981–82* (GPO, 1983), tables 5, 8.

fiscal equalization and enhanced local autonomy? Given the small size of the program relative to government expenditure levels, it should come as no surprise that the equalizing effects have been modest. The Congressional Budget Office estimated that, in 1982, interstate disparities in fiscal capacity were reduced by less than 2 percent by general revenue sharing.[8]

Tax Expenditures: An Implicit Grant

The federal government carries out many of its public policy goals through the use of tax expenditures. These expenditures are actually revenue losses that arise from federal tax laws that allow "a special exclusion, exemption or deduction from gross income" or provide "a special credit, a preferential rate of tax or a deferral of tax liability."[9] The value of tax expenditures is estimated as the level of direct budget outlays that would be required to provide the equivalent after-tax benefits.

As can be seen in table 3-4, tax expenditures arise from the deductibility of state and local taxes from federal taxation and the exclusion of interest income on many state and local bonds. Tax deductibility allows state and local units to raise a dollar of tax revenue at less than a dollar cost to their citizens. Interest exclusion enables states and localities to float debt at interest rates lower than would otherwise be the case.

A significant amount of state and local borrowing benefits quasi-public and private entities. Therefore, Congress in 1980 placed limits on tax-exempt mortgage subsidy bonds and on industrial development and revenue bonds. The very existence of tax expenditures aiding state and local governments was threatened in 1985 when the administration introduced a comprehensive tax reform plan that called for elimination of the deduction that taxpayers claim for state and local tax payments. But the House-passed tax reform bill (House Resolution 3838) preserved the deduction, with the Senate signaling its agreement.

Grant Features

Some federal grants are made on the condition that state or local governments pay a portion of program costs. Others require no such matching

8. Congressional Budget Office, *The Federal Government in a Federal System: Current Intergovernmental Programs and Options for Change* (GPO, 1983), p. 104.

9. Congressional Budget Act of 1974.

Table 3-4. *Federal Tax Expenditures Aiding State and Local Governments, 1984*
Millions of dollars

Type of expenditure	*Amount*
Deduction of taxes on	
Owner-occupied homes	8,930
Other, nonbusiness property or activities	21,000
Exclusion of interest on	
State and local debt for	
Public purposes	7,220
Rental housing	665
Private nonprofit educational facilities	120
Private nonprofit health facilities	1,090
Veterans' housing	225
Industrial development bonds for	
Energy facilities	145
Pollution control and sewage and waste disposal facilities	975
Mass-commuting vehicles	40
Airports, docks, and sports and convention facilities	330
Other	1,875
Subsidy bonds for owner-occupied mortgages	1,315
State and local bonds for student loans	220
Total tax expenditure[a]	35,690

Source: *Special Analysis, Fiscal 1986,* p. H-14.
a. Because of interactions among the tax expenditures, individual items cannot be added to obtain a total.

contribution. Another important distinction of grant programs is between those with fixed annual allocations—closed end—and those with indefinite, open-ended allocations.

Matching versus Nonmatching Grants

Both matching and nonmatching grants influence the behavior of recipients, but they do so in different ways. The matching grant effectively reduces the price of the program or activity to the receiving government. For example, a dollar-for-dollar match means that the state or local unit can provide a dollar of expenditure for only half a dollar.

The nonmatching grant simply provides the unit with more money. If it is a specific grant that must be spent on a particular program, then it will lead to a virtual one-for-one increase in expenditure on the designated activity. If it is a general nonmatching grant such as general revenue sharing, then the local unit is free to increase its efforts according to its own priorities.

Some observers have argued that the federal portion of a matching grant should be held to a minimum, leaving the state or local government to finance the bulk of the program costs. They claim that this will discourage wasteful overspending by the receiving unit. But such a view overlooks the relation between the matching rate (the price) and the amount of the activity that is provided. If the goal of the grant is to correct the inefficiencies caused by spillovers or to stimulate expenditure by local units with low fiscal capacity, then the matching rate should be set to achieve these objectives.

Open-ended versus Closed Grants

In most of its grant programs the federal government sets the annual amount of its expenditure; the grants are said to be closed. But a few of the federal government's largest programs—notably medicaid and public assistance—are open-ended. In these cases, "the federal government is committed to paying a fixed percentage of an indefinite total of program costs."[10] While it is possible for the federal government to influence the scale of its outlays by setting stringent eligibility criteria, once these are determined, the federal government relinquishes control over the amount of its spending.

From a budget perspective, the major open-ended grants that form the federal "safety net" reduce the ability of Congress to control its expenditures. When budget discipline is sought, funding cuts typically fall on the more controllable expenditures—such as closed-end grants.

Generally, grants in which the federal government provides matching funds should be open-ended. If federal monies were exhausted, the state or local unit would face the full price of providing the activity, thereby eliminating the federal government's ability to affect the behavior of the recipient.

Problems Raised by Grants

A persistent criticism of the categorical grant system is that the large number of grants has led to overlap and duplication of effort in many program areas. Yet the ACIR, in an assessment of the categorical grant system in 1977, strongly disagreed with this claim, citing instead exces-

10. ACIR, *Categorical Grants*, p. 169.

sive specificity as the primary problem. For example, in a single program area, separate grants often are made for administration, servicing, planning, demonstration, and training (transportation safety offers a good example, with nine categorical grants in which there is little overlap but much fragmentation). In merging grants it is important to find approaches that do not inhibit the capacity "to target, to foster equity, and to differentiate among wide-ranging governmental units."[11]

In addition, recipient governments often find their administrative and compliance problems greatly complicated by the enactment of "crosscutting" regulations that apply to all federal grants. Requirements relating to the environment, equal access to government services, and a host of other government objectives, while often serving worthy goals, have increased the complexity of the grant system.

Project grants are criticized because their proliferation has brought complexity, because they are seen as a threat to federalism, and because they infringe on horizontal equity (equal treatment of equals by government). The most commonly voiced, and well-documented, complaint is that their number and variety are so great that a premium is placed on the ability to know what is available, how to prepare applications, and how to lobby them to funding. This ability and these skills are unlikely to be correlated with governmental needs, with the result that poor governments, and citizens for whom they have responsibility, are neglected.

The most philosophical—and most fundamental—criticism of project grants is that the basis and logic of federalism have been threatened. Programs have been put in operation that conflict with the desires of responsible state and local officials. In such cases rational priorities to demands on limited community resources are difficult to frame; the decisionmaking function at state and local levels is eroded.

The rationale for project grants is that each is transient in its time period, self-limiting in scope, and so framed as to be capable of evaluation. However, project grants often continue long after their purpose of demonstration or experimentation, or innovation, has been fulfilled, thus infringing the principle of horizontal equity. They then render governmental services to people in certain geographical areas that are not rendered to similarly situated people in other areas.

To increase the effectiveness of categorical grants, the ACIR recommended that project grants be employed only when "funds are to be

11. Ibid, p. 290.

targeted precisely to a limited number of recipients having unusually great needs, when national objectives call for selective research and demonstration projects, or when appropriate formulas and eligibility requirements cannot be devised for systematic distribution of program funds." On the other hand, formula grants would be appropriate when "a federal program has nationwide applicability and when objective factors relevant to program needs and recipient jurisdictions' characteristics can be quantified appropriately and interrelated in a formula for the allocation of funds among recipients."[12]

In addition, the ACIR called for consolidation of grants where possible, periodic review, and sunset provisions to assure that programs not outlive their usefulness; greater attention to the timing of state and local budget cycles; exploration of the options for advance funding to enable longer-term planning efforts; rationalization of allocation formulas and maintenance-of-effort requirements; and simplification in the administration of crosscutting requirements.

Functions Aided by Grants

Grants have been used to support a wide variety of functions. The more important categories are grants for education (see chapter 11), for infrastructure, and for income security and health.

Highways

Grants for construction of highways began in 1916 under a formula that allocated funds among the states according to three factors: population, area, and rural delivery and star route mileage. Equal matching with state funds was required. A system of roads to be constructed with federal aid was marked out in the 1920s and a plan of federal supervision was developed. The highway grants became the most orderly part of the whole program of grants. During World War II, plans were made to expand the highway program to accommodate a great postwar increase in traffic and to give more attention to urban roads. The plans came to fruition in the Federal-Aid Highway Act of 1956 which established a trust fund to finance construction of a national system of interstate and defense highways of 41,000 miles (later raised to 42,900 miles).

12. Ibid, p. 294.

In addition, the trust fund provided a stable source of revenue for primary, secondary, and urban roads that are part of the federal-aid system. In addition to the interstate highways, the system includes 260,000 bridges, 260,000 miles of primary arterial roads, 400,000 miles of rural collector routes, and 125,000 miles of urban roads. Revenue to support the trust fund comes primarily from federal excises on motor fuels, tires, trucks, buses, and automotive parts—with users funding 95 percent of federal highway expenditures. The major source of revenue is the motor fuel excise, set at $0.09 per gallon by the Surface Transportation Assistance Act of 1982. The trust fund showed sizable surpluses in the early 1970s which made possible increased federal assistance to mass transit systems, but the energy crises and inflation late in the decade eroded the financial position of both federal and state highway funds. Because construction costs rose faster than the rate of inflation, while the increased costs of fuel encouraged conservation and thus reduced revenues, states and the federal government were forced to increase excises to support highway programs.

Federal expenditures since 1970 have accounted for 30 percent of total government spending on highways, with the states undertaking half of all government expenditures. In 1984 the federal government spent $10.8 billion on highways and highway safety.[13]

The federal contribution to the federal-aid system varies from 90 percent of construction costs for interstate highways to 75 percent for other roads in the system. The distribution of funds for interstate highways depends on each state's share in the total system. Funds for maintenance and repair of the interstate system are determined by age and wear, while allocations for primary and secondary roads depend on the area, rural population, and the mileage of rural and intercity mail routes.

Public Transportation

Federal assistance for transportation began in the early 1960s with efforts to help localities purchase failing private bus lines and upgrade their services. These lines had encountered financial difficulties as the upsurge in automobile use after World War II resulted in a 65 percent decline in ridership between 1945 and 1965.[14] Federal financing of public

13. CBO, *Federal Government in a Federal System*, p. 121; *The Budget of the United States Government, Fiscal Year 1986*, p. 5-69.

14. George W. Hilton, *Federal Transit Subsidies: The Urban Mass Transportation Assistance Program* (Washington: American Enterprise Institute, 1974), p. 3.

transportation increased dramatically in the 1970s; federal spending grew at a 40 percent annual rate through the decade. By 1984 the level had reached $3.8 billion, with approximately 75 percent going for capital programs and the remainder helping to cover the operating deficits of transit authorities.

Unlike federal highway assistance, in which funds are channeled to the states, virtually all aid for public transportation is received by local government transit operators. Six major cities in the 1970s received two-thirds of federal commitments and ten urban areas accounted for 80 percent of federal spending.[15] Federal grants for public transit require that state and local governments match federal funds, contributing at least 20 percent of capital expenditures and 50 percent of operating costs.

With the passage of the Surface Transportation Assistance Act of 1982, public transport secured a long-term source of funding as $0.01 of the increase in motor fuel tax was dedicated to public transit needs. The revenue available in 1984 amounted to $1.1 billion, committed to capital expenditures. Allocations were made by a formula based on population, population density, and mail route mileage.

Airports

Federal funds are made available to airport authorities through a system of matching grants in which the federal share for construction and rehabilitation has varied between 50 percent and 94 percent.[16] Federal support is made possible through a trust fund financed by fees imposed on domestic airline tickets (8 percent), jet fuel ($0.14 per gallon), and aviation gasoline ($0.12 per gallon).

Federal funds for major commercial airports are allocated by a formula that depends on passenger volume, while funds for small general aviation airports are channeled through block grants to the states. The federal share for capital spending has averaged 20 percent at large airports and around 85 percent at general aviation airports.[17]

15. Consad Research Corporation, *A Study of Public Works Investment in the United States,* prepared for U.S. Department of Commerce (GPO, 1980), vol. 3, pp. 52–53. In order of decreasing size of commitments, recipients include the tri-state area constituting New York City and environs, Boston, Chicago, Atlanta, San Francisco–Oakland, Washington, D.C., Philadelphia, Baltimore, Seattle, and Pittsburgh.

16. CBO, *Public Works Infrastructure: Policy Considerations for the 1980s* (GPO, 1983), p. 106.

17. CBO, *Federal Government in a Federal System,* p. 41.

Major U.S. airports suffer from severe congestion. In fact, 90 percent of passenger volume flows through 2 percent of the nation's airports. There have been few efforts to relieve congestion by employing user fees (with or without peak-load features) or by inducing greater use of the nation's 155 general aviation reliever fields. However, Congress made a major commitment in 1982 to increase capital expenditures at airports from the then current $410 million to $900 million by 1987.[18]

Waste Water Treatment

Federal programs to control water pollution began with the Water Pollution Control Act of 1956. Federal activity increased sharply in the 1970s as public concern focused on the nation's environmental and pollution problems. Since 1970, major responsibility for waste water treatment has been vested in the Environmental Protection Agency (EPA), with spending rising from $1.1 billion in 1971 to between $3 billion and $5 billion annually during the period 1975–84.[19]

Until 1985, EPA grants covered 75 percent of the costs of constructing and improving conventional publicly owned treatment works and 85 percent of the cost of an innovative or alternative waste water system. Thereafter, federal matching was slated to decline to 55 percent for conventional and 75 percent for the innovative systems. Localities receiving federal grants are responsible for operation and maintenance expenses.

Recently, states have become more involved in funding waste water treatment projects and have increased their grants to localities, primarily to assist them in meeting federal matching requirements. In 1982, thirty-two states extended grants to localities while thirteen offered loans.[20]

Community and Economic Development

In the Housing Act of 1949 a program of urban renewal was initiated. The program was slow to develop and critics declared that it put too much emphasis on downtown commercial redevelopment, that too much construction favored middle-income housing units, and that relocation was disruptive and costly for the poor. In an effort to meet the criticisms, a model cities program was added in 1966. It allowed selected communities

18. CBO, *Public Works Infrastructure,* pp. 103, 110.
19. CBO, *Federal Government in a Federal System,* p. 130.
20. CBO, *Public Works Infrastructure,* p. 58.

to focus attention on specific blighted areas within their boundaries, and supplementary grants of up to 80 percent of costs were approved for the program.

In 1971, President Nixon proposed special revenue sharing for urban community development. The objective of his better communities bill was to remedy two basic problems afflicting the existing system: excessive fragmentation of aid, and excessive federal controls on spending. This initiative and other pressures to improve the efficiency of federal involvement in redevelopment resulted in establishment of the Community Development Block Grant program (CDBG) in 1974. This program consolidated the major categorical grant programs dealing with urban renewal, neighborhood development, neighborhood facilities, open space, model cities, and water and sewer facilities. The strict requirements of the previous grants were replaced by a system in which localities took primary responsibility for framing and executing their programs, and the federal role was limited to setting broad guidelines and funding the programs. Between 1975 and 1982, $27 billion was spent under the program.[21] In 1983, the federal commitment rose to $4.5 billion, in part because funds were made available through the Anti-recession Jobs Appropriations Act.

The federal guidelines called for the funds to be used for elimination of blight and slums, to meet urgent community needs, and to benefit low-income households. In practice, funds have been used for community facilities, public works projects, social services, and economic development.

Old-Age Assistance and Aid to Families with Dependent Children

Grants for public assistance began with the Social Security Act of 1935 when the federal government gave grants to the states to provide for three categories of needy, unemployable persons—the aged, dependent children, and the blind. The grants reimbursed the states for one-half of their payments to the aged and the blind up to a $30 monthly ceiling, and one-third of their payments for children up to a ceiling of $18 for the first child and $12 for each of the others. As conditions of eligibility, the federal legislation specified citizenship, residency, and age (sixty-five years for old-age assistance, and sixteen years for child dependency). The major responsibility, however, for determining which persons should be put on the welfare rolls was left to the states.

21. CBO, *Federal Government in a Federal System*, p. 132.

The program was rapidly accepted. Soon more liberal federal grants were provided and the format was altered. New categories were added—the permanently and totally disabled in 1950, and medical assistance to the aged, the blind, and the disabled in 1960 and 1962—and the coverage of families with dependent children was enlarged in 1961. The grants were made variable by providing that the federal contribution would be a larger fraction of a low payment than of a high one, and that reimbursements on payments by poor states (those with a low per capita personal income) would be larger than those by rich states.

Very early in the life of public assistance it became clear that interstate differences in standards of eligibility existed that arose out of state differences in definition and appraisal of need, as well as from differences in need itself. It became clear also that limiting grants to specific categories of public assistance had induced states—especially poor states—to load ineligible recipients on the eligible categories in order to minimize their expenditure for general assistance. General assistance, which received no federal grants, was a catchall program covering unemployable persons under sixty-five years of age and not blind, retired persons not in receipt of adequate retirement pensions, or employable persons not covered by unemployment insurance or not in receipt of adequate benefits.

For the first two decades after 1935, grants for old-age assistance absorbed more than half the grants for public assistance and had by far the largest number of recipients. In 1950, however, the number of old-age recipients reached a peak and thereafter began a slow decline as old-age insurance (social security) came to provide for more retired workers. At about the same time, the number of recipients of aid to families with dependent children (AFDC) turned upward, rising from 2.5 million in 1958 to 11 million by the mid-1970s.

What brought the upsurge? The causes were multiple: the greater frequency of divorce, separation, and illegitimacy enlarged the base; and increased awareness of what the law allowed (because of the remarkable spread of legal assistance) and a liberalization of eligibility rules brought a substantial increase in applications.[22]

The growth in the number of eligible AFDC recipients slowed mark-

22. Two Supreme Court decisions helped liberalization. In *King* v. *Smith*, 392 U.S. 309 (1968), the Court held that states could not declare families ineligible because of the presence of a man in the house who was not married to the mother of the family. In *Shapiro* v. *Thompson*, 394 U.S. 618 (1969), the Court eliminated eligibility requirements based on the length of the residence period.

edly in the late 1970s and the number of recipients actually declined—to 10.4 million in 1982—in the aftermath of a tightening of eligibility requirements in the Omnibus Budget Reconciliation Act of 1981. The federal government now sets the categories of people who are eligible. However, it is the state that determines both the value of benefits and the income level that qualifies a family for the program. The federal government pays a share of a state's program costs, inversely proportionate to the state's per capita income, that varies between 50 percent and 78 percent. As a result of differences in state practices, similarly situated families can receive drastically different benefit levels. For example, a family of three with no other income would receive $96 per month in Mississippi but $513 in Connecticut.[23]

In 1973 the AFDC program consumed 64 percent ($7.2 billion out of $11.3 billion) of federal public assistance expenditures. By 1984, the proportion had fallen to 19 percent—$8.9 billion out of a total of $46.8 billion. The reason was the creation and growth of programs such as supplemental security income ($8.5 billion), food stamps ($12.4 billion), child nutrition ($5.7 billion), and housing assistance ($11.3 billion).[24]

Supplemental Security Income

Enacted under the Social Security Amendments of 1972 and put into effect in 1974, the supplemental security income program replaced old-age assistance, aid to the blind, and aid to the permanently and totally disabled. The number of people receiving SSI payments remained near 4 million, but the composition of the recipients shifted away from the elderly and toward the disabled who by 1984 accounted for nearly 60 percent of recipients.

This entitlement differs substantially from AFDC in that the federal government sets both eligibility standards and basic benefit levels and pays the entire amount of the grant. In 1984, individuals were entitled to $314 per month and married couples to $472. However, 42 states supplemented the federal payments, with the add-on going as high as $252 for an individual. Of the $8.5 billion of SSI payments made in 1984, the federal share was 80 percent. There is a significant variation among states in the amount of their payments to needy people.[25]

23. CBO, *Federal Government in a Federal System*, pp. 172–73.
24. *Budget of the United States Government, Fiscal Year 1986*, p. 5-117.
25. *Background Material and Data on Programs within the Jurisdiction of the*

Food Stamps

The original food stamp program, enacted into law in 1964, relied on federal funding but gave states some leeway in restricting eligibility. However, the inequities that arose as a result of differences in state practices induced the federal government to assume more control over the program. In 1971, the various state eligibility criteria were replaced by a uniform federal income standard and, in addition, the level of benefits was tied to the rate of food price inflation. In 1973, eligibility was expanded and coverage was extended to all areas of the country. In 1977 the purchase requirement, in which recipients paid a portion of their income to receive a higher value of food stamps, was replaced by a system in which the benefit was reduced by $0.30 for each dollar of adjusted income above a specified level.

The number of recipients increased from 4.3 million in 1970 to over 19 million in 1975. Severe recession and the 1973 expansion of coverage contributed to the rise, but the most important factor was the program's assumption of responsibility for those who had been served by the food distribution program. By 1978, the total number of recipients had fallen to 15.2 million, but the trend reversed and reached a new peak of 23 million participants in the recession year of 1981. The changes brought about by the Omnibus Budget Reconciliation Act of 1981 caused enrollment in the program to decline to approximately 20 million people.

Because the income measure that is used to determine benefits includes the cash value of payments under the AFDC and SSI programs, the food stamp allotment tends to be greatest in states where payments from these other entitlements are smallest. The average benefit in 1984 was about $50 per month while total expenditures on the program were $12.4 billion.

Housing Assistance

Established in 1937, the housing program is one of the oldest of federal assistance programs. The objective was to stimulate construction activity during the depression. About 460,000 units were constructed between 1937 and 1961. However, the program was not particularly successful in reaching the needy. In the 1960s Congress made public housing more

Committee on Ways and Means, Committee Print, House Committee on Ways and Means, 99 Cong. 1 sess. (GPO, 1985), pp. 433–35.

accessible to the needy through programs that subsidized operating as well as capital costs and by limiting rent payments to 25 percent of the tenant's income.[26]

The focus of federal assistance has changed over time, with the emphasis shifting away from government-sponsored construction and ownership to subsidies of rents on privately owned buildings. In 1984 only 22 percent of housing assistance went to public housing while the bulk of the remainder was used to underwrite rent assistance.[27]

This housing program is not an entitlement. In 1982 just over 21 percent of eligible recipients received housing assistance.[28] The Budget Reconciliation Act of 1981 targeted funds to low-income recipients and required tenants to pay 30 percent of their adjusted income for housing.

Public Health

After precarious beginnings in the years following World War I, a broad support program for health services was set up in 1935. Grants were provided for public health work, maternal and child health services, and so on. In 1946 another aid program was added. By the federal Hospital Survey and Construction Act (Hill-Burton), the states were given grants to make inventories of their facilities to determine their hospital needs, and further grants were provided to construct both public and nonpublic facilities. Appropriations started at $75 million a year and were soon enlarged in annual amount and scope. Allocations to the states were based on population and a variant of per capita income.

The largest program in the health area, however, is medicaid. Its beginnings can be traced to 1950, when Congress broadened the definition of public assistance to include vendor payments: direct payments by government to doctors and others for services rendered to persons on welfare rolls. A further step along the road of recognizing the medical needs of welfare recipients was taken when the Social Security Amendments of 1960—known as the Kerr-Mills Act—established a new category of medical assistance to the aged (MAA), offering to reimburse part of the cost of state programs that provide medical care for "medically indigent" aged persons. The indigent who were blind, and the disabled, were added in 1962. The federal matching ratios (ranging from 50 percent to 80 percent) were to be in inverse relation to state per capita income.

26. CBO, *Federal Government in a Federal System,* p. 180.
27. *Budget of the United States Government, Fiscal Year 1986,* p. 5–117.
28. CBO, *Federal Government in a Federal System,* p. 181.

The grants proved attractive mostly to governments of rich states, and this fault induced Congress, in 1965, to create medicaid, which extended the benefits of medical care to all recipients in federally aided state public assistance programs and also to the "medically indigent." The matching provisions of Kerr-Mills were, in general, carried over to medicaid.

States still have substantial leeway to influence both the number of recipients and the types of services that are offered. The federal government requires that all states provide certain minimum benefits, but beyond that many services that are eligible for federal matching are offered only at the option of the state. In addition, the states' freedom to determine eligibility for AFDC and SSI benefits means that the income levels at which the entitlement takes hold vary across states. In 1984, the average federal contribution was 59 percent, based on a state's per capita income; the contribution varied, however, from 50 percent for residents of some states to 78 percent for residents of others. Federal payments in 1984 totaled $20 billion to 22 million clients, with 45 percent of the funds going to the care of children (AFDC), 25 percent to adults (under AFDC), 15 percent to the aged, and 13 percent to the medically needy.[29]

Medicaid payments rose much faster than had been anticipated, primarily because of the increase in eligible recipients from 11 million in 1968 to 22 million in 1980. Addition of new services and inefficient delivery of some benefits helped to increase health care costs. In response to the rapid growth of medicaid payments—15 percent annually between 1975 and 1980—the Omnibus Budget Reconciliation Act of 1981 provided for reduction of federal matching payments to states that could not successfully reduce their error rates and the growth of vendor payments. States were also given greater flexibility in adopting new approaches to health care provisions such as alternative hospital reimbursement systems. And the Tax Equity and Fiscal Responsibility Act of 1982 permitted states to require recipients to make small copayments. These federal adjustments were preceded and accompanied by reductions in states' benefits, which were largely a result of their poor fiscal condition during the recession at the beginning of the 1980s.

Continuing Issues in Grant Design

It is plausible to argue that direct federal grants to local governments are not compatible with the logic of federalism and are, moreover, admin-

29. *Background Material and Data*, pp. 222–25.

istratively awkward. Not only are localities the legal creation of the states but to work through fifty would appear to be better than to work through thousands of local governments.

But both difficult cases and the desire by several administrations to improve the condition of urban centers and distressed areas have operated to impair this general position. For example, when the federal government, by extensive construction and operation of defense facilities in small geographic areas, swells the school enrollment while not adding to taxable local real property, federal grants to construct and operate schools seem justifiable. Debate over whether or not the state government should be the intermediary seems academic.

Other types of federal grants to local governments (listed in table 3-5) may seem to offer less plausible grounds for such direct action. But the fact is that the problems of urban renewal, mass transit, airport construction, and low-rent public housing are primarily local problems. In addition, both Democratic and Republican administrations have often viewed direct aid to localities as the preferred way of achieving their social objectives.

When Lyndon Johnson took office, federal grants-in-aid were confined to a few specific areas, with programs in transportation and income security consuming two-thirds of federal grant monies. But the pursuit of Johnson's Great Society program was to greatly expand and alter the form of federal transfers. In the two years from 1965 to 1967, the Eighty-ninth Congress increased the number of grant-in-aid programs from 221 to 379, relying almost exclusively on categorical grants. Landmark legislation was enacted in health (medicaid), education (Elementary and Secondary Education Act of 1965), manpower training (Economic Opportunity Act of 1964), and nutrition. Moreover, special emphasis was given to the needs of urban areas, with legislation aimed at the problems of inadequate housing and urban blight. President Johnson saw the elimination of these problems as a national goal and favored specific project grants as the primary way of achieving these objectives. During the Eighty-ninth Congress, over 80 percent of the newly enacted programs were funded by project rather than formula grants. With the emphasis on aid for cities, funds for model cities and urban renewal projects flowed directly to localities rather than through the states. Anxious to achieve the desired results, federal legislators gave little thought to the impact on state and local fiscal relations.

During the Nixon and Ford administrations, emphasis shifted from

Table 3-5. *Federal Intergovernmental Transfers to Local Governments, 1984*
Millions of dollars

Purpose	*Amount*
Education (impact aid and other)	1,376
Urban renewal and community development	6,012
Sewerage	386
Welfare	382
Health and hospitals	277
Highways	234
General local support	132
Other	7,574
All grants	16,372
General revenue sharing	4,540
Total	20,912

Source: Census Bureau, "Annual Survey of Governmental Finances, 1984"; data furnished by the Census Bureau.

categorical aid to forms of assistance that gave wider discretion to recipient governments. Perhaps surprisingly, however, most of the initiatives during the period tended to favor local rather than state governments. The two major block grants—for the CETA and CDBG programs—benefited localities rather than states, while Nixon's general revenue sharing gave two-thirds of the assistance to local units.

During the Carter administration, localities continued to receive large amounts of direct assistance, both as a result of previous programs and because of the president's concern about the problems of large cities. With the election of Ronald Reagan, however, the pendulum began to swing back toward an expanded role for the states and, like Presidents Eisenhower, Nixon, and Ford, President Reagan sought to alter the form of federal aid to give wider discretion to the recipient government. The major step was taken through the Omnibus Budget Reconciliation Act of 1981 in which numerous categorical programs were consolidated into block grants.

Another matter of continuing debate in grant design is the equalization brought about by the redistribution of income among the states. Two sets of forces are at work. One is tax equalization, the process by which money that is eventually spent as grants is collected through the federal tax system. The other is formula equalization, which Congress provides by its allocation of grants and by the matching requirements it sets. By making relative capacity a determinant in allocating grants or in setting matching requirements, federal formulas explicitly recognize differences in the fiscal capacity of states. A variable commonly used is per capita income;

grant allocation is larger, or matching ratio smaller, when per capita income is low than when it is high.

A rough measurement of the redistribution of income by states can be made from estimates of the incidence of federal taxes on the residents of each state. The Tax Foundation has developed data that allow the redistribution to be divided into the portions due to tax equalization and to grant equalization. In 1982, federal grants-in-aid to state and local governments averaged $369 per capita—ranging from $894 in Alaska to $244 in Texas (see appendix table A-11).

The tax burden of providing these grants does not fall evenly on the states. The Tax Foundation's calculations of the per capita tax burden of supporting the federal grant system in 1982 (assuming that for the United States as a whole that tax burden is equal to the value of grant payments) range from $548 in Alaska to $238 in Mississippi. The redistributive impact of the grant system depends on a state's grant receipts and tax burden relative to the national average. If each state received and financed $369 in grants per capita, then the redistributive impact of the program would be zero. Yet for a poor state such as Mississippi, per capita grants ($420) were greater than the national average while the tax burden ($238) was less. Mississippi received $51 more in grants per capita than the national average while its tax burden was $131 less, which together resulted in a total redistribution of $182 per capita in the state's favor. For a relatively rich state like Connecticut, however, whose grants receipts were $14 less and tax burden $127 more than the U.S. average per capita, there was a negative per capita redistribution of $141.

CHAPTER FOUR

State Intergovernmental Transfers

A SECOND broad stream of intergovernmental transfers flows from state to local governments. Local governments, constitutionally, are the creatures of the states, and the states have spawned a large progeny. When the first count was made, for the early 1930s, the total number of all types of governmental units in the United States was approximately 175,000. By 1967 it had fallen to 81,299 as a result of a steep decline in the number of school districts. But by 1982 the number had risen to 82,341, the reason being the growing number of special districts (see table 4-1). Undoubtedly, in many parts of the United States the number of governmental units is still excessive.

Structure of Local Governments

An important characteristic of many local governments is the overlapping of three or four—and occasionally seven or eight—layers of governmental units in the same geographic area. In addition to a local "general" government such as a township or municipality, there may be school districts, sanitary districts, counties, soil conservation districts, drainage districts, and so on. In terms of public finance, the diversity and proliferation seldom make sense. In rural areas, small and overlapping units often lack the resources to perform their functions efficiently.

In urban areas, governmental units of very unequal financial strength cannot provide a uniform level of service; the very poor ones cannot even provide the minimum level that the urban community as a whole requires. The problems are most acute and intractable in metropolitan areas, which are composed of a central city or cities and a variety of suburban units. In 1982 the 305 standard metropolitan statistical areas and New England county metropolitan areas of the nation had 29,861 local governments—more than one-third of all local governments in the nation. The Chicago metropolitan area alone contained 1,194 units, including 6 counties, 113

Table 4-1. *Number and Type of Governmental Units in the United States, 1957, 1967, 1977, and 1982*

Unit of government	Number of units				Change in number of units	
	1957	1967	1977	1982	1957–77	1977–82
National	1	1	1	1	0	0
State	48	50	50	50	2	0
County	3,047	3,049	3,042	3,041	−5	−1
Municipality	17,183	18,048	18,862	19,076	1,679	214
Township and town	17,198	17,105	16,822	16,734	−376	−88
School district	50,446	21,782	15,174	14,851	−35,272	−323
Special district	14,405	21,264	25,962	28,588	11,557	2,626
Total	102,328	81,299	79,913	82,341	−22,415	2,428

Sources: U.S. Census Bureau, *Census of Governments, 1957,* vol. 1, no. 1: *Governments in the United States* (Government Printing Office, 1958), p. 1; *1982,* vol. 1: *Governmental Organization* (GPO, 1983), p. vi, table A. In all tables years are fiscal unless otherwise noted and figures are rounded.

townships, 261 municipalities, 313 school districts, and 501 special districts.[1] While unification is understandably difficult and may not be wise, problems of sanitation, water supply, police, and transportation need coordination. In some areas, functional intergovernmental schemes that do not change the existing governmental structure have been put into operation—for example, the Metropolitan Water District of Southern California. More comprehensive structural integration is often desirable, but annexation, the integrating technique favored a few decades ago, has been halted in many states by the opposition of suburban areas.

The growth of special districts in recent years has been remarkable. These districts have peculiar features. They are created usually to perform a single function and they overlap geographically; 43 percent of special districts raise revenue through property taxation, while the remainder are funded by charging for services or are dependent on grants from other governments.[2]

The organization of local governments is not, to be sure, merely a matter of administrative and fiscal efficiency. In a democracy a wide variation in performance is—and should be—tolerated. However, the variation now exceeds acceptable limits. The obstacles to change here are patent and powerful: local loyalties, vested interests, urban-rural antagonisms, the inertia of the status quo. Most of the blame for the excessive

1. U.S. Census Bureau, *Census of Governments, 1982,* vol. 1: *Governmental Organization* (U.S. Government Printing Office, 1983), pp. xviii, 42; vol. 5: *Local Government in Metropolitan Areas* (GPO, 1983), p. 37.

2. Census Bureau, *Census of Governments, 1982,* vol. 1, p. xi.

amount of local government fragmentation is to be placed on the states. State constitutions and statutes have often made change difficult by placing inflexible restrictions on the power of localities to handle public services. Some state constitutions, for instance, prescribe a pattern of local government. Debt and tax limits for local governments are widespread, and their operation sometimes reinforces the maintenance of overlapping units whose separate limits add up to more than the amount the electorate might allow in consolidated government. Legislation limiting taxes and expenditures has also stimulated the use of special districts. The effect of these attempts to constrain general revenues and expenditures may be to shift responsibility for providing some services from general government to special districts.

The federal government must bear a portion of the blame because a good many special districts have been created through its "direct advocacy."[3] Specialists in the Department of Agriculture prefer to deal with officials of soil conservation districts (2,409 in 1982) rather than with county officers. Federal specialists in housing prefer to deal with officials of housing and urban renewal districts (3,296 in 1982) rather than with city officers. The pragmatic tendency of federal agencies to develop local counterparts has complicated local government structure and encouraged isolation of units within urban areas. Against the short-run convenience of special-purpose districts must be set the long-run confusion arising out of uncoordinated area development.

Finally, the system of federal and state grants to localities has often served as an impediment to local reorganization. Grants that support functionally distinct programs reduce pressure at the local level to consolidate responsibility for groups of programs. Careful consideration of the assignment of local responsibilities based on local needs and resources is discouraged, leading to inefficient and irrational local government structures and a weakening of accountability for local actions.

Yet, given the will, much can be done—witness the great decline in the number of school districts since 1957.[4] Another encouraging sign is the increased propensity of states to create some type of mechanism to study and advise on issues related to the viability and structure of local govern-

3. John C. Bollens, *Special District Governments in the United States* (University of California Press, 1957), p. 250.

4. See table 4-1. An emphatic warning against assuming that "fragmentation of authority and overlapping jurisdictions are the primary causes of urban ills," and that consolidation is the remedy, is given by Robert L. Bish and Vincent Ostrom, *Understanding Urban Government* (Washington: American Enterprise Institute, 1973), p. 1.

ments. Eighteen states have created advisory commissions on intergovernmental relations, and every state has conducted an interim study of some aspect of state-local relations.[5] States might consider removing the self-imposed constitutional and statutory inflexibilities that stand in the way of governmental reorganization. And they should consider making financial aid to local governments conditional on progress in structural reorganization. More efficient local governments would allow a larger measure of local financial responsibility in provision of local services. And it is a truth, as well as a truism, that only when local governments are strong does democracy flourish.

Transfers to Local Governments

The arguments for state grants to local governments are much the same as those for federal grants to subnational units. Through its grants the state can redistribute resources to aid localities with low fiscal capacities and can help in the provision of goods of local merit or those that have positive spillovers. Furthermore, the states' tax bases are generally more income elastic than those of localities and thus grants provide a means of achieving vertical balance.

There are two basic types of intergovernmental transfers from state to local governments: grants, or appropriated funds, and shared taxes—that is, portions of tax yields. State grants to local governments are straightforward transfers of funds. In the case of shared taxes, the level of government that is most fitted to collect a tax efficiently assigns all or part of the collections on some basis to the government that gives up the tax. For example, a state government might assume the sole right to tax the income from intangible property, promising to distribute all or some share of the proceeds to local governments according to the place of residence of the owners; or it might assume the sole right to tax motor vehicles as property, promising distribution of the proceeds to local governments according to where the vehicles were principally garaged.

Sharing of taxes frequently began when a state government withdrew some types of property that could not be efficiently or equitably taxed by local governments from the base of the general property tax. As a quid pro

5. Advisory Commission on Intergovernmental Relations, *State-Local Relations Bodies: State ACIRs and Other Approaches,* M-124 (Washington: ACIR, 1981), p. 45.

quo, revenue was assigned to local governments to make the move palatable. In the first instance the states tended to base their distributions on such criteria as location of the property, prior assessed value of the property, and prior local revenue from the property. Quite frequently it turned out that because of the greater efficiency of state administration, the amounts collected by the state were much in excess of the prior collections of the local governments. Moreover, distribution according to origin of the revenue favored rich localities. Accordingly, the basis for sharing was shifted, usually toward some measure of local government need, and specific directions for use of the revenue were added. A variety of formulas was framed, the particular outcome depending on the tug and pull between those local governments wanting to retain a favorable allocation and those wanting a change appropriate to their needs. As a result, the original basis for tax sharing has been overlaid by numerous modifications that usually tend to allocate the proceeds according to some measure of local need, and to commit them to designated purposes.

In these two respects the original logic of the shared tax has been impaired and shared taxes, as now used, have come to resemble conditional grants. An important difference is, however, that the annual amount of taxes shared depends on the amount collected. It is therefore unstable, being larger in boom and smaller in recession years. This is awkward for local governments, since their spending has the opposite variation. Moreover, in many states the criteria for sharing different taxes are varied and complicated. They have grown ad hoc over the decades. At the very least it would make sense to pool the state collections, to distribute them according to a single formula, and to reduce earmarking. Then the shared taxes would become an unconditional grant whose annual amount would depend on the amount of taxes collected, whereas the amount of a conventional grant would depend on an annual legislative decision.

The distinction between shared taxes and grants has become so blurred that the Bureau of the Census does not provide separate figures for them. Instead, figures for state payments to local governments are split into two categories, one for those that support general local government and another for those that support specific functions such as education, highways, and welfare. In terms of the amount of revenue collected, state sharing is important for income taxes, liquor store profits, motor vehicle licenses and registration fees, gasoline taxes, sales taxes, tobacco taxes, and pari-mutuel taxes.

Table 4-2 and figure 4-1 show that from 1948 until the mid-1960s, state

Figure 4-1. *Tax Collections and General Expenditure of State and Local Governments, 1948–84*

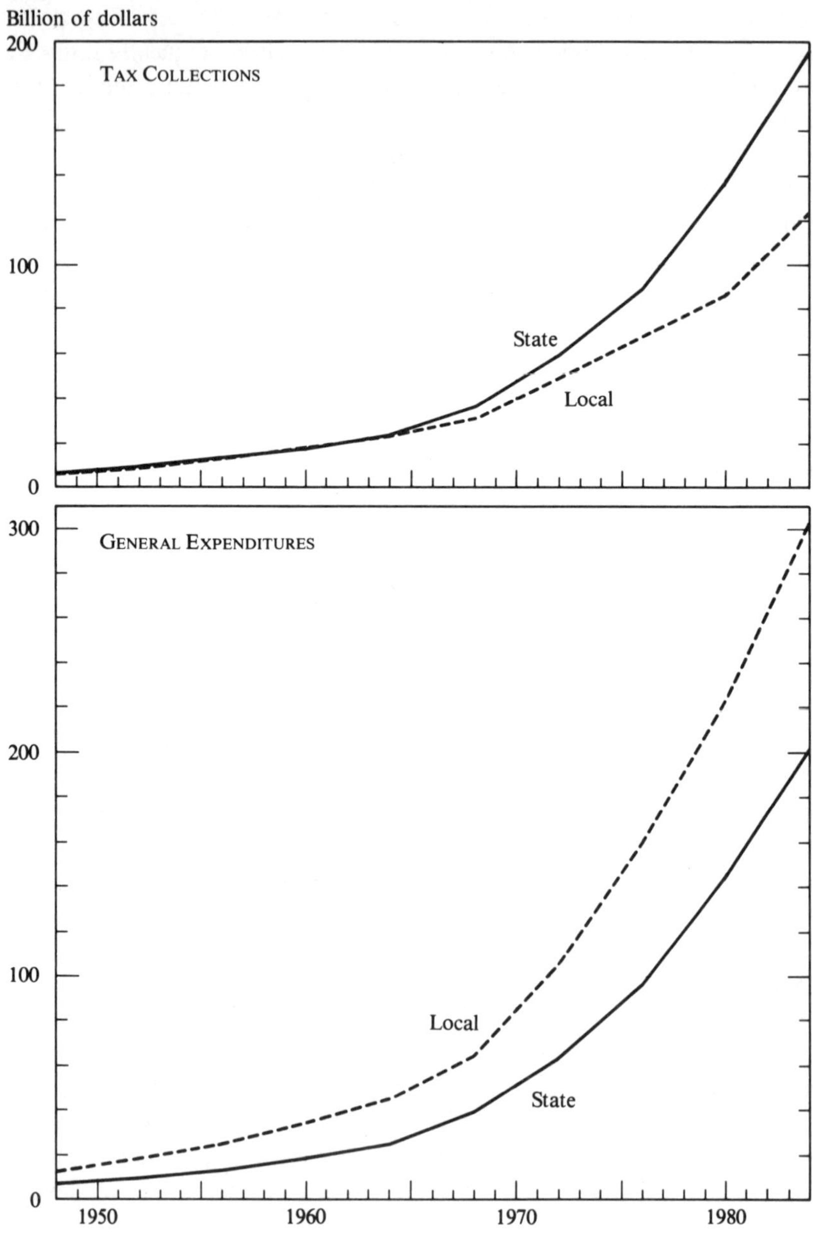

Source: Table 4-2.

Table 4-2. *Tax Collections and Direct General Expenditure of State and Local Governments, Selected Years, 1948–84*

Billions of dollars

	Tax collections			*Expenditures*		
Year	*State*	*Local*	*Total*	*State*	*Local*	*Total*
1948	6.7	6.6	13.3	6.2	11.5	17.7
1952	9.9	9.5	19.3	8.7	17.4	26.1
1956	13.4	13.0	26.4	12.3	24.4	36.7
1960	18.0	18.1	36.1	17.9	33.9	51.9
1964	24.2	23.5	47.8	24.3	45.0	69.3
1968	36.4	31.2	67.6	38.4	64.0	102.4
1972	59.9	48.9	108.8	62.1	104.8	166.9
1976	89.3	67.6	156.8	95.8	159.7	255.6
1980	137.1	86.4	223.5	143.7	223.6	367.3
1984	196.8	123.4	320.2	201.3	302.0	503.3

Sources: Census Bureau, *Historical Statistics of the United States: Colonial Times to 1957* (GPO, 1960), pp. 727–30; Census Bureau, *Governmental Finances in 1983–84* (GPO, 1985), tables 4, 6, and earlier issues.

and local governments ran neck and neck in terms of overall tax collections. Since then state collections have outpaced local, and the likelihood is that the spread will increase. And yet, in terms of expenditure, local governments have always outstripped the state governments.

The gap between local revenue and expenditure—$178.6 billion in 1984—has been largely filled by intergovernmental grants from both the state and federal levels. In effect, these higher-level governments have taken over from localities much of the financial responsibility for functions such as education, highways, and welfare, leaving administration and performance of the programs primarily in local hands. The aid in such cases serves as an alternative to state assumption of full responsibility for the particular service. Centralization at the state level is often not the best move. State aid offers a middle course; it leaves performance of the specific governmental activity in local hands, while providing state financial assistance and a modicum of overall direction. Table 4-3 shows the total amount and breakdown by function of state transfers to local governments in 1984.

Intergovernmental expenditure by states on a significant scale is a phenomenon of the 1930s, although a structure had been built up earlier. In 1902, the first year for which the Bureau of the Census supplies figures, state intergovernmental expenditure was $52 million. It is a mark of the limited scope of state governmental activities that this sum amounted to 38.8 percent of total state direct general expenditure (see table 4-4). Local governments were then relatively much more important, and the $52 mil-

Table 4-3. *State Intergovernmental Payments, by Purpose, 1984*
Billions of dollars

Purpose	*1984*
Specific	97.6
Education	67.5
Public welfare	13.6
Highways	5.7
Other[a]	10.8
General (local government support)	10.7
Total	108.3

Source: Appendix table A-12.
a. Includes housing and urban renewal, libraries, correction, hospitals, airports, and others.

Table 4-4. *State Intergovernmental Expenditure, State Direct General Expenditure, and Local General Revenue, Selected Years, 1902–84*

				State intergovernmental expenditure as a percent of	
Year	*State inter-governmental expenditure (millions of dollars)*	*State direct general expenditure (millions of dollars)*	*Local general revenue (millions of dollars)*	*State direct general expenditure*	*Local general revenue*
1902	52	134	854	38.8	6.1
1927	596	1,380	5,903	43.2	10.1
1938	1,516	2,576	6,651	58.9	22.8
1948	3,283	6,186	11,373	53.1	28.9
1957	7,440	13,647	25,531	54.5	29.1
1967	19,056	34,249	58,235	55.6	32.7
1978	67,287	112,515	194,783	59.8	34.5
1984	108,373	201,310	323,236	53.8	33.5

Sources: Census Bureau, *Historical Statistics*, pp. 728–29; Census Bureau, *Governmental Finances in 1984*, tables 5, 13, and earlier issues.

lion received by them from state governments amounted to only 6.1 percent of their general revenue. By 1927, state intergovernmental payments had risen to $596 million—totaling 43.2 percent of total state expenditures and 10.1 percent of local general revenue. The 1930s and the postwar period brought further absolute increases. In recent years state intergovernmental expenditure has been more than half of state direct general expenditure and over 30 percent of local general revenue. This development has been a mixed blessing from the viewpoint of local governments. While grants have filled the gap between local revenues and the costs of providing local services, they have also reduced the discretionary authority of local officials. Typically, the uses of grant funds are tightly cir-

Figure 4-2. *Distribution of State Intergovernmental Expenditure, by Function. Selected Years, 1902–84*

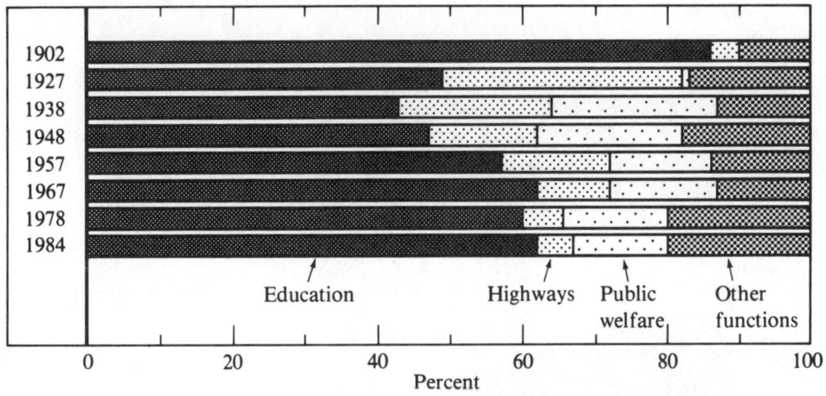

Source: Appendix table A-12.

cumscribed while even broad-based grants carry "crosscutting" requirements.

Significant changes have taken place, over the decades, in the functional distribution of specific-purpose state aid (see figure 4-2). In 1902 education was the major recipient—86 percent of the total. In 1984 it was still the function receiving by far the largest slice—62 percent. But public welfare began to secure important state aid in the 1930s and by 1984 accounted for 13 percent of total state aid.

These developments mean, of course, a great increase in state-local collaboration. Figure 4-3 shows that state governments now provide a good slice of the finance of important functions of local governments—in 1984, over 87 percent of public welfare, 53 percent of education, and 35 percent of highways—and they give a good deal of direction as well. Some states have gone so far as to assume complete control of some functions.

In terms of general-purpose aid, as table 4-3 shows, state governments provided $10.7 billion to local governments in 1984 (9.9 percent of all state intergovernmental payments). This type of aid has grown relatively in recent years. Here again a wide variation prevails in state practice. In 1984, two states gave no general-purpose grants, while at the other end of the range, five gave over $150 per capita (Wyoming and Alaska gave $311 and $281 per capita, respectively). Thirty-two states gave per capita grants

Figure 4-3. *State Intergovernmental Expenditure as a Percent of Local Expenditure, by Function, Selected Years, 1902–84*

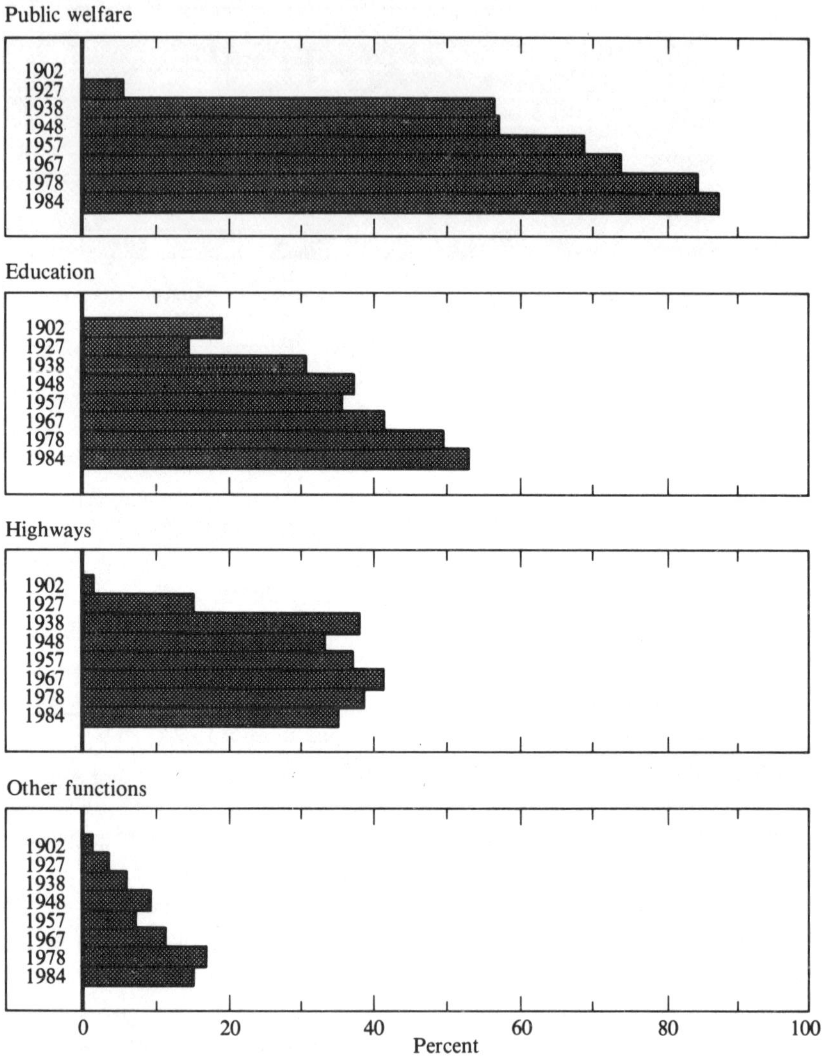

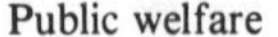

Source: Appendix table A-13.

ranging up to $50 and eleven grants of $50–$150.[6] The source of these grants is always shared taxes.[7]

Conclusion

Sometimes states, through intergovernmental transfers to existing local governmental organizations, have perpetuated the lives of inefficient units and placed barriers in the way of desirable reform. State governments should be alert to couple aid with reorganization whenever reorganization has merit.

The clutter of grants and shared taxes that make up state intergovernmental payments is an untidy accumulation that should be consolidated. No pattern for the conversion can be prescribed that would be suitable for all states; diversity is appropriate. In states that are compact in size and homogeneous in economic structure, a centralizing program with a bias toward direct state performance of services and collection of revenues is feasible and desirable. In large states, on the other hand, strengthening of local governments is likely to be a better alternative, and here state grants are a useful instrument. The distribution formulas for many specific-purpose grants now in use are faulty. They should be reshaped by precise definition of the services for which they provide support. In addition, the local ability to finance a program for a service should be defined and measured. Adequate and objective evidence on which to base a quantification of need and ability is not easy to secure. State governments can, however, make greater use of general-purpose grants, for they can serve to equalize the revenue capacities of similar types of local governments.

6. Census Bureau, *State Government Finances in 1984* (GPO, 1984), tables 14, 36.

7. For details see ACIR, *Federal-State-Local Finances: Significant Features of Fiscal Federalism, 1973–74 Edition* (GPO, 1974), tables 53–56.

CHAPTER FIVE

State Taxes on Individual Income and Sales

Whoe'er expects a faultless tax to see
Expects what neither is, nor was, nor e'er shall be.

John Ramsay McCulloch

BEFORE the twentieth century, taxation of individual incomes by the states had a long and unsuccessful history. So marked was the failure that many eminent students of public finance expressed the opinion that failure was inevitable. The key to the failure was ineffective administration. One economist, T. S. Adams, believed that "past failure did not preclude future success," and his faith was justified by the marked success of the Wisconsin tax of 1911. This success rested on "two administrative innovations": centralized administration and use of information-at-source returns.[1] Moreover, the Wisconsin tax, be it noted, antedated the Sixteenth Amendment to the Constitution which made a federal income tax possible.

Taxes on Individual Incomes

Despite the enactment of a federal tax on individual incomes in 1913 and the remarkable extension of federal coverage and rates during World War I, state income taxes at this time experienced a wave of popularity. By 1920, nine states and Hawaii were levying the tax. In the next decade five more states were added; by 1940 the total was thirty-one states plus Hawaii. In the next two decades only Alaska (1949) joined the ranks. Since 1961, eleven states have instituted the tax and one (Alaska, 1979) has dropped it. The total as of 1984 was forty-three, of which forty could be described as broad-based.[2]

1. Clara Penniman and Walter W. Heller, *State Income Tax Administration* (Chicago: Public Administration Service, 1959), pp. 5–6.

2. Plus the District of Columbia, which enacted an income tax in 1939. See Advisory Commission on Intergovernmental Relations, *Significant Features of Fiscal Federalism, 1984 Edition* (Washington: ACIR, 1985), p. 124.

Individual income taxation currently ranks second as a producer of state revenue. In 1973 it produced approximately 23 percent of state tax collections; by 1984 this proportion had increased to 30 percent. Several factors explain the increasing importance of the state income tax. Higher tax rates, a broad base, effective administration (especially through withholding), and a relatively high income elasticity have combined to produce an important revenue raiser for states.[3]

Diversity in State Yields

Reliance on revenue from taxing income varies among the states. For Oregon in 1984 it accounted for 65.8 percent of all tax collections and, as table 5-1 shows, it provided 40.7 percent or more of tax collections for seven other states. On the other hand, for some states the yield was very modest.

This same diversity is displayed by per capita figures (table 5-1). Per capita collections for the highest state, Delaware, were many times those of states such as Louisiana and New Mexico where relatively little use had been made of the tax. The eight states with the highest per capita collections accounted for over half of total collections although their population was only one-third of the total population of the forty-three states that have a general income tax. Per capita figures do not, of course, take account of the inequality of the states in tax base, rate structure, exemptions, deductions, and so on.

The value of personal exemption level varies rather dramatically among states. In ten states the value is $1,000, similar to the exemption level under the federal personal income tax. But in seven states and the District of Columbia it is less than $1,000, and in other states considerably higher. In Mississippi, for example, the exemption value is $6,000.[4]

It is the normal situation to double the exemption level for those filing joint returns. However, it is not uncommon to set the exemption level for dependents at a lower level than that applicable to the head of household. Also, in a number of states the exemption is provided by means of a tax credit rather than as a dollar amount. In California, for example, the

3. U.S. Census Bureau, *Governmental Finances in 1983–84* (U.S. Government Printing Office, 1985), table 4. Estimates of the income elasticity (that is, the responsiveness of state income tax revenues to changes in gross national product) can be found in ACIR, *State-Local Finances in Recession and Inflation*, A-70 (GPO, 1979), p. 24.

4. ACIR, *Significant Features, 1984*, pp. 73–74. Seven states allow a tax credit rather than an exemption.

Table 5-1. *State Individual Income Tax Collections, Highest and Lowest States, 1984*

Individual income tax as source of revenue	*Percent of state's total tax revenue*	*Individual income tax collection per capita*	*Amount per capita (dollars)*
Highest states		*Highest states*	
Oregon	65.8	Delaware	560.28
New York	49.8	Minnesota	556.55
Delaware	48.2	New York	528.56
Massachusetts	47.8	Massachusetts	481.21
Minnesota	45.6	Wisconsin	457.81
Virginia	43.3	Oregon	455.44
Wisconsin	42.6	Hawaii	387.70
Maryland	40.7	Michigan	372.87
Lowest states[a]		*Lowest states*[a]	
New Mexico	5.4	New Mexico	52.57
North Dakota	10.8	Louisiana	91.24
Louisiana	13.0	Mississippi	100.10
Mississippi	14.9	North Dakota	107.80
Arizona	20.9	Alabama	156.18
Alabama	23.0	Arizona	173.03
West Virginia	23.0	Missouri	180.43
Oklahoma	24.7	Arkansas	184.77

Sources: Appendix tables A-10, A-14. In all tables years are fiscal unless otherwise noted and figures are rounded.
a. Excludes Alaska, Tennessee, New Hampshire, and Connecticut, where income taxes were limited in scope.

exemption is a $40 tax credit. How much is such a credit worth? For people whose income is taxed at marginal rates of 1 percent it is equivalent to an exemption of $4,000; for those in the 2 percent tax bracket it is equivalent to an exemption of $2,000.

The variety of personal exemptions can be explained partly on the basis of history. States, when they first enacted their tax, would adopt an exemption acceptable at the time. Thereafter, different sets of forces and needs would operate on them, making for diversity.

The statutory rates of the state taxes are graduated to a modest level, the highest being 16 percent (Minnesota).[5] Many have several brackets, the top one including a wide range of income—for example, in Oklahoma "over $15,000," in New York "over $23,000."[6] The lower brackets are, therefore, relatively narrow and the effective rates of progression, at first quite steep, soon flatten out.

A good many federal practices find their way, with a considerable lag, into the state laws. Thus, in 1984, most states (and the District of Colum-

5. Ibid., table 53.
6. Ibid.

bia) allowed a variety of standard deductions as an alternative to itemizing, provided an optional tax table, and had adopted withholding. Withholding, which was pioneered by Oregon in 1948, serves to locate taxpayers who otherwise might not file; it reduces delinquency by keeping taxpayers current and it collects without a lag from a growing tax base.

There are important differences between the federal and the state definitions of taxable income, of which the most difficult arise out of the allocation of interstate income and definition of residence. Less vital differences occur with respect to income splitting, dividend credits, capital gains, and variations in allowed deductions. Most of the variation rests on no better basis than inertia; some is an expression of state experimentation; some, especially with respect to income arising outside the state, grows out of the insoluble problem of state boundaries and a desire to define taxable income so as to tax nonresidents. The inconvenience to the taxpayer receives slight consideration.

Residence and Origin of Income

The question of residence arises for the federal tax only with respect to foreign income, since the federal definition of income applies over the nation. However, for the states the question is important. The classic solution, proposed in the model plan of the National Tax Association in 1919, was that the residence of the taxpayer should govern; individuals should be taxed on their entire net incomes by their home states.[7] Nonresidents would not be taxed on income earned within the state.

The other approach, pioneered by Wisconsin, was to levy a tax on all income arising in the state whether earned by residents or nonresidents; income accruing to residents from outside the state was not taxed. Either plan would eliminate most discriminatory taxation of individual income, the latter favoring states whose residents had large investments outside the state, the former those in the opposite situation.

In law, most states claim the right to tax the total income of a resident, whatever its origin, and also to tax income originating in the state and going to nonresidents. In practice, the states, while casting a wide net, have moderated the discrimination inherent in their laws through crediting and reciprocity provisions by which they allow a credit for income taxes

7. National Tax Association–Tax Institute of America, *Proceedings of the Twelfth Annual Conference on Taxation, 1920* (Columbus, Ohio: NTA-TIA, 1921), pp. 401–03; *Twenty-sixth Conference, 1934,* pp. 365–74.

paid by their residents to other states or exempt, on a reciprocal basis, each others' residents.[8]

Taxes on Sales

Taxation of consumption has taken the form of taxes on particular commodities (selective sales), and on general sales, mostly imposed at the retail level.

Selective Sales Taxes

Selective sales, or excise, taxes are predominantly of two types: benefit taxes, notably those on motor fuel, and sumptuary taxes, those on liquor, tobacco, and pari-mutuels, for example. The rationale of benefit taxes is that they are a quid pro quo for public services that yield particular and measurable benefits to individuals. Failure to levy them would be to allow receipt of particular services without particular payments; the cost of such services would then be borne by the community as a whole through general taxes (this subject is examined in greater detail in chapter 8). The rationale of sumptuary taxes on liquor, tobacco, and pari-mutuels is more illusive. The taxes penalize consumption of these things and should fulfill the sumptuary purpose of diminishing their consumption. In fact, in an affluent society the taxes are not pushed hard enough to secure much diminution but do secure a large revenue. The compromise rationale seems to be that if particular consumers care to pay a penalty tax, the proceeds to be used for collective purposes, they may continue to consume.

Table 5-2 shows state revenue in 1984 from selective sales taxes. Taxation of motor fuel is common to all the state governments, and so is taxation of liquor, cigarettes, and insurance. Thirty states tax pari-mutuels and forty-one tax public utilities by excises, although only a few secure a substantial revenue thereby.

MOTOR FUEL. The first taxes on commodities widely used by the states were on gasoline and tobacco products (especially cigarettes). In 1919 Oregon imposed a gasoline tax, and it proved so productive and acceptable that by 1929 it was used by every state in the union. During the 1930s and

8. Clara Penniman, *State Income Taxation* (Johns Hopkins University Press, 1980), p. 260.

Table 5-2. *State Revenue from Selective Sales Taxes, 1984*

Tax	*Amount (millions of dollars)*	*Percent of total selective sales tax collections*
Motor fuel	12,396	37.3
Alcoholic beverages	2,900	8.7
Tobacco products	4,149	12.5
Insurance	3,974	12.0
Public utilities	5,875	17.7
Pari-mutuels	739	2.2
Others	3,205	9.6
Total	33,238	100.0

Source: U.S. Census Bureau, *State Government Finances in 1984* (U.S. Government Printing Office, 1985), table 6.

early 1940s it was the most important tax source of state governments, yielding one-quarter or more of their tax revenues (see chapter 2). Gasoline rationing during World War II cut the yield, and taxes on general sales became the leading revenue producer, a position that they have not relinquished.

The rates at which the states tax motor fuel are fairly diverse. In December 1984 two states had gasoline tax rates of 5–7.5 cents per gallon, fourteen of 8–10 cents, twenty-one of 11–13.8 cents, eleven of 14–16 cents, and two of 17–18 cents per gallon.[9] There is diversity also in the exemptions and refunds they allow. Moreover, in thirteen states, local as well as state gasoline taxes are levied.

Federal use of the gasoline tax began in 1932 amid strong state protest at federal trespass. This time the protest rang true. The states had made vigorous use of the tax; their administration of it was reasonably efficient and had brought no significant jurisdictional conflicts. The issue of federal trespass was therefore a real one, and state pressure for federal withdrawal had merit. The issue was, however, sidetracked when Congress, in 1956, not only enlarged federal aid for highway construction but also provided that, for sixteen years, large slices of revenue from the federal motor fuel tax (as well as from other highway user taxes) be placed in the new Highway Trust Fund and spent for an expanded program of highway construction.

TOBACCO. In 1921 Iowa enacted a cigarette tax, and by 1929 seven other states had followed suit. The depression of the 1930s accelerated adoption of this tax (or a tax on tobacco products). By 1961 all the states and the District of Columbia taxed cigarettes.

9. ACIR, *Significant Features, 1984,* table 65.

In taxing cigarettes the states encountered important administrative difficulties because they had to collect from wholesalers and jobbers within their jurisdiction, not as the federal Treasury does from a small number of manufacturers. State taxes could be evaded either by smuggling or by purchase in interstate commerce. An early device to defeat evasion was enactment of a state use tax, a levy on commodities purchased outside a state but brought into it for use. Applied first to gasoline and then extended to other commodities, the tax gave administrators a legal base for enforcement, leaving unsolved the task of finding the commodities on which the tax had not been paid.

The states turned to interstate cooperation, especially by providing lists of consignees to tax administrators in states that cigarettes were shipped to. The device was useless, however, when sales came from states that did not tax these items, since no basis for reciprocity existed. Moreover, cigarettes could be shipped by parcel post (as gasoline could not), and dealers, protected by the privacy of the United States mails, did not declare such shipments. The Post Office resisted schemes that would have required it to provide information to the states concerning shipments of tobacco products.

But after World War II, as the number of states imposing taxes on tobacco products grew, pressure for federal help mounted, and in 1949 Congress required sellers of cigarettes in interstate commerce to send to state tax administrators copies of invoices of every tobacco shipment into their state. This effectively closed a major loophole.

Since the 1960s a major problem faced by state tax administrators has been organized large-scale cigarette smuggling. This criminal activity became profitable as large differences in state cigarette tax rates arose. The Surgeon General's warnings concerning the health hazards of smoking encouraged states to increase their taxes on cigarettes, with some states increasing their rates more than others. The Advisory Commission on Intergovernmental Relations has estimated that the revenue loss to state and local governments in 1975 from cigarette tax evasion was about $400 million and there was little that state law enforcement officials could do about it. However, reasonable control of the problem was achieved in 1978 when Congress enacted Public Law 95-575, the Contraband Cigarette Act. This law prohibited the transportation, receipt, shipment, possession, distribution, or purchase of more than sixty thousand cigarettes not bearing the tax indicia of the state in which the cigarettes were found. The law seems to have worked well, but as long as cigarette taxes stay high and large interstate rate differentials exist an encouragement to smuggling will remain.[10]

Tobacco taxes in 1982 produced 7.9 percent of state general tax revenue collections. In thirteen states they represented 2 percent or less of the total general sales taxes collected, in thirty-four states 2–4 percent, in two 4–6 percent, and in one state at least 8 percent.[11]

ALCOHOLIC BEVERAGE. The third bundle of commodities subject to state excises is liquor. After repeal of Prohibition the states chose two different methods of controlling and gathering revenue from the liquor business. In 1984 thirty-three states used the license system, raising revenue mostly from a gallonage excise and license charge; seventeen had chosen the monopoly system of state stores, raising revenue chiefly from profits. In 1984 the revenue from state excises on alcoholic beverages, including licenses and permits, was $3,161 million; from state-run stores the net contribution to general funds was $338.4 million. Local governments collected $481 million from liquor store revenues.[12]

The interstate tax conflict and trade barriers have raised intricate problems. The states used the freedom given them by the Twenty-first Amendment to the Constitution, which excluded alcoholic beverages from the protection given to interstate commerce, to levy liquor taxes and license charges as trade barriers in order to protect local producers and distributors. A counteragitation developed against such practices that halted the growth of discrimination, although it did not remove that already in existence.

General Retail Sales Taxes

The success of selective excises as revenue producers (particularly excises on motor fuel) held back the development of state taxes on general retail sales. In addition, the states were afraid that taxation of sales might cause migration into tax-free states and they were conscious of the Supreme Court's zealousness in barring taxation of all transactions of an interstate character. Sales made by merchants to customers outside a tax-

10. ACIR, *Cigarette Tax Evasion: A Second Look,* A-100 (Washington: ACIR, 1985), pp. 1–2.

11. Tax Foundation, *Facts and Figures on Government Finance, 1983* (Washington: Tax Foundation, 1983), pp. 254–55, 274.

12. U.S. Census Bureau, *State Government Finances in 1984* (GPO, 1985), table 6; Census Bureau, *Governmental Finances in 1983–84,* table 4.

ing state, and sales made by merchants who were outside a taxing state to customers in a taxing state, could not be taxed. The effect of this strict Court interpretation was to discriminate in favor of interstate commerce.

The depression of the 1930s broke through some of the obstacles. The states perceived that a general sales tax was a source of revenue that, unlike income taxation, held up in bad times. Moreover, Congress indicated clearly in 1931–32 that a federal sales tax was unacceptable. The states, worried by the collapse of the property tax and the desperate plight of local governments, saw sales taxes as a means of financial salvation. Mississippi adopted a sales tax in 1932. In 1933 thirteen states enacted a general tax on retail sales,[13] and by the end of 1938 nine more states and Hawaii had followed suit. World War II halted the swing, but afterward, as states prepared to finance the backlog of demands bottled up during the war, there came a second wave of sales taxes. In 1944 the general retail sales tax became the most important tax source of state governments, and its preeminence has remained since. In 1984 forty-five states (plus the District of Columbia) imposed the tax, and it accounted for 32 percent of their tax collections.

Figure 5-1 and tables 5-3 and 5-4 give an indication of the interstate variation in the significance of the tax. In 1984, general sales taxes produced over $200 per capita in tax revenue for thirty-nine states; individual income taxes produced this amount for twenty-nine states. The range of sales tax rates—from 2 percent to 7.5 percent—is shown in table 5-4.

Meanwhile, local governments have utilized the tax, following the examples of New York City in 1934 and New Orleans in 1938 (see chapter 8). After World War II, local sales taxes spread and as of October 1984 were utilized in twenty-six states (although in six by only a few local governments).[14] About 6,400 local governments, most notably in California, Illinois, Texas, Oklahoma, and Washington, imposed the tax. In many states with local general sales taxes, administration is by the state (piggyback). While the aggregate revenue secured—$12.6 billion or 10.2 percent of local tax revenue in 1984—may seem modest, the tax brings in 20–30 percent of the total tax collections of the large cities of Los Angeles, Washington, Dallas, and Houston, and 40–60 percent of smaller cities such as Phoenix, Omaha, and Denver.[15]

13. Includes Indiana which taxes gross income only but is usually included in tabulations of sales taxes.

14. ACIR, *Significant Features, 1984,* table 61.

15. Census Bureau, *City Government Finances in 1983–84* (GPO, 1985), table 5.

Table 5-3. *Distribution of States by General Sales Tax and Individual Income Tax Collections Per Capita, 1984*

	Number of states	
Dollars collected per capita	*Sales tax*	*Income tax*
Under 100	0	3
100–149	2	2
150–199	4	7
200–249	15	13
250–299	10	5
300–349	5	1
350–399	3	4
400–449	3	0
450–499	1	3
500 and over	2	3

Source: Appendix table A-14.

Some Characteristics

The state (and local) governments chose retail sales as the base of their sales tax. Some states have few manufacturing concerns, and others many, that ship across state lines. A sales tax at the manufacturing level would burden these concerns compared with competitors outside the state; it would, besides, raise complications concerning interstate commerce. Taxing at the retail level avoids or limits these difficulties. The tax as employed is, therefore, approximately a single-stage tax on retail sales. Sales for resale are excluded, either by an ingredient test or by a direct-use test. The ingredient test removes from the tax base property that becomes an ingredient of a product to be sold; the direct-use test removes property used directly in producing goods to be sold. But neither rule excludes completely from the tax base sales of supplies used in industrial processes. Sales of office supplies and of fuel, for example, are included in the base. Although complete exemption of goods that have an industrial consumption or production use would not be justified, the result of inclusion in the base is multiple taxation. The tax on goods used in production is shifted forward and becomes a cost of the relevant consumer goods which, in turn, are taxed when sold at the retail level.

A general retail sales tax should logically include services in the base. In fact, most services are excluded, and thereby a considerable slice of consumers' expenditures is not taxed. It is, however, common to include in the base admissions, transient lodging, meals served in restaurants, and public utility services such as gas, electricity, and telephone. Some states, on grounds of equity, exclude specific categories of tangible consumer

Figure 5-1. *Distribution of States by General Sales Tax and Individual Income Tax Collections Per Capita, 1984*

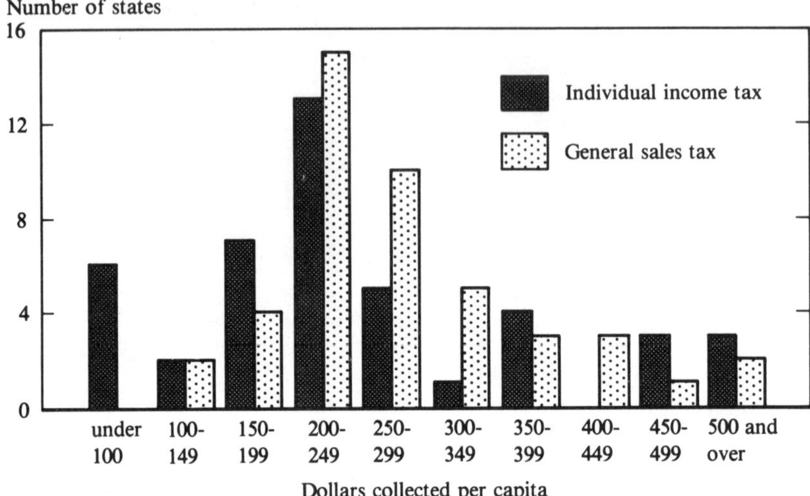

Source: Table 5-3.

goods—in 1984 prescription drugs were exempt in forty-four states and the District of Columbia, and expenditures on food for home consumption were not taxed in twenty-nine states and the District of Columbia. Less than half a dozen states exempt clothing.

All the sales-tax states have supplementary use taxes, applicable to goods bought outside the state and brought into it for consumption. In 1937 the Supreme Court upheld the use tax, declaring that it was not a tax on interstate commerce, but on the privilege of use after commerce had ended.[16] Since then the constitutional basis of sales and use taxes has been so greatly broadened that serious concern is now expressed that the states will put discriminatory burdens on interstate trade.

Information concerning the costs of administering and complying with sales tax laws is spotty. Compliance costs fall mostly on retailers, rather than on consumers, and studies in the 1950s and 1960s indicated that about half the states compensated them for their costs to the extent of 1–5 percent of the tax obligation. Administrative costs reported by the states have run at less than \$2 per \$100 of sales tax revenue.[17] State governments

16. *Henneford* v. *Silas Mason Co.*, 300 U.S. 577 (1937).

17. John F. Due and John L. Mikesell, *Sales Taxation: State and Local Structure and Administration* (Johns Hopkins University Press, 1983), p. 325.

Table 5-4. *Distribution of States by General Sales Tax Rate, as of December 1984*

Tax rate (percent)	*Number of states*	*Tax rate (percent)*	*Number of states*
2.000	0	4.750	1
3.000	7	5.000	12
3.500	1	5.500	1
3.750	1	5.750	1
4.000	11	6.000	5
4.125	2	6.500	1
4.625	1	7.500	1

Source: Advisory Commission on Intergovernmental Relations, *Significant Features of Fiscal Federalism, 1984 Edition* (Washington: ACIR, 1985), p.88.

spend too little in seeing that firms remit payment of tax at the required time. A more serious administrative weakness is states' failure to audit tax collections carefully. The size and technical training of audit staffs are usually inadequate.

The Charge of Inequity

Beyond question the most weighty criticism of the sales tax has been its inequity. The tax is on consumption, and since consumption must absorb a higher percentage of income for poor than for rich persons, a tax that rests on consumption is regressive. Its rate, as a percentage of income, is higher for the poor person than for the rich. The extent of the regression depends on the coverage of the sales tax. Exemption of food and medicine reduces regression simply because low-income persons spend a relatively high proportion of their income for these items. Exemptions narrow the tax base and discriminate in favor of persons who consume relatively large amounts of the untaxed items. This discrimination may accord with social policy, but it complicates administration and therefore induces or allows evasion of taxes. A firm that sells exempt and nonexempt articles must distinguish between them in its accounts. Besides, definition of food, medicine, and so on, raises borderline cases that require arbitrary decisions. And every exemption is, of course, a subsidy to consumers of the untaxed product, and therefore requires justification.

General sales tax payments as a percentage of family income are lower at higher levels of income, as the following rough estimate of the incidence of state and local general sales taxes for a family of four in 1980 indicates:[18]

18. ACIR, *Significant Features of Fiscal Federalism, 1980–81 Edition* (Washington: ACIR, 1981), p. 49.

Family income (dollars)	*Tax burden (percent of income)*
Average—21,500	1.1
Twice the average—43,000	0.9
Four times the average—86,000	0.6

The effective rate of the sales tax, however, has an unfortunate tendency to increase as the size of the family grows. The potential magnitude of these inequities is softened when food is exempt from the tax base.[19] Several states have provided a sales tax credit against income tax liability, and the plausible argument is advanced that such a credit is superior to an exemption on grounds of equity, revenue productivity, and compliance costs.[20] States with both an income tax and sales tax should, therefore, prefer the credit to exemption of food (and other) purchases.

Regressivity of sales taxes is concerned with vertical equity, measured usually by the relation of average tax payments of families by income classes. Horizontal equity, or equality of treatment based on the characteristics of the family, has been neglected. Horizontal equity may be measured by the standard deviation in an income class, "computed from the differences between the effective tax rate for each family and the average effective rate of each family."[21] Tax credits so arranged as to take account of family characteristics, notably family size, improve horizontal equity; indeed, "for the majority of taxpayers, effective tax rate differentials result from differences in consumption patterns which are explained primarily by factors other than income."[22]

The equity argument, whatever weight is given to it, should be placed in perspective by relating the sales tax burden to the total tax burden borne by taxpayers. The fact that one tax is regressive or progressive has significance only with respect to its weight in the total system of taxes. The sophisticated and abstract argument that has been developed by economists concerning tax sacrifice among individuals assumes a summation of the sacrifices imposed by the whole system of taxes. For decisive practical reasons, local governments tend to utilize regressive taxes. State governments have more freedom, but their choice concerning tax progression is

19. Reed R. Hansen, "An Empirical Analysis of the Retail Sales Tax with Policy Recommendations," *National Tax Journal,* vol. 15 (March 1962), pp. 1–13. Also see J. Richard Aronson, *Public Finance* (McGraw-Hill, 1985), p. 476.

20. ACIR, *Significant Features, 1983,* pp. 58–59.

21. James A. Papke and Timothy G. Shahen, "Optimal Consumption-Base Taxes: The Equity Effects of Tax Credits," *National Tax Journal,* vol. 25 (September 1972), p. 481.

22. Ibid., p. 486.

narrowly limited because taxpayers subjected to high rates in one state can move to others where the rates are lower. The national government has much greater freedom, since moving outside the national boundaries in order to avoid taxes imposes other costs, many of them nonmonetary.

The relevant issue, then, is the incidence on individuals of total taxes—federal, state, and local. Table 5-5 shows estimates of federal and state-local taxes under the most progressive set of assumptions used in Joseph Pechman's comprehensive study of tax incidence and under the least progressive set of assumptions.[23] Federal taxes appear progressive under one set of assumptions but not the other. Where the corporation income tax is assumed to fall on corporate owners and property income recipients, the tax burden appears progressive; however, under the least progressive, half of the corporation income tax is thought to be passed on to consumers and as a result the federal tax burden appears roughly proportional. The distribution of state-local taxes is quite sensitive to the incidence assumptions used. Under the most progressive, where property taxes on improvements fall on property income, the distribution follows a U-shaped pattern. Under the other set of assumptions, when the property tax on improvements is assumed to be passed on to consumers, state-local taxes exhibit a regressive pattern.

The potential degree of overall progressivity should not be exaggerated. "The tax system in 1980," according to Pechman, "was only mildly progressive or slightly regressive, depending on the incidence assumptions. Under the most progressive set of assumptions examined in this study (variant 1c), taxes reduced income inequality by 2.5 percent; under the least progressive assumptions (3b), income inequality was increased by about 0.8 percent."[24]

Some awkward, if abstruse, questions remain unanswered. Should it be assumed that Congress determines the progression of the federal tax system after consideration of the evidence concerning the incidence of state and local taxes? Does Congress use the federal tax system as an instrument

23. Joseph A. Pechman, *Who Paid the Taxes, 1966–85?* (Brookings, 1985). This study s a successor to Joseph A. Pechman and Benjamin A. Okner, *Who Bears the Tax Burden?* (Brookings, 1974).

24. *Who Paid the Taxes?* p. 60. Pechman uses Gini coefficients to measure the distribution of income. An alternate view of the progressivity of the tax system, provided by Browning and Johnson, suggests a high degree of progressivity exists. Under their analysis sales and excise taxes fall on people not in relation to their consumption but rather according to income. Edgar K. Browning and William R. Johnson, *The Distribution of the Tax Burden* (Washington: American Enterprise Institute, 1979); Aronson, *Public Finance*, pp. 508–24.

Table 5-5. *Incidence of Federal and State-Local Taxes under Most Progressive and Least Progressive Assumptions about Tax Burdens, by Income Class, 1980*

Percent

Adjusted family income (thousands of dollars)	*Most progressive assumptions*[a]			*Least progressive assumptions*[b]		
	Federal tax	*State-local taxes*	*Total taxes*	*Federal tax*	*State-local taxes*	*Total taxes*
0–5	80	244	128	161	358	219
5–10	69	108	80	85	140	102
10–15	75	96	81	86	115	95
15–20	82	93	85	90	106	95
20–25	89	92	90	94	105	97
25–30	92	93	92	96	104	98
30–50	98	96	97	101	103	101
50–100	108	99	105	105	96	102
100–500	108	108	108	97	78	92
500–1,000	103	119	107	79	67	75
1,000 and over	121	129	123	84	65	79

Source: Joseph A. Pechman, *Who Paid the Taxes, 1966–85?* (Brookings, 1985), p. 60.
a. See ibid., table 3-1, variant 1c, p. 35.
b. See ibid., variant 3b, p. 35.

to secure the right—the desired—total incidence? Evidence in support of the opinion that Congress does so act would be difficult to produce, and yet no more difficult than evidence concerning how Congress resolves many major decisions concerning spending and taxing.

Another difficult, if more niggling, question is: How can Congress make an adjustment in the progression of federal taxes so as to fit the different tax systems of fifty states? A scale of federal progression suitable as an instrument of adjustment to the tax systems of states where taxes on consumption are dominant would be less suitable for states where they are not. Congress must, it seems, be assumed to aim at adjusting to a hypothetical average state and local tax system. This interpretation of the procedure adopted, of necessity, by Congress brings to light a fault of a markedly regressive (or progressive) state tax system. If Congress adjusts the progression of federal taxes to an average state system, citizens in a state with a system that diverges markedly from this average secure an imperfect adjustment.

Sales Tax or Income Tax?

For most states there is no longer a question of whether they should use a sales tax or an income tax; most states must employ both. Yet, there remains the problem of balance. How much reliance should be placed on one or the other of these two sources of revenue?

A practical issue of some consequence is the comparative effect of sales and income taxes on interstate movement. A state income tax on top of a heavy and steeply progressive federal income tax may seem oppressive and even confiscatory to a high-income person. A shift in domicile to avoid the state tax is something to fear. Proponents of state income taxes sometimes brush aside this possibility by demonstrating the ameliorative effect on progression and on total income tax of federal deductibility—payments of state income tax may be deducted from the base of the federal tax. In short, the base of federal tax is income after deduction of state income tax payments (and many other items). The federal Treasury, therefore, collects less federal tax from a taxpayer in an income tax state. If, for example, a married taxpayer in 1984 had taxable income of $11,900 in a state with no income tax, his federal tax would be $1,149, but in a state that collected $146 in income tax from him, his federal tax would be reduced to $1,126 (the tax on $11,900 minus $146), and he therefore would pay only an additional $123 as a result of the state income tax.

The federal income tax law allows individuals to deduct state and local sales taxes as well as income taxes from adjusted gross income. Therefore, taxpayers in the state that had no income tax could reduce their federal income tax by deducting their sales tax payments. The relevant comparison is between the aggregate tax levels (federal and state) of taxpayers in the two states. Is it favorable to one or the other?

It is easy to show that for two states with the same total revenue, a differential would exist that would be favorable at the bottom end of the scale to residents of the income tax state and at the upper end to residents of the sales tax state. Since income tax payments are progressive, and sales tax payments regressive, the deductible amounts in the sales tax state will be relatively large for low- and middle-income taxpayers, and relatively small for high-income taxpayers. Conversely, in the income tax state, deductible amounts will be relatively small for low- and middle-income taxpayers, and relatively large for high-income persons, those most likely to migrate to avoid taxation. Therefore, a state legislature might choose to enact a sales tax rather than an income tax; it might worry more about interstate migration than equity.

Finally, with respect to costs of administration, the income and sales taxes may be roughly equivalent. For each, costs probably fall in the range of 1.0–2.5 percent of revenues.[25] With respect to compliance, the income tax puts costs chiefly on the payers of the tax, while the sales tax puts them

25. See Due and Mikesell, *Sales Taxation*, pp. 323–25; Penniman, *State Income Taxation*, pp. 266–69.

on retailers. Sales taxation has sometimes been favored because part of it can be shifted out of state—to tourists, visitors, and out-of-state buyers of the products of a state. But states also use the income tax to tap nonresidents, as when New York levies a tax on the income earned in the state by commuters from New Jersey and Connecticut. While some states have more ability than others to exact such tribute, the net amount of the tribute is probably not great.

The sales tax and income tax differ significantly in revenue stability. The yield of a progressive income tax will vary more over the business cycle than that of a general sales tax, both because the base of the income tax is more variable and because its rates are progressive. State and local governments favor taxes with stable yields because, in recession, they cannot easily borrow to finance deficits. And yet an income tax with high built-in revenue flexibility promotes national economic stabilization.

In the 1930s and immediately after World War II, when sales taxes were being adopted by many states, sales taxation and income taxation were widely regarded as alternatives. Debate over the two is still sometimes couched in these terms, even though it has come to be quite unrealistic. Today only New Hampshire has neither a general retail sales tax nor an individual income tax. Forty-four states employ an individual income tax; forty-five states use a general sales tax; and thirty-five states have both. Will states rely more on one source than the other in the future? In recent years greater reliance has been placed on the income tax and this was convenient during times of strong economic growth. The increased elasticity of the tax structure, however, is not an unmixed blessing. It has made states more fiscally vulnerable during recession. As a result, they may be reluctant to tilt the revenue structure more toward the income tax.

CHAPTER SIX

Other State Taxes

But you must confine yourself within the modest limits of order.

Twelfth Night

THE IMPERFECT RATIONALE for state taxation of business income is some version of a benefit theory. Business, it is held, owes taxes because of benefits received from the jurisdiction where business is carried on. The tax can come in the form of either a direct tax on net income or an excise on the privilege of doing business and measured by or according to net income.[1]

Corporation Income Tax

The modern version of a state tax on corporation income, like that on individual income, started with the Wisconsin tax of 1911. Thereafter, most states, when they enacted income taxes, taxed both individual and corporate income. Between 1911 and 1920, nine states adopted a corporation income tax; in the 1920s eight states did so, in the 1930s fifteen, in the 1940s two, in the 1950s two, in the 1960s six, and in the 1970s three.[2] In 1984, forty-five states (and the District of Columbia) had a corporation income tax. Twenty-nine states (and the District) use flat rates—4.5 percent to 11.5 percent—and sixteen use graduated rates. These taxes in 1984 produced 7.9 percent of total state tax collections, while license taxes on corporations in general produced an additional 1.1 percent. As always,

1. Of the states that levy no corporation income tax, one (Texas) raises considerable sums by annual license taxes on corporations in general, and the others raise modest amounts using these taxes. Some states with corporation income taxes (Delaware, Alabama, Ohio, Pennsylvania, New Jersey, Louisiana, North Carolina, Tennessee) raise significant additional amounts in a similar way. See U.S. Census Bureau, *State Government Finances in 1984* (U.S. Government Printing Office, 1985), table 6.

2. Advisory Commission on Intergovernmental Affairs, *Significant Features of Fiscal Federalism, 1983 Edition* (Washington: ACIR, 1984), table 66. The Hawaii tax, enacted in 1901, is counted in the first nine.

Table 6-1. *Distribution of States by Collections Per Capita from State Corporation Income Taxes, 1984*[a]

Collections per capita (dollars)	*Number of states*
0–20	0
20–40	9
40–60	21
60–80	6
80–100	3
100–120	1
120–150	4
Over 150	1
Total	45

Source: U.S. Census Bureau, *State Government Finances in 1985* (U.S. Government Printing Office, 1985), tables 6, 36. In all tables years are fiscal unless otherwise noted and figures are rounded.

a. Nevada, South Dakota, Texas, Washington, and Wyoming had no general corporate income tax in 1984.

variation among the states was significant. The distribution of collections per capita by states for 1984 is shown in table 6-1. Colorado, Florida, and Hawaii collected only $28, $33, and $36, respectively, in corporation income tax; Alaska, on the other hand, collected $609, and Michigan, California, Massachusetts, and Connecticut took in $142, $126, $126, and $127, respectively.[3]

As can be seen from table 6-2, the corporate income tax as a proportion of state revenue has hovered in the 7–10 percent range in the last three decades. Corporate income is quite responsive to economic growth and inflation and corporate tax revenues tend to follow the path of economic activity. Collections rose in the late 1970s as inflation increased nominal corporate income, then fell during the two recessions at the beginning of the 1980s, and began rising again with economic growth after 1982.

In 1964, the ACIR observed that states were "moving toward greater reliance on the Federal tax base for State corporate income taxes as well as for individual income taxes."[4] Thirty-three states were using the federal base in 1973, but by 1984 the trend toward conformity with federal practice had been reversed. Many states used the federal framework, but modifications in their tax codes weakened the link between federal and state practice. By 1984, the corporate tax systems of only six states showed no significant departures from that of the federal government.[5]

A major factor in prompting states to tax corporate income differently than the federal government was the anticipated impact of the accelerated

3. Census Bureau, *State Government Finances in 1984,* tables 6, 36.

4. ACIR, *Tax Overlapping in the United States, 1964* (GPO, 1964), p. 142.

5. *All States Tax Handbook, 1984 Edition* (Prentice-Hall, 1984), p. 124.

Table 6-2. *State Corporation Income Tax Revenue, Selected Years, 1948–84*

Year	*Millions of dollars*	*Percent of state tax collections*	*Year*	*Millions of dollars*	*Percent of state tax collections*
1948	585	8.7	1976	7,273	8.1
1956	890	6.7	1978	10,738	9.5
1964	1,695	7.0	1980	13,321	9.7
1968	2,518	6.9	1981	14,143	9.4
1970	3,738	7.8	1982	14,006	8.6
1972	4,416	7.4	1983	13,153	7.7
1974	6,015	8.1	1984	15,511	7.9

Source: Advisory Commission on Intergovernmental Relations, *Significant Features of Fiscal Federalism, 1982–83* (Washington: ACIR, 1984), table 24; Census Bureau, *State Government Finances in 1984*, table 6.

cost recovery system (ACRS) embodied in the Economic Recovery Tax Act (ERTA) of 1981. States that accept this extremely rapid depreciation of buildings and machinery can expect their revenues from the corporate tax to be reduced. Fifteen states have thus "decoupled" from the federal tax base and have maintained or adopted less generous depreciation schedules for their own tax structures.[6]

Corporations may deduct all payments of state corporate income taxes in computing their net income for federal corporate income tax purposes. During the 1970s, the federal corporate tax generated approximately seven times as much revenue as the total of states' corporate taxes. Since the federal yield was so high and states' rates so nearly uniform, overall tax differentials between states were not large. But the revenue productivity of the federal corporate tax has fallen, largely as a result of features enacted under the ERTA, and federal corporate revenues in 1984 were only about three and a half times as great as state collections.[7] At the same time, the variation among states' tax rates has grown. The result has been an increase in the state-by-state variation of effective corporate income tax rates.

Interstate Allocation of Income

Thousands of companies do business and earn income in more than one state. On what basis should each state reckon its tax share of the net income base? Three rules for division are used: formula apportionment, specific allocation, and separate accounting. Separate accounting, while

6. Four states that adopted the ACRS (Indiana, Iowa, Nebraska, Wisconsin) increased their corporate tax rates to offset the revenue loss from generous depreciation allowances. See ACIR, *Significant Features, 1982–83*, table 49.

7. Census Bureau, *Governmental Finances in 1983–84* (GPO, 1985), table 4.

permitted by most states, has only limited application. It assumes that the operations of a multistate business can be split into pieces; in fact, most such businesses are unitary.[8] Specific allocation, provided by all except six states, means that some items of income are regarded as nonapportionable—for example, dividends and interest—and must be allocated wholly to one state or another. But the states differ on the kinds of income to be so allocated, and also on where a particular kind of income has its source. Specific allocation, it should be appreciated, applies only to part of the income of a business; it is used mainly as an adjunct to formula apportionment.

The dominant approach to income allocation is formula apportionment, under which each state uses a formula designed to determine what portion of a corporation's total income should be assigned to it. The most common formula, which is incorporated in the Uniform Division of Income for Tax Purposes Act (UDITPA), is one that uses three factors—sales, payroll, and property. For example, the state calculates the ratio of the corporation's in-state sales to its total sales and uses the same procedure to calculate the ratios for payroll and property. The arithmetic average of the three ratios is used to determine the portion of the corporations' taxable income that is subject to taxation by the state. In applying the apportionment formula, roughly one-half of the states look beyond the legal fiction of separate incorporation and combine the income (and apportionment factors) of entities that are deemed to be part of a unitary business enterprise. While states' interpretations of what constitutes a unitary enterprise differ, the usual attributes are common ownership, functional integration, centralization of management, and economies of scale.

If all states used the same apportionment formula and applied it to a commonly accepted definition of corporate income, then all the income earned by corporations would be apportioned among the states, no more and no less. But, in practice, states apply different apportionment formulas to different definitions of income. This may result in either underapportionment or overapportionment of actual corporate income.[9] It has been claimed that states sometimes choose their formulas to maximize their

8. While businesses may be incorporated separately, the concept of a unitary enterprise recognizes the interdependence of affiliates that are under common control and management and that may realize cost savings from integration and economies of scale.

9. Overapportionment is the assignment of a taxable income base to a corporation that is larger than the amount of income actually generated by the corporation in that state. Of course, overapportionment of a corporation's income in one state does not preclude overapportionment in other states as well.

revenue from the tax. For example, in a state where corporations produce goods that are primarily consumed in other states, the state's tax revenue would be increased if in its apportionment formula a greater weight were given to payroll and property and less to sales.

To what extent can corporations' taxable income be overapportioned by states choosing apportionment formulas that try to maximize their revenue from the corporate tax? The first effort at measuring overapportionment, carried out for the Judiciary Committee of the House of Representatives, concluded that "contrary to common belief . . . the choice among formulas studied is not an issue involving great amounts of money."[10] A later attempt to answer the question, using 1980 data, found that for all states taken together, there was the potential for apportioned corporate income to be 6 percent greater than actual corporate income. That study also estimated the level of overapportionment that might occur if states, with an eye toward maximizing tax revenue, applied different apportionment formulas to different industries. For all industries in the sample examined, overapportionment could be as high as 17 percent, and the amount of overapportionment would vary significantly among industries. The most severe case of overapportionment would occur in mining industries if the states in which production takes place use a payroll-based formula and other states employ a sales-based formula.[11]

Which Formula to Use?

On economic grounds, which formula is to be favored? Until recently most observers took a "supply-side" approach, arguing that income should be apportioned on the basis of where it was earned, that is, based on the location of the factors that create the income. As C. Lowell Harris argued: "Income is created by human and material resources. The resources utilized by a business as a whole in producing its income can be measured reasonably well by what is paid for them. Moreover, the places where the resources have been producing during a year can be determined on a consistent, though not completely unambiguous basis."[12]

10. *State Taxation of Interstate Commerce,* H. Rept. 1480, 88 Cong. 2 sess. (GPO, 1964), vol. 1, p. 530.

11. Steven M. Sheffrin and Jack Fulcher, "Alternative Divisions of the Tax Base: How Much Is at Stake?" in Charles E. McLure, Jr., ed., *The State Corporation Income Tax: Issues in Worldwide Unitary Combination* (Hoover Institution Press, 1984), pp. 192–227.

12. "Interstate Apportionment of Business Income," *American Economic Review,* vol. 49 (June 1959), p. 400.

Under this view, property and payrolls should count. Opinions differ on what property should be included and what standard of valuation should be used, as well as on the composition of payrolls and the state in which payrolls are located. But these issues can be resolved without great difficulty.

Taken a step further, the argument would be that a workable formula should not give sales a separate or distinct place. Sales effort would be represented merely by the cost of the economic resources used in selling; it would not be represented by the value of sales made in a state. But those who favor a separate sales component make two points. As a practical matter, inclusion of a sales factor is the best way to reserve a significant share in the tax base for the market states. And on theoretical grounds it is argued that the interaction of supply and demand, and not supply alone, creates value. Thus a sales factor, which reflects the demand component, should play some role in determining the apportionment of corporate income among states.

It has been argued that inclusion of a sales factor increases the costs of compliance of the corporate income tax. Computation of a property factor is, the Judiciary study finds, "relatively simple if property is valued either at original cost or at adjusted basis for Federal tax purposes," and computation of payroll factors is "generally quite simple." But a sales factor, especially for smaller firms, is costly to compute and these compliance costs are "wholly disproportionate to the tax liabilities involved."[13] Indeed, any formula that attempts to apportion income over a large number of states, as a sales destination factor must often do, is bound to bring either high cost of compliance, or else noncompliance.

Incidence of the State Corporation Income Tax

It is tempting to analyze the incidence of the state corporate income tax in much the same way as a federal tax on corporate income. If it could be assumed that all states levied a uniform tax on a uniform base, then this approach would make sense. Yet, even in such a case, hard-and-fast answers would be hard to come by since the incidence of the federal corporate income tax is itself controversial.

Theoretically, the incidence of the corporate income tax depends on whether markets are competitive or not. Under competitive conditions, the short-run burden is likely to fall on owners of capital in the corporate

13. *State Taxation of Interstate Commerce*, H. Rept. 1480, pp. 562–63.

sector, but in the longer run the burden is likely to be shared by owners of capital in the noncorporate sector as well. In addition, as production shifts out of the taxed (corporate) sector, there may be further effects on the returns to labor and capital, depending on the intensity with which the factors are used in the taxed and untaxed sectors. Finally, the long-run effect of a lowering of the return to capital might be to discourage capital formation, inducing a decline in the wage rate.[14]

If markets are oligopolistic or prices are administered, then there is an increased likelihood that a portion of the tax can be passed forward to consumers. Furthermore, if corporations do not follow strict profit-maximizing behavior but instead attempt to maximize sales or engage in mark-up pricing, there is the possibility that the tax can result in higher prices to consumers.

Finally, the analysis of the incidence depends on whether capital is internationally mobile. If the United States alone were to increase the rate of corporate taxation, capital might flee abroad and, by reducing the available stock of capital, lower the real wage of American labor.[15]

With all of these theoretical possibilities, it is the empirical evidence that must determine who bears the federal corporate income tax. Unfortunately, however, definitive answers have not emerged from the numerous studies that have been conducted and further work remains to be done.

But drawing an analogy between the incidence of a state and federal corporate income tax is dangerous and perhaps misleading. State corporate tax systems are not uniform, rates and bases vary from state to state, and apportionment formulas are not uniform. In the face of such complexity, one alternative is to examine the incidence of the corporate tax from the viewpoint of a particular state.

Charles E. McLure, Jr., has shown that corporate taxation based on an apportionment formula (such as the UDITPA formula) is correctly viewed as "a composite of taxes levied on whatever factors are employed in the states' apportionment formula."[16] The extent to which the tax is distributed among these factors—commonly, property, payroll, and sales—

14. J. Richard Aronson, *Public Finance* (McGraw-Hill, 1985), chap. 15; it contains references to the theoretical and empirical literature.

15. See Arnold C. Harberger, "The State of the Corporation Income Tax: Who Pays It? Should It Be Repealed?" in Charls E. Walker and Mark A. Bloomfield, eds., *New Directions for Federal Tax Policy for the 1980s* (Ballinger Publishing, 1983), pp. 161–81.

16. "The Elusive Incidence of the Corporate Income Tax: The State Case," *Public Finance Quarterly* (October 1981), pp. 395–413.

depends on their relative mobility. The potential to relocate when the burden of the tax is placed on a particular factor shields it from absorbing the burden. For example, an attempt by a corporation to lower wages when labor is mobile will cause labor to leave, forcing the corporation to bid up wages to retain workers—in effect forcing it to rescind its attempt to pass on the burden of the tax through lower wages. On the other hand, immobile labor is likely to absorb a portion of the tax.

Similarly, if the goods produced in the state are mobile, either in the sense that they face competition from goods produced elsewhere or they are sold in competitive national markets, then it is unlikely that the tax can be shifted forward to consumers. Rather it will be borne by immobile factors within the state.

State Taxation of Multinational Corporate Income

The spirited discussion in recent years concerning state taxation of corporate income has included an even more heated issue than what formula should be used for the interstate apportionment of the tax base. That issue deals with the methods of determining the tax base of firms with international operations.

APPORTIONMENT FORMULAS FOR WORLDWIDE INCOME. By the start of 1984, eleven states had extended the apportionment concept to the worldwide operations of unitary business enterprises. Under this approach, known as worldwide unitary combination, the state determines a firm's taxable income by applying an apportionment formula to the company's worldwide income (and factors). This approach makes consistent the state's tax treatment of domestic and international corporations. Use of this technique is supported by the Supreme Court's ruling in the *Container* case that the worldwide unitary combination method violated neither the due process clause nor the commerce clause of the U.S. Constitution.[17]

The alternative to formula apportionment of the worldwide income of multinational firms is separate accounting. Under separate accounting, the income of a corporation is computed independently of the income of its affiliates. The major operational problem is to allocate the income of a commonly controlled corporate group among the various affiliates. To prevent the shifting of income to low-tax jurisdictions through manipula-

17. *Container Corporation of America* v. *Franchise Tax Board*, 463 U.S. 159 (1983).

tion of transfer prices or overhead costs, transactions within the group must be carried out at prices that would exist if the corporations were unrelated. Where no market prices are available, it is permissible to apply resale price or a cost-plus measure.

When applied to the taxation of multinational corporations, separate accounting implies that the income factors of overseas affiliates are not included in calculating apportionable domestic income of U.S. parent firms (this "water's edge" approach combines a formula apportionment of domestic income with separate accounting for foreign income). Similarly, only the earnings of foreign-owned companies' subsidiaries located in the United States are subject to apportionment among the states. The apportionment cannot be based on the worldwide income of the foreign-owned multinational firm.

ARGUMENTS AGAINST WORLDWIDE UNITARY COMBINATION. In the debate about the appropriate method of taxing corporate income, worldwide unitary combination has been attacked as producing an erroneous measure of corporate income, resulting in extraterritorial taxation of foreign-source income. It is argued that the inclusion of foreign payroll in the apportionment formula (where foreign wages are lower than those paid in the United States) results in a greater portion of income being attributed to the corporation's domestic operations.

Businesses have argued that the lack of a clear definition of the criteria that make a corporation and its foreign affiliates a unitary enterprise has led to business uncertainty and often resulted in inequities in the tax treatment of corporations. Furthermore, worldwide unitary combination is considered to be in violation of U.S. international tax treaties, which are based on separate accounting principles. The model tax treaties of the Organization for Economic Cooperation and Development and the United Nations, which are the basis for international practice, endorse the separate accounting, or water's edge, approach.

Because multinational firms that are foreign-based have a greater share of their operations outside the United States than do those that are American-based, worldwide unitary combination may place the foreign firms at a competitive disadvantage. The payroll factor in the apportionment formula in this instance may overstate the portion of their income that is generated in the United States. Foreign multinational corporations must, in addition, bear a heavy administrative burden if they are forced to translate their international operating results into dollar terms and conform to the reporting requirements of the taxing states.

ARGUMENTS AGAINST SEPARATE ACCOUNTING. Opponents of separate accounting claim that it creates the potential for tax avoidance through the shifting of profits to low-tax jurisdictions. The auditing and enforcement effort needed to police multinational corporations is simply beyond the resources of the states. State officials are inclined to oppose separate accounting because they believe that it will not generate as much tax revenue as would worldwide unitary combination.

A further complaint is that when a business enterprise is truly unitary, shared expenses, overhead, and economies of scale may make it impossible in principle to separate the income of the affiliates. For example, economies of scale allow a more than proportionate increase in output for a proportionate increase in inputs. There may be no accurate way to allocate among the affiliates the "surplus" generated by the economies of scale.

OVERSTATING CORPORATE INCOME. Would the worldwide unitary method result in an overstatement of corporate income relative to what that income would be under a separate accounting approach? An examination of the one hundred largest U.S. manufacturing firms, which in line with standard reporting requirements allocate profits, sales, and assets between U.S. and foreign sources, found it would. Profits calculated using a worldwide apportionment formula exceeded book profits—representing separate accounting results—by approximately 13 percent. Most of the measured overapportionment occurred in the petroleum and automobile industries, where domestic earnings were weak but profits from overseas operations were strong.[18] A follow-up study of ninety-one large U.S. manufacturing firms (which accounted for over 60 percent of U.S. manufacturing pretax profits) over the period 1979–81 confirmed those findings. Apportioned profits exceeded book profits in all three years, with the difference ranging from 8.7 percent to 0.4 percent.[19] Again, the discrepancy was accounted for predominantly by the automobile and petroleum industries. In fact, when these industries were excluded from the calculations, book profits actually exceeded apportioned profits slightly in both 1980 and 1981.

18. Sheffrin and Fulcher, "Alternative Division of the Tax Base." Two points of caution should be emphasized. First, the study compared apportioned profits to book profits, which can differ significantly from the relevant measure—taxable profits. Second, lacking data on foreign versus domestic payroll, apportionment formula included only sales and assets.

19. Steven M. Sheffrin and Jack Fulcher, "The *Container Case:* Can We Identify the Winners and Losers?" National Tax Association–Tax Institute of America, *Proceedings of the Seventy-sixth Annual Conference on Taxation, 1983* (Columbus, Ohio: NTA-TIA, 1984), pp. 34–35.

Perhaps the major lesson is that the use of one approach or the other can lead to substantial variation in the treatment of particular industries.

INCLUSION OF DIVIDENDS IN TAXABLE INCOME. Whether or not dividends received by a corporation should be included in its taxable income is another controversial issue. The treatment of dividends varies significantly from state to state. Dividends received from a domestic corporation are subject to taxation in thirty-seven states, but full or partial deductions for these dividends are often allowed. Foreign-source dividends are treated in ways ranging from full taxation to full exemption to allocation to the state of commercial domicile.

States' taxation of intercorporate dividends raises conceptual difficulties. The state corporate income tax is based on the principle of taxation at source. Accordingly, separate accounting and formula apportionment (the unitary method) have a common goal, to assign income to its source for purposes of taxation. When states tax intercorporate dividends arising outside their jurisdiction, they violate this source principle and create the potential for the multiple taxation of income as when a foreign subsidiary is taxed by the host country and its repatriated dividends by the states.

In addition, the taxation of dividends paid by one affiliate to another runs against the logic of the unitary approach. If an enterprise is truly unitary, taxation should be based only on the consolidated statement of the unitary enterprise. The inclusion of interaffiliate dividends in the income to be apportioned runs counter to this principle.

Recommendations of the Worldwide Unitary Taxation Task Force

In 1983, President Reagan appointed a working group of representatives from the administration, the states, and business to analyze the issues and recommend a solution to the controversy surrounding the worldwide unitary combination method. This initiative was taken in the wake of the Supreme Court's 1983 *Container* decision upholding the constitutionality of California's worldwide unitary combination method of taxing corporate income. The administration had come under pressure from foreign governments and multinational firms to take action against states, either by filing an amicus curiae brief in support of the Container Corporation's petition for a rehearing or by supporting federal legislation that would curtail states' use of the method. Being sensitive to states' prerogatives to determine their fiscal affairs, the administration hoped that the work of the task force would eliminate the need for further confrontation.

The major controversy seemed to center on the use of formula apportionment versus separate accounting. Yet, to the surprise of many, the task force was able to agree on separate accounting beyond the water's edge while leaving the question of taxation of intercorporate dividends unresolved. The working group agreed in 1984 that the federal government would provide administrative assistance and cooperation to the states "to promote full taxpayer disclosure and compliance," and that the Internal Revenue Service would increase its auditing of multinational corporations, and federal tax information would be made more accessible to states. The states, in turn, would aim their tax policies at maintaining "competitive balance among all business taxpayers, including foreign multinationals, U.S. multinationals, and purely domestic business."[20]

Participants representing state interests were adamant about maintaining the right to tax foreign-source dividends. As a practical matter, foreign dividends are a significant component of corporate income and thus tax revenues would be reduced significantly by their exclusion from the tax base. They rejected the argument that taxation of corporate dividends represents an unwarranted additional layer of taxation. Their view was that state and federal tax systems are concurrent rather than competing and the fact that dividends may have already been taxed at the national level is irrelevant for their right to tax these same dividends. They also argued that dividends should be included in the state corporate tax base because, particularly in the foreign context, they can be surrogates for interest or royalties or for reductions in the cost of goods sold. Thus, unless dividends are included in the tax base, firms will have an easy avenue to tax avoidance.

Spokesmen for business, on the other hand, claimed that taxation of dividends amounts to multiple taxation of corporations' income and puts them at a competitive disadvantage vis-à-vis foreign-based businesses whose dividends are not taxed. Recognizing that the exemption of foreign-source dividends from state taxation would bring a significant revenue loss to some states, businesses have expressed a willingness to work with states to develop nondividend sources of revenue.

Immediately after the release of the working group's report in May 1984, it was clear that the controversy had not been resolved. State governments were making acceptance of a water's edge approach contingent

20. Department of the Treasury, Worldwide Unitary Taxation Working Group, *The Final Report of the Worldwide Unitary Taxation Working Group* (Treasury Department, 1984).

on their right to tax foreign-source dividends. Businesses, however, continued to lobby against the inclusion of these dividends.

In spite of the deep disagreement, several states moved to replace their use of the worldwide unitary combination with the water's edge concept. Certainly, an important factor in these decisions was the promise in the working group agreement of federal support in auditing the tax returns of multinational companies. But perhaps as significant was the "divide and conquer" technique used by foreign-owned companies. They threatened to withhold further investment from states using the unitary method and in several well-publicized instances they made plant location decisions conditional on the state's willingness to abandon worldwide unitary combination.[21]

Within six months, Oregon, California, Florida, Indiana, Massachusetts, North Dakota, Utah, and Colorado had taken legislative or administrative action aimed at implementing the water's edge approach. And several states had moved away from the strong position they held on the taxation of foreign-source dividends during the working group deliberations. Florida adopted separate accounting exclusive of foreign-source dividends and increased the corporate tax rate to make up for the revenue loss. In California a bill was introduced that would exclude 85 percent of foreign-source dividends from taxation.

Death and Gift Taxes

Death and gift taxes are not an important source of state tax revenue—in 1984 they provided only 1.1 percent of total state collections. Twenty-one states and the District of Columbia in 1984 levied inheritance taxes, which are applied to individual bequests. Nine states used estate taxes, which are levied on the entire estate. Both inheritance and estate taxes have a progressive rate structure. In many states the rate on the inheritance varies depending on the relation of the deceased to the recipient. As might be expected, several states completely exempt surviving spouses from inheritance tax. Nineteen states had only pick-up taxes, which are employed to

21. To foreign-based multinational firms, the worldwide unitary versus water's edge question is the dominant issue. Under the water's edge approach, the dividends paid by U.S.-based subsidiaries to the foreign parent are irrelevant for U.S. tax purposes. In fact, if states retained taxation of U.S. firms' foreign-source dividends, the foreign-based companies would gain a competitive advantage (in violation of the working group agreement).

capture the credit allowed on federal taxes. Nine states levied taxes on gifts.[22]

There is, of course, a marked variation in yield among the states. For twenty-one states, death and gift taxes in 1984 provided less than $6 per capita of tax revenue, for thirteen between $6 and $10, for eight between $10 and $15, and for four between $15 and $20. For four—Connecticut, Massachusetts, New Jersey, and Pennsylvania—these taxes supplied over $20 per capita.[23]

The Federal Tax Credit

The state governments have used death taxes much longer than the federal government. On three occasions before 1916 a federal tax was used as an emergency device—1798–1802, 1861–70, and 1898–1902—and repealed when the emergency need had passed. A few state governments levied inheritance taxes early in the nineteenth century, but by 1891 less than ten states were using these taxes, all of them with low flat rates. Thereafter the need for revenue and an agitation against concentration of wealth combined to popularize the tax. By 1916 forty-two states were levying it (all but Florida, Mississippi, New Mexico, Nebraska, South Carolina, and Alabama), usually at low progressive rates, raising $30.7 million or 8.4 percent of their tax revenue. Almost all of the taxes were on inheritances.

In 1916 the federal government imposed an estate tax, a claim against the entire net estate left by a decedent. The state governments, by virtue of long prior occupancy, regarded death taxation as their preserve, and they resented federal intrusion. Further, the states advanced the legal theory that they—and not the federal government—had the right to regulate the descent and distribution of property at death. In the 1920s, when federal finances eased and those of the state governments tightened, agitation for federal repeal mounted. In 1924, a curious compromise emerged. Congress raised the rates of the federal estate tax, but it also provided for a credit of up to 25 percent against the federal tax for death taxes paid to the states. If, for example, the federal tax on an estate was $100 and the state tax $25, the total tax, after credit, would be $100 rather than $125.

22. Census Bureau, *State Government Finances in 1984,* table 6; Federation of Tax Administrators, *Tax Administrators News* (Chicago: FTA, May 29, 1985).

23. Census Bureau, *State Government Finances in 1984,* tables 6, 36. For the United States as a whole, per capita collections on death and gift taxes in 1984 were $9.45.

At this time (1924) three states—Florida, Nevada, and Alabama—were without a death tax. Florida had never had such a tax, but in November 1924, by constitutional amendment, it forbade enactment of either inheritance or income taxes. The purpose of this move was only too apparent; by supplementing the attractions of its climate with the establishment of a tax haven, Florida hoped to induce rich people to choose Florida as their home. Since domicile for the purpose of taxation was easy to establish, the other states had reason to fear the migration of estates beyond their jurisdiction. Nevada promptly met the threat, or rather imitated Florida, by passing a similar constitutional amendment in July 1925; California, which had up to this time been the natural competitor of Florida as a domicile for retired millionaires, discussed the need for parallel action.

Nothing more was needed to bring home the realization that the future of death taxes as a source of state revenue was in serious jeopardy. At the very time when many state officers were urging federal withdrawal from the field, here were illustrations of the inability of the states to use a system of death taxation with success.

In an attempt to stifle the anarchistic moves of Florida and Nevada, and to apply pressure on the states generally to reform their taxes, a committee of federal and state representatives was formed to consider remedies for the existing difficulties over death taxation. The major recommendation, which was subsequently enacted by Congress, was to increase the federal tax credit from 25 percent to 80 percent. By this step the tax advantages sought by Florida and Nevada were largely canceled, since the estate of a decedent in those states would pay the full federal tax.

This was the turning point of the movement for repeal of the federal tax. Many state officials were, on the one hand, pacified by the 80 percent credit, and on the other hand, timid about the prospect of federal withdrawal. For a few years progress toward reform was made.[24] In 1931 federal credits for state taxes offset, on the average, 75.6 percent of the federal tax liability; the number of states using the estate tax only had risen from two in 1925 to seven in 1932, and the number using estate and inheritance taxes jointly had risen from three to twenty-seven.

But in 1931–32 all such progress stopped because of the depression. Congress underscored this retreat when, in 1932, it enacted a supplemen-

24. The reform came through decisions of the Supreme Court that limited the situs of intangible goods to the domicile of the decedent, and through adoption of reciprocity (that is, state A would exempt intangible goods of nonresident decedents provided that state B reciprocated).

tary estate tax (with an exemption of $50,000) against which no credit for state taxes was provided. The provisions were retained, including the 80 percent credit, but the idea of repeal was no longer contemplated. On several later occasions Congress increased the federal rates and altered the exemptions in order to increase federal collections. As a result, the federal tax credit, which in 1931 came to nearly 76 percent of the federal tax liability, had declined by 1942 to 10 percent. The aim of providing the states with a larger share of death tax revenue was sidetracked.

In 1984 the federal government received 73 percent of all death and gift taxes, with the remaining 27 percent going to states.[25] With the effective average federal credit for state death taxes near 27 percent, a strong incentive exists for interstate competition. The result has been decreased reliance on state death taxes. Between 1979 and 1984, inheritance taxes were repealed in Colorado, Maine, Missouri, Texas, Washington, and Wyoming. In the same years, Arizona, North Dakota, Utah, Vermont, and Virginia repealed their existing estate taxes. In every state, the old law was replaced by a pick-up tax provision. Thus the states can receive the full amount allowable as a federal tax credit and avoid having residents flee their jurisdiction because of the death tax. With a pick-up tax, the total (federal plus state) death tax is the same as if the state had no death tax. Without the pick-up tax, all of the revenue would go to the federal government.

Conclusion

The weight of the arguments in favor of federal withdrawal from death taxes has diminished over the decades. After nearly seventy years of unbroken federal occupancy, the historical plea of prior state occupancy seems unconvincing, and while property does pass at death under state law, the constitutional right of the federal government to tax transfer of property at death is now beyond dispute.

The primary question is whether or not death taxation is a logical or promising source of state revenue. Death tax revenue from its very nature is unstable for the nation as a whole. This instability increases when the taxing unit is a state because, in such case, the yearly number of returns is small and the composition of taxable estates is highly variable from state to state. The sources of private wealth recognize no state lines, and the

25. Census Bureau, *Governmental Finances in 1983–84,* table 4.

basis on which the states mainly rest their right to tax—domicile of the decedent—is often quite unrelated to the geographic origin of a decedent's wealth. In short, for most states the death tax is not now, and cannot be, a satisfactory revenue source. The recent trend toward decreased reliance on death taxes and the use of pick-up taxes is evidence of this reality.

CHAPTER SEVEN

The Property Tax

A tax as ancient as that on property tends to become an institution and to accumulate fondly clinging traditions as it evolves over the years.

ACIR, *The Role of the States in Strengthening the Property Tax*

DURING most of the history of the nation, the property tax has been, by a wide margin, the most important tax revenue source. Table 7-1 shows that in 1902 it provided 51 percent of total federal, state, and local tax collections. No other tax even approached it in importance. As late as 1940 the property tax provided nearly 35 percent of total tax collections; the second-ranking tax, on corporation income, provided 10 percent. With World War II, however, the property tax lost ground. By 1944 it provided only 9 percent of total collections and was outranked by the revenue from taxes on individual and corporate income.[1] A major reason for the shift was, of course, the vast expansion of *federal* tax collections to which the property tax made no contribution, since it was, and always had been, wholly a source of state and local funds.[2] After the war the property tax regained some ground, but its relative importance began to fall again in the 1970s and by 1984 it provided only 13 percent of total tax collections.

Significance to State and Local Governments

The significance of the property tax as a source of state and local tax revenue is indicated in table 7-1. Completely dominant in 1902, and only slightly less so in the 1920s, the property tax lost relative ground in the 1930s and during World War II, which it never regained. In 1984 property

1. U.S. Census Bureau, *Historical Statistics of the United States: Colonial Times to 1957* (U.S. Government Printing Office, 1960), p. 722.

2. The so-called direct tax levied by the federal government in 1798, 1814–19, and 1861 might be regarded as a property tax, since it was levied chiefly against property. See Paul Studenski and Herman E. Krooss, *Financial History of the United States*, 2d ed. (McGraw-Hill, 1963), pp. 50–51, 76–78, 92, 141.

Table 7-1. *Property Tax Collections and Total Federal, State, and Local Tax Collections, Selected Years, 1902–84*

	Tax collections (millions of dollars)			Property tax collections as a percent of	
Year	*Federal, state, and local*	*State and local*	*Property*	*Federal, state, and local tax collections*	*State and local tax collections*
1902	1,373	860	706	51	82
1927	9,451	6,087	4,730	50	78
1938	12,949	7,605	4,440	34	58
1948	51,218	13,342	6,126	12	46
1957	98,632	28,817	12,864	13	45
1967	176,121	61,000	26,047	15	43
1978	465,161	193,642	66,422	14	34
1984	735,023	320,194	96,457	13	30

Source: Appendix table A-2. In all tables years are fiscal unless otherwise noted and figures are rounded.

taxes provided only 30 percent of the total state and local tax collections. The reason for the decline was that state governments replaced the property tax with other revenue sources, chiefly sales and income taxes.

Hastening the adoption of alternative revenue sources was the administratively awkward arrangement through which states received property tax revenue. State governments did not assess and collect property tax through state officers; instead they apportioned to their local governments a yearly sum that the local governments were instructed to secure and turn over to the state treasury. This procedure was not popular and when in the 1930s delinquency in property tax payments became large, the state tax was bitterly resented. As a measure of relief to local governments, many state governments discontinued their tax; collections, which were 23 percent of state taxes in 1927, fell to 4 percent in 1948 (see appendix table A-2). The downward trend has continued; in 1984, the figure was 2 percent. The general property tax has become a local tax. The proposition that state and local sources of taxation should be separate, rather than overlapping, found practical application here.

Not only has the general property tax become local, but in terms of revenue productivity it is the dominant local tax. In 1984 it provided about 75 percent of local tax revenue. The efforts of local governments during the past forty years to develop other taxes have borne some fruit. And nontax revenues have been found that help finance local governments—notably state and federal aid and charges collected for services. As table 7-2 shows, these nontax revenues provided about one-quarter of local

Table 7-2. *General Revenue of Local Governments, 1927 and 1984*

Millions of dollars and, in parentheses, percent of total

Source	*1927*	*1984*
Tax revenue		
Property tax	4,360 (74)	92,595 (29)
Other taxes	119 (2)	30,804 (10)
Nontax revenue		
State and federal aid	605 (10)	126,732 (39)
Charges and miscellaneous	819 (14)	73,105 (23)
Total general revenue	5,903 (100)	323,326 (100)

Sources: U.S. Census Bureau, *Historical Statistics of the United States: Colonial Times to 1957* (U.S. Government Printing Office, 1960), p.729; Census Bureau, *Governmental Finances in 1983–84* (GPO, 1985), table 23.

funds in 1927; in 1984 they provided more than 60 percent. Therefore, if attention is concentrated on all general revenue, the importance of the property tax to local governments has diminished.

Local governments are of many types, and the property tax is not of the same importance to all of them. As table 7-3 shows, the dependence of school districts on the property tax is nearly complete—it provides 97 percent of their tax revenue—and that of counties, townships, and special districts is also great. Municipalities, however, have managed to secure half of their tax revenue from other sources.

The extreme dependence of local governments on the property tax rests on one ineluctable fact—lack of option. No other tax is available for such productive use. Local taxation of income, sales, or business would induce shrinkage in the tax base and, therefore, bring serious injury to the locality. But real property is quite immobile.

If property tax changes are fully capitalized into property values, then an owner has no financial incentive to relocate, since the windfall loss on the sale of his property would exactly reflect the differential in property levies between his present residence and other jurisdictions. Moreover, manufacturing establishments, once committed, tend to stay put, since even severe property taxes are a modest part of their total costs. In short, real property offers a base on which local governments can safely levy taxes.

The yield of the tax since World War II has been quite significant, responding well in the aggregate to increases in gross national product, as well as to increases of population. Recent evidence of the underlying strength of the property tax may be found in the tax-limitation movement. In several states, techniques have been devised to curb the rising revenues generated by the property tax (see chapter 12).

Table 7-3. *Local Government Property Tax, Tax Revenue, and General Revenue, by Type of Govermental Unit, 1984*

	Amount (millions of dollars)			Property tax as a percent of	
Governmental unit	*General revenue*	*Tax revenue*	*Property tax*	*General revenue*	*Tax revenue*
All units	323,236	123,399	92,595	29	75
Counties	77,142	27,901	21,343	28	76
Municipalities	104,856	43,719	22,061	21	50
School districts	109,645	41,633	40,341	37	97
Townships and special districts	39,315	10,146	8,852	23	87

Source: Census Bureau, *Governmental Finances in 1983–84,* table 23.

Incidence and Economic Effects

How should the property tax be rated in terms of the principles of taxation? Does it conform to standards of equity? How does its incidence compare with that of other taxes? What are its economic effects? To make this appraisal, let it be assumed that administration of the property tax conforms to good current practice (now achieved in somewhat less than one-half of all local areas). In particular, let the assumption be made that the assessment of real property (the mainstay of the tax) is quite uniform within each taxing jurisdiction and levied on the gross value of real property.

This definition itself brings into view some obvious problems. The base of the tax is gross value, rather than an individual's net worth, and this is characteristic of an impersonal tax that is levied against things. Against this gross value a proportional tax rate is levied. If equity is held to indicate that tax payments be proportional among income groups (not to say progressive) in relation to net wealth, the impersonal property tax is defective.

Incidence

One estimate of the incidence of the property tax, based on 1980 data, indicates that the level of the effective property tax rate across income classes follows a U-shaped pattern with a regressive range running up to those people with family income of about $30,000. The estimates, developed by Joseph Pechman according to traditional or orthodox assumptions concerning the shifting and incidence of these taxes, are shown in table 7-4. Under the traditional approach, the property tax is treated as two separate taxes on land and on improvements. The shifting assumptions are that the tax on land falls entirely on the landlord (that is, taxes are fully capitalized in the price of land) and that the tax on improvements is reflected in higher prices for shelter and other goods. The relative rates presented in table 7-4 show the variation—in either direction—from the average tax rate for property taxes (the value of 100 is assigned to the average effective tax rate).[3]

The alternative view is that the tax burden falls on property income rather than being shifted forward to consumers in the form of higher prices for goods. The property tax is seen as a tax on capital income and falls most immediately on owners of capital in the taxing jurisdiction. But, over time the tax imposed by one jurisdiction will cause adjustments that spread the burden to all owners of capital. Capital will be redeployed to low-tax jurisdictions until after-tax return to capital is equal across locations.[4] Under the alternative incidence assumptions in table 7-4, the tax burden appears to be quite progressive.

Which view, the traditional or the alternative, provides the more accurate picture of the incidence of property taxes? The answer lies somewhere between the two. The use of current rather than permanent income does overstate the regressive nature of the tax. The more crucial problem, however, is measuring the elasticity of the supply of capital. The traditional view assumes an elastic supply of capital, the alternative view an inelastic supply. Unfortunately the empirical evidence on this point is meager and a definitive answer to the question is unavailable.[5]

Some writers have argued that the property tax is a benefit levy and should be regarded as a payment by individuals for services rendered. This

3. Critics point out that the use of current income rather than average or permanent income in the calculation of effective tax rates overstates the regressivity of the property tax. In any given year some people experience unusual gains and others unusual losses. Thus, two families with the same permanent income who perhaps consume the same amount of housing may have different amounts of current income. Dividing property tax payments by current income produces a regressive tax distribution. See Henry J. Aaron, *Who Pays the Property Tax? A New View* (Brookings, 1975), pp. 27–32.

4. For a detailed description and analysis of the various views of property tax incidence, see George F. Break, "The Incidence and Economic Effects of Taxation," in Alan S. Blinder and others, *The Economics of Public Finance* (Brookings, 1974), pp. 154–68; Aaron, *Who Pays the Property Tax?* chap. 3; J. Richard Aronson, *Public Finance* (McGraw-Hill, 1985), chaps. 16, 17.

5. Aaron, *Who Pays the Property Tax?* pp. 49–50.

Table 7-4. *Estimated Effective Property Tax Rates under Two Sets of Incidence Assumptions, by Income Class, 1980*

Percent

Adjusted family income (thousands of dollars)	*Orthodox incidence assumptions*[a]	*Alternative incidence assumptions*[b]
0–5	343	50
5–10	130	30
10–15	104	45
15–20	91	45
20–25	91	50
25–30	91	60
30–50	96	70
50–100	100	110
100–500	96	195
500–1,000	96	260
1,000 and over	100	290
All classes	100	100

Source: Joseph A. Pechman, *Who Paid the Taxes, 1966–85?* (Brookings, 1985), p. 56.

a. The tax on land is borne by landowners; the tax on improvements is shifted in the form of higher prices of shelter and consumption.

b. The burden of property taxes on both land and improvements is apportioned according to property income.

argument is most plausible with respect to such local governmental services as fire protection, street improvements, sewerage construction and operation, and street lighting. But even here general benefits, which spill over to the community, are present. And education expenditure, the most important component of local budgets, is not related in any meaningful sense to property taxes. The benefits from primary and secondary education spread far beyond the recipients, and assessment of property tax for it is, moreover, quite unrelated even to the direct benefits that accrue to recipients. The general property tax is, then, only partially a benefit tax.

Economic Effects

What are the economic effects of the property tax? Since it is levied on ownership of property (especially real property) rather than on current economic effort, it does not adversely affect labor incentives. But the tax must discourage private spending for housing and thus reduce the housing supply by some unascertainable amount. Similarly, it has adverse effects on business investment in taxable property. In urban areas the property tax, combined with fragmentation of governmental units, has a distorting effect on land-use patterns. When property taxes are not fully capitalized into property values, heavy taxes on property in core cities induce business and people to move to the suburbs, and the migration of relatively wealthy individuals and on-going businesses from the core city increases the pressure on cities to raise taxes further.[6]

Judged, therefore, in terms of equity and economic effects, the property tax cannot be awarded a high position. As a source of state income, it has no attraction, because other broad-based and productive taxes are in successful use. But for local governments the property tax provides a large, predictable, certain, and elastic revenue.

The Base of Property Taxation

During colonial times and the early years of the Republic, property was taxed selectively and at nonuniform rates. But with the nineteenth century a strong swing began toward inclusion of all property in the tax base, and toward taxation within each jurisdiction at a uniform rate. Governmental property was exempt and so also was the property of religious, charitable, and educational establishments. The main component in the tax base was real property—land and its improvements. But personal property—tangible and intangible—was another component. Tangible personal property includes machinery, inventory, livestock, motor vehicles, furniture, jewelry, and so on; here the significant split is between business property (including farms) and household effects. Intangible personal property consists of legal rights to valuable things—stocks, bonds, mortgages, bank deposits, and the like. Most of these are "representative" of real property or of tangible personal property; a few—such as patents and copyrights—are nonrepresentative; and sometimes intangible assets are mixed. Inclusion in the tax base of both the representative property and the real property on which the representative property rests is clearly duplicative.

In 1981, 90 percent of the $2,799 billion value of locally assessed

6. Jesse Burkhead, *State and Local Taxes for Public Education* (Syracuse University Press, 1963), p. 106, suggests that "although imperfections remain, property tax resources do tend to be more uniformly distributed among the municipalities within a given metropolitan area over time." For a less optimistic view, see Dick Netzer, *Economics of the Property Tax* (Brookings, 1966), pp. 67–85. For an analysis of how taxes and expenditures affect the distribution of population in metropolitan areas, see J. Richard Aronson and Eli Schwartz, "Financing Public Goods and the Distribution of Population in a System of Local Governments," *National Tax Journal*, vol. 26 (June 1973), pp. 137–60.

property was real, as the following comparison of assessed values in recent years indicate:[7]

Property	Assessed value (billions of dollars)			Percent of total		
	1956	*1973*	*1981*	*1956*	*1973*	*1981*
Real	209.8	704.6	2,514.9	81.3	86.6	89.8
Personal	48.3	108.7	284.2	18.7	13.4	10.2

Residential (nonfarm) property was the most important contributor to the real tax base. Assessments on personal property applied almost wholly to tangible goods.

Tangible personal property in 1981 was legally exempt from taxation in eight states (Delaware, Hawaii, New York, Illinois, New Hampshire, North Dakota, South Dakota, and Pennsylvania); general coverage prevailed in ten states, and partial coverage elsewhere. The disappearance from the assessment rolls of some kinds of tangible property, such as household effects, is notorious, even though state law has not always recognized this fact. Assessors cannot ascertain the existence of such property by acceptable administrative techniques, and they cannot accurately value it when ascertained.

Commercial and industrial tangible personal property was legally taxable in forty-three states in 1981, household personal property in sixteen states, and motor vehicles in nineteen states. This listing exaggerates the taxation of household personal property, since many of the sixteen states provided partial exemptions. But it underestimates the taxation of motor vehicles, since some states that exempt them from local general property tax apply a special property tax, and most of the remaining states apply some other form of taxation. Commercial and industrial property is generally the most important component of personal property.

Two kinds of tangible personal property—one, machinery and equipment, the other, inventory—are used in business. The former has been a more satisfactory component of the property tax than the latter. Inventory is movable, its amount is often highly variable over the year, and its turnover is different from industry to industry (and even among firms in

7. Census Bureau, *Census of Governments, 1957,* vol. 5: *Taxable Property Values in the United States* (GPO, 1959), p. 22; *1982,* vol. 2: *Taxable Property Values and Assessment-Sales Price Ratios* (GPO, 1982), p. 2. Census Bureau, *Property Values Subject to Local General Property Taxation in the United States: 1973* (GPO, 1974), p. 32.

the same industry). Inventory can, therefore, be manipulated for the purpose of tax avoidance and its removal from the property tax base has considerable appeal. Intangible property was legally part of the local general property tax base in thirteen states in 1981, but it does not represent a significant part of total assessed personal property. Louisiana had the highest ratio of intangible property to total personal property (almost 9 percent).[8]

When real property is compared with other types of property, discovery and assessment seem relatively easy. Adam Smith observed that "the quantity and value of the land which any man possesses can never be a secret, and can always be ascertained with great exactness."[9] While the history of property taxation in the United States makes this generalization seem oversanguine, the fact remains that real property can more readily be discovered and assessed than other kinds of property. In this area, administrative abuse is least defensible; and here abuse must be rooted out if the property tax is to be retained as the mainstay of local revenues.

Assessment

The most publicized and the most serious administrative fault of the general property tax is inaccurate assessment. The inaccuracy may result either from underassessment or from deviation of individual property values from the general assessment ratio of the taxing jurisdiction.

Underassessment

The *Census of Governments,* undertaken every fifth year since 1957, includes incisive and cogent materials concerning the valuation of real property across the nation. The Census Bureau has developed extensive tabulations of assessment-to-sales-price ratios on this most important component of the general property tax. The numerator of the ratios is assessed value, "as shown on local tax records prior to the sale"; the denominator is "measurable sales"—the price paid for properties "changing hands on an ordinary market basis."[10] In 1981 the average assessed value of locally assessed taxable real property was 40 percent of market value as indicated

8. Census Bureau, *Census of Governments, 1982,* vol. 2, pp. xviii, 260.

9. *The Wealth of Nations,* bk. 5, chap. 2, pt. 2.

10. Census Bureau, *Census of Governments, 1962,* vol. 2: *Taxable Property Values* (GPO, 1963), p. 9.

Table 7-5. *Distribution of States by Ratios of Assessed Value to Sales Price of Real Property, 1956, 1966, 1971, and 1981*

Assessments as a percent of sales	*1956*	*1966*	*1971*	*1981*
		Number of states		
0–9	2	1	5	13
10–19	16	17	11	8
20–29	16	10	9	7
30–39	4	7	10	5
40–49	7	6[a]	8[a]	1
50–59	2	6	4	5
60–69	1	2	1	7[a]
70 and over	0	2	3	5
		Percent		
Average	30.0	32.8	32.7	40.0

Sources: Census Bureau, *Census of Governments, 1957,* vol. 5: *Taxable Property Values in the United States* (GPO, 1959), p. 81; *1967,* vol. 2, table 9; *1972,* vol. 2, pt. 2: *Assessment–Sales Price Ratios and Tax Rates* (GPO, 1973), table 2; *1982,* vol. 2: *Taxable Property Values and Assessment–Sales Price Ratios* (GPO, 1984), pp. 20–25.

a. Includes the District of Columbia.

by measurable sales (see table 7-5). The state ratios ranged from 0.5 percent in Vermont to 78.9 percent in Kentucky. The actual level of assessment ratios is generally well below that prescribed by law.

Undervaluation in itself is not inequitable. If all property were assessed at some uniform percentage of true value, the result would be simply a higher rate of tax. In practice, however, general undervaluation induces inequity in individual assessments; it also impairs or defeats the objectives of other state financial legislation.

Inequity in Individual Assessments

More than half a century ago, Charles J. Bullock diagnosed the failure of uniform and general undervaluation:

> If the practice is to assess realty at its true value, the assessor has a definite mark at which to aim, and the citizen a definite standard by which he can compare his assessment with his neighbor's; but when the opposite practice prevails, assessor and taxpayer alike are left in uncertainty. Absolute accuracy, of course, is not to be expected, but errors can be more readily detected if the standard is full valuation. If two buildings worth $100,000 each are assessed, the one for $20,000 and the other for $18,000, the discrepancy seems to be but $2,000; in reality it is $10,000, since it represents one-tenth part of the tax burden.[11]

11. "The General Property Tax in the United States," in Charles J. Bullock, ed., *Selected Readings in Public Finance,* 3d ed. (Ginn, 1924), p. 293.

Table 7-6. *Illustrative Calculation of a Coefficient of Dispersion for Nine Properties*

Property	*Assessed value (dollars)*	*Assessment ratio*	*Deviation from median assessment ratio*[a]
A	6,400	32.0	18.0
B	7,400	37.0	13.0
C	8,000	40.0	10.0
D	8,800	44.0	6.0
E	10,000	50.0	0.0
F	11,000	55.0	5.0
G	11,600	58.0	8.0
H	12,800	64.0	14.0
I	13,200	66.0	16.0
Total	...	...	90.0[b]

Source: Frederick L. Bird, *The General Property Tax: Findings of the 1957 Census of Governments* (Chicago Public Administration Service, 1960), p. 54.

a. Negative signs are disregarded here.

b. Average deviation = 90.0/9 = 10.0. Coefficient of dispersion = (average deviation/median assessment ratio) × 100 = 20 percent.

Among the statistical evidence on the extent of undervaluation collected in the *Census of Governments* are assessment-to-sales ratios for census years since 1956, collected in over a thousand "selected areas" for non-farm houses, a class of property that is large and relatively homogenous.[12] The Census reckoned a median ratio for each area. Individual ratios would, of course, differ from the median, and an average of the difference can be computed. In illustrative table 7-6, the median assessment ratio of the nine properties is 50.0, and the average deviation is 10.0. Another area with the same average deviation of 10.0 might have a much lower median ratio, however—say, 25.0. To secure comparability between the ratios in different areas, the deviation from the median ratios within an area should be expressed in relative—not absolute—terms. This is accomplished by dividing the average deviation by the median assessment ratio. This measure—the coefficient of dispersion—is 20 percent for the series of properties with a median assessment ratio of 50.0 and an average deviation of 10.0, and 40 percent for the properties with a median assessment ratio of 25.0 and the same average deviation. The relative dispersion in the latter instance is greater than in the first.

Table 7-7 shows the median assessment ratios for nonfarm houses and their coefficients of dispersion for selected local areas in several recent years. The general relationship has been inverse: as assessment ratios rise, and assessments come closer to sales prices, the coefficients tend to

12. Census Bureau, *Census of Governments, 1982,* vol. 2, p. 49, and earlier issues.

Table 7-7. *Coefficients of Intra-area Dispersion for Principal Median Assessment Ratios for Nonfarm Houses, Selected Local Areas, 1956, 1966, 1971, and 1981*

Median assessment ratio	*Coefficient of dispersion*			
	1956	*1966*	*1971*	*1981*
Under 20.0	37.3	26.1	27.2	31.9
20.0–29.9	32.0	20.7	21.3	23.0
30.0–39.9	25.1	18.7	21.4	18.0
40.0 or more	22.2	15.8	16.6	16.1

Source: Census Bureau, *Census of Governments, 1957,* vol. 5, table 17; *1967,* vol. 2, table 14; *1972,* vol. 2, pt. 2, table 7; *1982,* vol. 2, table 16.

decline, and the relative deviation from the average diminishes. It seems, then, that severe undervaluation is unlikely to be uniform, and for this reason it engenders inequities in individual assessments.

Undervaluation has other faults. It obscures unequal assessments and thereby prevents a taxpayer from being aware that his assessment is out of line with that of other properties. He may suffer from an undervaluation illusion. Since the assessed value of his property is below market value, he may believe that he is especially favored and therefore be silent. Even if he is under no illusion, he will have difficulty in securing a review of his assessment. When the law specifies full value, acceptable evidence of undervaluation in support of an appeal for adjustment is not easy to obtain.

Impairment of Other Financial Objectives

Assessed valuations carried out by local governmental units have often been incorporated into state financial legislation.

Some state grants-in-aid and state-collected taxes distributed to local governments use assessed values as an indicator. For example, in allocating educational grants it is assumed that a low assessed value per child of school age indicates a low financial ability. But unless intra-area valuations are uniform, this is faulty evidence. In short, assessed value has been and is an elastic measuring stick.

State governments, perceiving this defect, have instituted state equalization of local assessments as a remedy. No attempt is made to value individual properties, but state officers estimate aggregate property values for each local unit, using these to secure an interarea standard for allocation. This technique, whatever its merits, does nothing to rectify inaccurate values of particular properties or to push localities toward full-value assessment. The two broad uses of assessed valuation by the state governments pull local governments in opposite directions. A locality is tempted to set a low valuation in order to reduce its share of county tax assessment and to set a high valuation in order to secure larger shares of state grants or of state distributions of taxes.

The state equalization process has often been crudely executed, resting on subjective and personalized decisions of a few state officers. In recent years, the sales-sampling technique has been developed. The ratios of sales price to assessed value are determined for a sample of recently sold properties, and these ratios constitute the basis for updating and equalizing the assessments of different localities. If the sample is adequate and representative, this method has merit.

Local assessed valuations have been used widely in state constitutions or in state legislation as the measure for ceilings on local debt and property tax rates. Extensive and variable underassessment means that regulatory policy is determined by the assessor as well as the constitution or statute. For example, if assessment ratios decline while tax and debt limit ratios remain fixed, the effective taxing and borrowing power of a governmental unit is reduced.

Tax exemptions are another instance in which the apparent objective of state legislation is distorted by general undervaluation. The homestead and the veterans' exemptions—the two common types—are usually specified in dollars. Thus, the greater the degree of underassessment, the more valuable is the exemption. For example, a flat $10,000 exemption is potentially twice as valuable to beneficiaries if the assessment ratio is 50 percent rather than 100 percent.

The remedy for the defects arising from underassessment is, in principle, quite obvious. Assessed values should be used only as the base for property taxes; constitutional and statutory requirements that they be used for other purposes should be abolished. A less sweeping remedy, assuming that state governments wish to continue partial property tax exemptions as well as local tax and debt limits, would be to specify that full value, rather than assessed value, should be the base.[13]

Uniformity of Intra-area Assessments

The goal of assessment should be uniformity within an area at some figure not much below fair value. Since perfection here is an aspiration

13. Advisory Commission on Intergovernmental Relations (ACIR), *The Role of the States in Strengthening the Property Tax* (GPO, 1963), vol. 1, pp. 60–61.

Table 7-8. *Distribution of Selected Local Areas by Coefficient of Intra-area Dispersion for Assessment Ratios of Nonfarm Houses, 1956, 1966, 1971, and 1981*

Coefficient of dispersion	*Percent of areas*				*Cumulative percent*			
	1956	*1966*	*1971*	*1981*	*1956*	*1966*	*1971*	*1981*
Under 15.0	7.9	28.2	24.6	29.4	7.9	28.2	24.6	29.4
15.0–19.9	12.5	25.2	24.3	17.9	20.4	53.4	48.9	47.3
20.0–29.9	29.7	27.1	30.2	23.8	50.1	80.5	79.1	71.1
30.0–39.9	21.1	9.8	11.8	11.9	71.2	90.3	90.9	83.0
40.0 and over	28.7	9.8	9.1	17.0	100.0	100.0	100.0	100.0

Source: Census Bureau, *Census of Governments, 1957,* vol. 5, table 19; *1967,* vol. 2, table 16; *1972,* vol. 2, pt. 2, table 9; *1982,* vol. 2, table 18.

only, the question arises: What standard of uniformity is achievable? What degree of variation is tolerable within each assessment area? Frederick L. Bird has suggested a coefficient of dispersion of 20.0 percent.[14] The cumulative percentages in table 7-8 show that the tolerable limit of coefficients of dispersion for nonfarm houses in 1956 was met by only 20.4 percent of the areas, in 1966 by 53.4 percent, and in 1981 by 47.3 percent. The marked improvement in assessment uniformity in the ten-year period from 1956 to 1966 was followed by a slight worsening in the degree of uniformity from 1966 to 1981. Table 7-9 shows the distribution of states by coefficients of intra-area dispersion. In 1966 two states had coefficients of dispersion over 30 percent. Again the trend appears to be marked improvement from 1956 to 1966 and then some regression during the period 1966–71. Between 1971 and 1981, however, as the table shows, there appears to have been a serious deterioration in assessment standards.[15]

14. *The General Property Tax: Findings of the 1957 Census of Governments* (Chicago: Public Administration Service, 1960), p. 54. The general property tax has the peculiarity that its base, and therefore the amount of the tax liability, is determined by administrative decision. Tax liability for retail sales tax or individual income tax is determined by the taxpayer, subject to the possibility of audit by administrators. Figures showing the results of state audits are rare and, for this reason, coefficients of dispersion for state retail sales and individual income taxes cannot be computed as they have been by the Census Bureau for assessments of nonfarm houses. Thus it is not possible to say whether such coefficients, if computed, would be larger or smaller than those for nonfarm houses. Other experts suggest that the benchmark for uniformity in assessment be a coefficient of dispersion of 10–15 percent. See John O. Behrens, "Taxable Property Values 1-6—Matters of De Facto," National Tax Association–Tax Institute of America, *Proceedings of the Seventy-seventh Annual Conference on Taxation, 1984* (Columbus, Ohio: NTA-TIA, 1985), pp. 2-3.

15. What can account for the deterioration in assessment results? It may be that with inflation, property values in general were increasing more quickly and unevenly than in the previous decade. Thus, even if reassessments were being carried out more often than in

Table 7-9. *Distribution of States by Coefficient of Intra-area Dispersion for Nonfarm Houses, 1956, 1966, 1971, and 1981*

Median area coefficient of dispersion	Number of states			
	1956[a]	*1966*	*1971*	*1981*
Under 15.0	1	5	5	8
15.0–19.9	2	19	13	8
20.0–24.9	5	14	14	13
25.0–29.9	10	10	14	5
30.0–34.9	11	2	2	10
35.0–39.9	11	0	1	3
40.0 and over	5	0	1	3

Sources: Same as table 7-8.
a. Not computed for Arizona, Delaware, Nevada, Hawaii, and Alaska.

The Role of the States in Reform

What part should state governments play in improving assessment procedures and, indeed, in reforming the property tax?

Six decades ago the theory in vogue was that separation of state and local sources of revenue would bring about the reform of the property tax, especially of assessment. State governments would withdraw from the property tax, leaving it wholly in the hands of local governments, and thereby remove the incentive for competitive undervaluation. E. R. A. Seligman argued also that real estate, the backbone of the tax, could "far better be valued by officials of the neighborhood who are cognizant of the local conditions."[16]

The argument in favor of state withdrawal was strongly reinforced by the desire of local governments to gain full control of property tax revenue, and in the 1940s state withdrawal became a fact. The evidence is strong that harm resulted. Local governments, in sole possession of general property taxation, did not improve administration; instead, standards of equity and assessment deteriorated. Moreover, the property available to local units as a tax base did not match particular local needs for expenditure. State governments were persuaded to provide financial assistance to poor localities. But sometimes this aid was misdirected; it went to units with no rational basis for existence, or to units whose fiscal ability, measured by property valuation, was misjudged.

1956–66, the new increased rate of change in values might still be reflected in higher coefficients of dispersion.

16. *Essays in Taxation*, 9th ed. (Macmillan, 1921), p. 353.

In what ways might greater state responsibility be displayed? One extreme would be for a state agency to assess all real property, collect the revenues, and turn over the collections to the local governments. Hawaii, which had used such a system, shifted to county assessment of property in the 1960s. It is unlikely that other states will attempt statewide assessment. But there are other reforms that are possible.[17]

States must continue to encourage if not mandate that assessors be professionally trained. There is some evidence that progress along these lines has been made.[18]

In 1973, the ACIR published twenty-nine recommendations for property tax reform.[19] Since then, numerous improvements have been made in property tax administration and assessment procedures.[20] States have been particularly active in computerizing the administration of the tax and many states conduct their own assessment-sales price ratio studies. Yet most observers agree that the task of property tax reform is still far from complete.[21]

Erosion of the Tax Base

Reform of the property tax, so that it may become a more powerful source of local revenue, will require that erosion of the base of the property tax be halted and even reversed. This also is mainly a task for state governments. Some of the erosion is so long established and so widespread as to be almost "impervious to question."[22] Exemption of the property of nonprofit religious, charitable, and educational institutions rests on the opinion that they render semigovernmental services and promote the public welfare. The total value of all such excluded property nationwide is unknown. However, the value of excluded property in

17. In 1973 Montana moved all assessing to the state level and Maryland began a three-year phasing-in period to do so. See ACIR, *The Property Tax in a Changing Environment: Selected State Studies* (GPO, 1974), p. 17.

18. Attendance by assessment personnel at professional development courses has been increasing in recent years. See International Association of Assessment Officers, "Report on the Fiscal Year 1984 Education Program" (Chicago: IAAO, 1985); IAAO, "Education Department Attendance History 1975–1984" (Chicago: IAAO, 1985).

19. See ACIR, *Role of the States*, p.104; ACIR, "The Property Tax—Reform and Relief—The Legislator's Guide" (Washington: ACIR, 1973).

20. See Behrens, "Taxable Property Values," p. 12.

21. Steven D. Gold, *Property Tax Relief* (Lexington Books, 1979), pp. 1–28.

22. ACIR, *Role of the States*, p. 83.

twenty-three states and the District of Columbia reported in the *1982 Census of Governments* showed $15 billion for religious institutions, $22 billion for educational, and $15 billion for charitable, accounting for 6 percent, 9 percent, and 6 percent, respectively, of the total value of exempted property. The most important category was the property holdings of governments themselves, which was valued at $128 million and accounted for 49 percent of the total reported (another $79 million, or 31 percent, could not be allocated).[23]

Tax base erosion occurs because property values are either removed or excluded from the base. In general, property value removed from the base refers to portions of otherwise taxable value that are exempt from taxation.[24] The exemption of major classes of property—intangible and some types of tangible personal property—has often been undertaken as a step in the reform of the general property tax; this erosion is often justifiable. But erosion by state legislation to provide hidden subsidies to private persons or firms is highly questionable. The property tax is paid directly only by owners, and property tax concessions cannot, therefore, be assured for a veteran or an aged person who is not an owner-occupant of real property. A tax concession to a class of persons—the aged—assumes that all of them are in need, and this is not so.

Business Exemptions

Exemption of certain types of industrial property from the local property tax for a specified period has, intermittently, been tried in many states. The aim is to induce investment in the locality by new firms, and some states permit existing firms to share in the subsidy by exempting additions to plant and equipment. Quantitative evidence concerning the effects of the exemption is scanty and unsatisfactory, partly because administration is usually by local governments with no central recording of the relevant data, and partly because data concerning investment and locational decisions by firms are often unreliable. Even if positive advantages are secured by a particular locality, these are offset by the injury to competitors elsewhere and to taxpayers in the locality. In a national sense, the exemption is bound to be injurious.

23. Census Bureau, *Census of Governments, 1982,* vol. 2, p. xlvii. The states were Arizona, California, Colorado, Florida, Georgia, Hawaii, Idaho, Indiana, Iowa, Kansas, Maine, Maryland, Massachusetts, Michigan, Minnesota, Nevada, New Jersey, New Mexico, New York, Ohio, Oregon, Rhode Island, West Virginia.

24. Ibid.

Table 7-10. *Homestead Exemptions in Twenty States and the District of Columbia, 1981*

State	*Assessed value removed by homestead exemptions (millions of dollars)*	*Percent of gross assessed value*
Alabama	1,595	17.5
California	29,138	4.4
Delaware	86	2.1
District of Columbia	626	3.3
Florida	36,595	14.7
Georgia	2,947	6.3
Hawaii	2,235	11.0
Idaho	1,133	4.6
Indiana	86	0.3
Kentucky	2,432	4.2
Louisiana	2,395	24.2
Mississippi	1,160	21.9
Nebraska	1,251	3.4
New Hampshire	135	0.9
North Carolina	1,017	0.9
North Dakota	7	0.8
Oklahoma	681	8.5
Oregon	161	0.2
Washington	966	0.8
West Virginia	474	3.3
Wyoming	103	1.6
Total	85,223	2.9

Source: Census Bureau, *Census of Goverments, 1982,* vol. 2, tables U, 2.

Homestead and Veterans' Exemptions

Twenty states and the District of Columbia allow some exemption from the local property tax to owner-occupied homes or farms (see table 7-10). Many states also grant some kind of property tax exemption to veterans. Only California, Indiana, Maine, and Rhode Island exempted a substantial amount of veterans' property—$302 million, $109 million, $116 million, and $108 million, respectively—in 1981; three other states exempted a total of $104 million.[25]

The pattern of tax relief provided by the homestead exemption can be criticized for its failure to take into account the financial situation of the individual, and there can be little justification in a plan that distributes rewards to veterans according to their ownership of property. Programs to

25. Nevada, New Mexico, and Wyoming; Connecticut, New York, Oklahoma, Texas, and Utah also granted exemptions to veterans, but the amount is not separately available. Ibid., p. xlix.

benefit veterans should rest on the need and merit of these individuals and be financed from the general revenues of the state. In general, property tax relief, whether for special groups or not, should take account of the individual's ability to pay. This has been the purpose of the circuit-breaker device.

Circuit Breakers

The ACIR describes circuit breakers as "tax relief programs designed to protect family income from property tax 'overload' the same way that an electrical circuit-breaker protects the family home from current overload."[26] That is, when the property tax burden on an individual exceeds a predetermined percentage of personal income, the circuit breaker goes into effect to relieve the excess financial pressure.

By 1984 thirty-two states and the District of Columbia had enacted circuit-breaker programs.[27] The ACIR has classified three types of circuit breakers—basic, expanded, and general—based on extent of coverage. Basic coverage provides relief to elderly homeowners and is used in six states. Expanded coverage offers relief to all of the elderly (either homeowners or renters) and is used in eighteen states. General circuit breakers are comprehensive in that the relief program applies to all overburdened taxpayers. That is, any family meeting the state income criteria may qualify for relief.[28]

One of the two methods used in designing the relief formula is the threshold approach. Under this scheme an acceptable level of taxation is defined as some fixed percentage of household income. The amount by which the actual property tax exceeds this level qualifies for relief. The other method is the sliding scale approach, under which a fixed percentage of property tax is rebated to taxpayers within each eligible income class; the higher the income class, the lower the percent of the property tax rebatable.[29]

26. ACIR, *Property Tax Circuit-Breakers: Current Status and Policy Issues* (Washington: ACIR, 1975), p. 2.

27. For a comprehensive listing of property tax relief policies for homeowners and renters, see ACIR, *Significant Features of Fiscal Federalism, 1982–83 Edition* (Washington: ACIR, 1984), table 69.

28. ACIR, *Property Tax Circuit-Breakers*, p. 3.

29. Ibid., pp. 3–4. For a family with an income of $10,000 and a property tax burden of $600, the property tax relief would be $100 under a threshold approach that fixed the acceptable tax level at 5 percent ($600 burden minus $500). But under a sliding scale

Generally the circuit breaker is built into the state income tax system. Either rebates are credited against the individual's state income tax liability or refund checks are sent. Although there are other techniques for administering the circuit breaker, the ACIR feels "this method is not only efficient, its confidentiality preserves the dignity of the recipient."[30] An ACIR survey for 1984 reports that about $1,401 million in total benefits was provided.[31]

The circuit breaker has two advantages over traditional homestead exemptions. First, in the distribution of benefits an attempt is made to take account of the individual's ability to pay. Second, the circuit breaker provides its relief without eroding local governments' property tax base.

The circuit-breaker idea, however, has not been free of criticism. Circuit breakers tend to subsidize those people with high ratios of property to current income and people with fluctuating incomes.[32]

An overall appraisal of the circuit-breaker device depends not only on whether the incidence of the property tax is thought to be regressive or progressive but also on how well it fits into the nation's system of income maintenance programs. There is no doubt that certain technical faults exist in circuit-breaker programs (for example, current income rather than permanent income is used to measure ability to pay). Nevertheless, circuit breakers provide cash payments to relatively poor people, and until a negative income tax or some other comprehensive income maintenance plan is established, the device has a place in the state tax structure.[33]

The States' Responsibility

Most of the erosion of the local property tax base is a matter of state decision; state legislatures have thereby subsidized worthy purposes or groups at the indirect expense of local governments. This form of subsidy fails to provide equitable benefits since provision is denied to members of

---

approach that allowed rebates of 15 percent for families with $7,000–$9,000 income, 12 percent for those with $9,000–$11,000, and 10 percent for those with $11,000–$13,000, the same family would be entitled to a $72 rebate (12 percent of $600). If the family's income were $12,000, the rebate would be $60.

30. Ibid., p. 2.

31. ACIR, *Significant Features, 1984,* table 71.

32. Aaron, *Who Pays the Property Tax?* pp. 71–91.

33. For an extensive discussion of circuit breakers, see Gold, *Property Tax Relief,* pp. 55–80.

the group who do not own real property and quite often given to those who do, regardless of their need; it fails also in the equitable distribution of costs, since the amount of property removed from the tax base of a locality is unrelated to its total financial situation. How, then, can one explain the use of property tax exemptions? State legislatures, responsive to organized pressure, use property tax exemption as a way to act without placing an expenditure in state (or local) budgets. But a slice is taken from the tax base of local governments. The indicated conclusion is that, if a state subsidy is to be offered, its weight should be on state rather than on local resources. An obvious step, when the subsidy takes the form of a property tax exemption, is reimbursement to local governments for the shrinkage in their tax base.

State Assessment of Property

Some kinds of property are quite unsuitable for local assessment. Such an instance emerged in the nineteenth century with the railroads. Valuation of the operating property of a railway, piece by piece, made no sense; the valuation had to be of the whole system or at least of the part lying within a state. As a result, most states decided to centrally assess railway property and most public utility property. Local governments, however, often are allowed to assess nonoperative property, that is, property within their jurisdiction that is owned by a utility but not part of its business operations. In 1981 state-assessed property amounted to $159 billion out of a total of $2,837 billion of taxable property.[34] The shift toward state assessment has not been easily achieved; it had to overcome "both the hostile presumption against any state agency and the natural inertia supporting the local assessor."[35] And the movement does not follow any simple patterns. Sometimes states not only value but tax the property for their own use; sometimes they apportion the centrally assessed valuation for taxation by local units.

34. Census Bureau, *Census of Governments, 1982,* vol. 2, table 2. Nine states and the District of Columbia have no state-assessed property; in twenty-two states, under 10 percent of total local taxable assessed value is represented by state-assessed property; in eight, 10–20 percent; in six, 20–30 percent; in another three, 30–40 percent; in one, 40–50 percent; and in one, 70–80 percent.

35. Jens P. Jensen, *Property Taxation in the United States* (University of Chicago Press, 1931), p. 420.

Conclusion

Unresolved problems remain in estimating the burden of distribution of the property tax among income groups. Whether the burden is regressive or progressive depends on whether it is assumed that the tax on capital improvements is shifted forward to consumers in the form of higher prices or the tax on property is felt primarily in the form of reduced income from capital. Whatever the incidence, however, continued improvement in the administration of the tax remains important. State supervision of local performance of many governmental functions—education, health, welfare—is already extensive. But a state government must be concerned with efficient performance of all duties by all its governmental units. State interest in establishing and maintaining reasonable standards of property tax administration should be as vital as the state's interest in public education. Moreover, efficient local use of the property tax will simplify for state governments the problems of financial transfers to localities.

In addition, state governments must admit that even perfect rehabilitation of the property tax would not provide many local governments with financial means adequate to their needs. It is the duty of each state to see that the level of performance of governmental services is adequate everywhere within its boundaries, and this may require extensive use of intergovernmental transfers. Efficient use of the property tax will help rather than hinder this process. Besides supplying localities with a substantial portion of the revenue that they need, it will establish a fair base from which additional financial needs can be measured.

CHAPTER EIGHT

Nonproperty Taxes and Nontax Revenue

After all the proper subjects of taxation have been exhausted, if the exigencies of the state still continue to require new taxes, they must be imposed upon improper ones.

The Wealth of Nations

THE DOMINANCE of the property tax as a source of tax revenue for local governments rests chiefly on the scarcity of alternatives. A local government has a limited and artificial territorial jurisdiction; movement of persons and of some types of property beyond its boundaries is easy, and this movement may be induced by differential local tax rates. But real estate—land and improvements—is largely immobile, and it can therefore be taxed by local governments with a less acute fear of consequences.

These simple generalizations are, however, less forceful and applicable for some types of local governments than others. A large city may, in some cases, have advantages as a center for distribution or manufacturing that are not greatly impaired by a city sales or income tax. A large city will, moreover, have administrative resources that may enable it to handle taxes quite beyond the capacity of a small city.

Local Nonproperty Taxes

It is not surprising that the first major employment of local nonproperty taxes was made by large cities. In 1934 New York City adopted a retail sales tax, and in 1938 New Orleans followed suit. Philadelphia in 1939 varied the pattern by adopting an earnings tax. The urgent and decisive force behind these experiments was the impact of severe depression. New York City was spending heavily for relief, and opposition to a sales tax was appeased by declaring the tax revenue to be "a contribution to relief." In Philadelphia similar financial pressures led, in 1938, to enactment of a sales tax; it was, however, repealed in less than a year because of the belief that trade was being diverted from the city. A flat-rate (1.5 percent) tax on income earned in Philadelphia by individuals and unincorporated businesses was accepted as a substitute. Dividends, interest, and corporate profits were not taxable.

These examples awakened the interest of city governments over the nation, an interest revivified after World War II by the accumulation of a large backlog of desired public services. In two states, Ohio and California, "home rule" statutes allowed extensive tax powers to local governments; specific enabling legislation for such localities was not necessary. Accordingly, in 1945–46, five California cities enacted sales taxes, and other California cities soon followed. Before long these cities were imposing use taxes in attempts to protect the trade of their own merchants. Businesses that sold in many municipalities found it nearly impossible to comply with the numerous and dissimilar local requirements. The confusion was resolved in 1955 by converting local taxes to a 1 percent tax supplement to the state sales tax. In Ohio, a local income tax was adopted by Toledo in 1946 and other cities followed.

In 1947 the state government of Pennsylvania authorized local governments to utilize any tax not used by the state. The response was so exuberant that the state legislature was forced to draw up ground rules for the local use of taxing powers because many of the smallest jurisdictions levied income taxes. No adequate appraisal of the Pennsylvania experience is available, but it seems likely that the "tax anything" law was not one that should be copied.

The great surge in the use of local sales and income taxes occurred in the 1970s, with their relative importance increasing into the 1980s (table 8-1). The availability of these nonproperty taxes has allowed local governments to diversify their revenue sources. Property tax revenues, which accounted for about 87 percent of local tax collections in 1960, accounted for only 75 percent in 1984.

The general sales tax is the most productive of local nonproperty taxes and has gained in relative importance in the last decade. As table 8-2 shows, general and selective sales taxes accounted for 54 percent of local nonproperty tax revenue in 1973 but had risen to nearly 60 percent in 1984. The most important of the selective sales taxes is that on the gross receipts of public utilities. Income taxes, which accounted for 13 percent of nonproperty tax revenue in 1966, provided almost 27 percent of the total in 1973 and about 23 percent in 1984. The change since the 1960s is due mainly to the increased number of jurisdictions that tax income.

Table 8-1. *Percent of Local Tax Revenue Collected from Various Sources, Selected Years, 1948–84*

	Tax				
Year	*Property*	*General sales*	*Selective sales*	*Income*	*All others*
1948	88.6	3.2	2.9	0.7	4.6
1956	86.8	4.2	2.6	1.3	5.1
1960	87.4	4.8	2.6	1.4	3.8
1968	86.1	3.9	2.3	3.5	4.3
1972	83.7	5.5	3.1	2.5	3.3
1978	79.7	7.7	3.9	5.1	3.6
1982	76.0	9.9	4.4	5.9	4.7
1984	75.0	9.7	4.8	5.6	4.8

Source: Advisory Commission on Intergovernmental Relations, *Significant Features of Fiscal Federalism, 1984 Edition* (Washington: ACIR, 1985), table 39. In all tables years are fiscal unless otherwise noted and figures are rounded.

Table 8-2. *Local Nonproperty Tax Revenue, by Type of Tax, 1973 and 1984*

Millions of dollars and, in parentheses, percent of total

Type of tax	*1973*	*1984*
General sales	3,199 (35.3)	12,648 (41.1)
Selective sales	1,725 (19.0)	5,648 (18.3)
Motor fuel	65 (0.7)	160 (0.5)
Alcoholic beverages	78 (0.9)	249 (0.8)
Tobacco products	174 (1.9)	178 (0.6)
Public utilities	1,005 (11.1)	3,583 (11.6)
Other	403 (4.4)	1,477 (4.8)
Income	2,406 (26.6)	7,215 (23.4)
Licenses and all other	1,731 (19.1)	5,293 (17.2)
Total	9,061 (100.0)	30,804 (100.0)

Source: U.S. Census Bureau, *Governmental Finances in 1983–84* (U.S. Government Printing Office, 1985), table 4, and *1972–73* issue.

Because of the uneven distribution of nonproperty taxes among individual government units, aggregate figures of collections for all local governments, or even all cities, obscure their importance for some local governments. Table 8-3 lists twenty-one cities for which, in 1973, nonproperty taxes amounted to more than 40 percent of their tax collections. Notice that for all but one, nonproperty taxes grew in relative importance between 1973 and 1984. At the same time, these cities' dependence on the property tax lessened.

Local General Sales Tax

After the property tax, the general sales tax is the largest producer of revenue for local governments. And since 1970 its importance has grown

Table 8-3. *Local Nonproperty Taxes as a Share of Total Local Tax Collections, Selected Cities, 1973 and 1984*

Percent

City	*1973*	*1984*	*City*	*1973*	*1984*
Columbus	84	91	Cleveland	56	77
Toledo	83	89	Seattle	54	69
Kansas City	76	86	Oklahoma City	53	83
Philadelphia	71	78	San Jose	50	69
St. Louis	71	85	Los Angeles	49	66
Washington	71	72	San Diego	46	66
Tulsa	69	92	Detroit	45	62
Phoenix	67	67	New York	43	58
Cincinnati	64	79	Omaha	41	52
New Orleans	63	69	Pittsburgh	41	56
Denver	59	70			

Source: Census Bureau, *City Government Finances in 1983–84* (GPO, 1985), table 7, and *1972–73* issue.

in both absolute and relative terms. In 1972, local general sales taxes generated $2.7 billion of revenue and accounted for 5.5 percent of all local taxes. By 1984, revenues from this source were $12.0 billion and made up 9.7 percent of local tax revenues. In addition, local excise taxes levied on selected goods generated another $6.0 billion, accounting for 4.8 percent of local tax collections.[1]

Local general sales taxes were employed in twenty-six states in 1984 and were authorized in five others where municipalities had not made use of this source. Table 8-4 reports the taxing units and their rates for each of the twenty-six states. Most states authorized sales taxation in the 1960s, and the latest authorizations occurred in 1974. In all of the states except Alaska where local taxes are employed, the state also levies its own sales tax, and the state often administers the local tax as well as its own. While some localities define a tax base that differs from the state's definition, the most common practice is to adopt the state base.

In 1984, 6,492 localities levied a general sales tax. Of this number, 5,341 were municipalities, 1,070 were counties and boroughs, and 65 were school districts (in Louisiana only), while 16 transit districts levied a sales tax in support of their operations.[2] There is wide diversity in the rates they set. The highest municipal rates were 5.0 percent in Alaska, 4.0 percent in Colorado and Oklahoma, and 3.5 percent in Louisiana.[3] For all

1. Advisory Commission on Intergovernmental Relations, *Significant Features of Fiscal Federalism, 1984 Edition.* (Washington: ACIR, 1985), table 39.

2. Ibid., table 61.

3. Ibid., table 62.

Table 8-4. *Local General Sales Taxing Units and Their Rates, by State, 1984*

State and local units	*Units levying tax*		*Sales tax rate (percent)*
	Number	*Percent of eligible units*	
Alabama	...	...	4.0
Counties	43	64	0.5–3.0
Municipalities	310	71	0.5–3.0
Alaska	...	...	0.0
Municipalities	92	65	1.0–5.0
Boroughs	7	88	1.0–4.0
Arizona	...	...	5.0
Municipalities	70	92	1.0–2.0
Arkansas	...	...	4.0
Counties	16	21	1.0
Municipalities	44	9	1.0–2.0
California	...	...	4.75
Counties	58	100	1.25
Municipalities	434	100	1.0
Transit districts	5	n.a.	0.5
Colorado	...	...	3.0
Counties	29	47	0.25–3.00
Municipalities	175	66	1.0–4.0
Transit district	1	n.a.	0.6
Georgia	...	...	3.0
Counties	132	84	1.0
Transit district	1	n.a.	1.0
Illinois	...	...	5.0
Counties	102	100	1.0
Municipalities	1,249	46	0.5–1.0
Transit districts	2	n.a.	0.25–1.00
Kansas	...	...	3.0
Counties	52	50	0.5–1.0
Municipalities	87	4	0.5–1.0
Louisiana	...	...	4.0
Municipalities	158	52	0.3–3.5
Parishes	30	48	1.0–5.0
School districts	65	98	0.5–3.0
Minnesota	...	...	6.0
Municipalities	2	*	1.0
Missouri	...	...	4.125
Counties	81	32	0.375–1.000
Municipalities	406	44	0.5–1.0
Nebraska	...	...	3.5
Municipalities	12	2	1.0–1.5

Table 8-4 *(continued)*

State and local units	*Units levying tax* Number	*Units levying tax* Percent of eligible units	*Sales tax rate (percent)*
Nevada	...	...	5.75
County	1	6	0.25
New Mexico	...	...	3.75
Counties	22	67	0.125–6.250
Municipalities	98	100	0.250–1.125
New York	...	...	4.0
Counties	57	100	1.0–3.0
Municipalities	29	5	1.0–3.0
Transit district	1	n.a.	0.25
North Carolina	...	...	3.0
Counties	100	100	1.0–1.5
Ohio	...	...	5.0
Counties	62	70	0.5–1.0
Transit districts	3	n.a.	0.5–1.0
Oklahoma	...	...	2.0
Counties	6	8	1.0
Municipalities	441	76	1.0–4.0
South Dakota	...	...	4.0
Municipalities	82	22	1.0–2.0
Tennessee	...	...	4.5
Counties	94	100	0.75–2.25
Municipalities	8	29	0.25–2.25
Texas	...	...	4.125
Municipalities	1,117	100	1.0
Transit districts	3	n.a.	0.5–1.0
Utah	...	...	4.625
Counties	29	100	0.750–0.875
Municipalities	219	98	0.750–0.875
Virginia	...	...	3.0
Counties	95	100	1.0
Municipalities	41	100	1.0
Washington	...	...	6.5
Counties	39	100	0.5–1.0
Municipalities	267	100	0.5–1.0
Wyoming	...	...	3.0
Counties	15	65	1.0

Source: ACIR, *Significant Features, 1984,* tables 61, 62.
n.a. = not available.
* = less than 1 percent.

local units, the tax has grown in importance, particularly for transit districts and counties. In 1972, 8.9 percent of county tax revenue was derived from general or selective sales taxes. By 1982, this proportion had almost doubled to 16.0 percent.[4]

With both counties and cities using the general sales tax, the problem of tax overlap naturally arises. There are several ways to deal with this issue. In Utah, the county tax applies only outside the city limits, while in California and Washington the existence of a municipal tax lowers the county tax in that area. For the most part, however, the mechanism is more informal, with county and municipal officials discussing rate structures in light of both the revenue needs of the governments and the burden on taxpayers. However, there are six states where local taxes are levied independently and true overlap exists.[5]

Most states limit their local units' power to tax sales. Of the thirty-one states where local sales taxation is authorized, twenty-three limit the level of municipal rates while three set the limit on how high the combined rate may reach when overlapping jurisdictions employ the tax. Only five states set no limit on sales tax rates, and, unsurprisingly, it is in these states that the rates are highest. Yet another constraint used in most states is a requirement of voter approval or referendum to enact rate increases. Voter approval is usually required in states that also limit the level of the tax rate.

Many large cities make use of the general sales tax, and the nation's largest cities have become increasingly reliant on it. Yet there is a great diversity in the extent to which cities depend on this tax. At one extreme is Tulsa, Oklahoma, which in fiscal 1981 derived 77 percent of its local revenue from general sales and gross receipts taxes while, on average, the twenty-four largest cities that use these taxes derived 21 percent of their tax revenue from it.[6]

Upon what principles can a local sales tax be justified? The benefit principle can be employed when the proceeds are used to aid commerce. Perhaps the clearest example of this is a sales tax levied by a transit authority. The availability of good public transport is a boon to customers and businesses alike. More and more, localities are dedicating new or increased sales taxes to commerce-related activities. Public sentiment seems to support the growing role played by the local sales tax. In a 1983

4. ACIR, "Sales Taxation" (Washington: ACIR, November 15, 1984), p. 4.

5. The states are Alabama, Arkansas, Kansas, Missouri, New Mexico, and Oklahoma. Ibid., p. 5.

6. Ibid., table 2.2.

poll conducted by the ACIR, respondents cited the tax as the least objectionable form of taxation.[7]

The local sales tax, however, has two potential defects. The first concerns its equity, the second its efficiency. An unmodified and broad-based sales tax is regressive. This effect can be reduced by excluding necessities from the tax base. But improvement in the distribution of the tax burden is achieved at the expense of weakening the revenue productivity of the tax. The second problem arises because individuals and firms can avoid local sales taxes that are high in relation to those in nearby communities. Shoppers may choose to do business and merchants to locate elsewhere. And differentially high rates might even affect where people choose to live. In some states this problem has led legislatures either to refuse authorization for local use of the sales tax or to restrict the permissible tax rates (see table 8-4).[8] In other states, it is up to local officials to anticipate the consequences of their actions.

Local Income and Wage Taxes

Local wage and income taxes are the third most important source of local tax revenue behind the property and sales taxes. Eleven states have authorized their local governments to levy wage or income taxes. As can be seen from table 8-5, use of the tax is concentrated in Pennsylvania and Ohio. In terms of revenue collections, New York City and Philadelphia account for over half the total.

Five of the states define income narrowly and tax only wage income (at flat rates).[9] The tax base in the other six states is the state's definition of taxable income. Yet there is diversity in how this base is taxed. Three states apply a flat rate to the state definition of taxable income. On the other hand, localities in Maryland and Iowa attach a surcharge to the state personal income tax. Since these two states base their tax on both wages and certain nonwage income and the state tax is graduated, the local surcharge shares these attributes. Finally, New York City applies its own graduated rate scale to the state definition of taxable income.

Large cities rely heavily on wage and income taxation and their depen-

7. ACIR, *Changing Public Attitudes on Governments and Taxes, 1983* (U.S. Government Printing Office, 1983), p. 1.

8. In the Northeast, where localities are more concentrated and the potential for border problems is great, state legislatures have been reluctant to authorize the tax.

9. ACIR, *Significant Features, 1984,* table 55.

Table 8-5. *Local Income Taxing Units and Their Rates, by State, 1984*

State	*Number of local units levying tax*	*Rate (percent)*
Alabama	8 municipalities	1.0–2.0
Delaware	1 municipality	1.25
Indiana	43 counties	0.2–1.0
Iowa	57 school districts	2.00–17.75
Kentucky	9 counties	0.1–2.2
	61 municipalities	0.5–2.5
Maryland	24 counties	a
Michigan	16 municipalities	1.0–3.0
Missouri	2 municipalities	1.0
New York	2 municipalities	1.9–4.3
Ohio	460 municipalities	0.25–2.50
	6 school districts	0.5–1.0
Pennsylvania	2,644 municipalities, school districts, boroughs, and towns[b]	0.25–4.31

Source: ACIR, *Significant Features, 1984,* tables 54, 55.
a. Surcharge of 20–50 percent on state income tax.
b. Estimated.

dence has increased over time, as is evident among the eleven cities shown in table 8-6 that made greatest use of the tax. And there is great variation among these cities. Columbus derived 86 percent of its revenue from income taxes in 1984 as compared to 20 percent for Baltimore.

As can be seen in table 8-1, the local income tax has gained in importance, rising from 3.5 percent of total local revenues in 1968 to a high of 5.9 percent in 1982 before falling to 5.6 percent in 1984. Because income tax revenues rise with income and inflation, and the 1970s was a period of rapid price increases, income tax collections went up in step. In the early 1980s, in the wake of two recessions, however, the income tax declined in importance. This fluctuation in revenue reflects the high income elasticity of this tax—estimated to be between 1.3 and 2.4.[10]

A broad-based local income tax could potentially be a progressive element in the overall local tax structure. And the degree of progressivity could be increased by using a graduated rate structure or by including personal exemptions similar to those included in state and federal income taxes. However, as in the case of the local sales tax, care should be taken not to enact a local rate structure that induces disruptive or inefficient migration.

10. ACIR, *Local Finances in Recession and Inflation,* A-70 (GPO, 1979), p. 24. For an elasticity value of 2.0, each 1 percent rise in income could be expected to increase income tax revenues by 2.0 percent.

Table 8-6. *Reliance on Local Income or Wage Taxes, by Selected Large Cities, 1972 and 1984*

City	Income taxes as a percent of all taxes	
	1972	1984
Baltimore	14.2	20.2
Cincinnati	57.7	69.0
Cleveland	47.8	74.7
Columbus	78.2	86.1
Detroit	35.1	48.7
Kansas City	37.0	31.2
New York	21.0	28.7
Philadelphia	62.5	65.2
Pittsburgh	16.8	29.6
St. Louis	29.4	31.3
Toledo	74.9	83.6
All large cities[a]	16.8	21.0

Source: Census Bureau, *City Government Finances in 1983–84*, table 7, and *1971–72* issue.
a. Cities with at least 300,000 residents.

Nontax Revenue

State governments first ventured extensively into commercial enterprises in the 1820s. By this time population had moved westward, and streams of internal commerce had begun to take shape. Internal improvements would swell this commerce; they would, moreover, enhance the economic growth of states served by them. But the improvements were too risky and required too much capital for private enterprise to handle.[11] Why might not large-scale improvements be federal? Because the Constitution had made no provision for federal expenditure of this sort. To use the welfare clause as justification for federal action might endanger the Union because it would obliterate the functional boundaries between federal and state responsibility.

Since federal intervention was debarred, use of direct state enterprise or state guarantees seemed indicated. It happened that, at this very time, state governments could borrow with unprecedented ease. The nation was prosperous, and foreign capital (especially British capital) was flowing into the United States. The safest use of this capital was in federal securities, but in the 1820s they were being retired out of federal surpluses at a remarkable

11. At this time no industrial enterprise in the nation had capital of as much as a million dollars.

rate. What was more natural than that foreign investors, unacquainted with the intricacies of federalism, should regard state securities as a close substitute for federal? Accordingly, the issuance of state debt for internal improvements found a ready market.

Almost all of the state enterprises proved unprofitable. And when, after 1837, the nation suffered first a severe economic crisis and then a prolonged depression, states that had borrowed for internal improvements suffered acute financial difficulties. Some defaulted, and in all of them a revulsion of opinion led citizens to amend state constitutions to prohibit the use of state credit for business undertakings.

Public Service Enterprises

When interest in public ownership revived, local rather than state governments were to be the instruments. A keen debate developed late in the nineteenth century over public versus private ownership of public service industries—the supply of water, gas, electricity, transportation, and so on. These enterprises were "natural" monopolies. Competition in the supply of such services was not sensible. The choice was either to make the activity a public function, or to assign it to a private company subject to public regulation. John Stuart Mill stated the alternatives clearly in 1848:

> When, therefore, a business of real public importance can only be carried on advantageously upon so large a scale as to render the liberty of competition almost illusory, it is an unthrifty dispensation of the public resources that several costly sets of arrangements should be kept up for the purpose of rendering to the community this one service. It is much better to treat it at once as a public function; and if it be not such as the government itself could beneficially undertake, it should be made over entire to the company or association which will perform it on the best terms for the public.[12]

In reality, regulated enterprises are a mix of public and private ownership. The best example of publicly owned municipal utilities is water systems. The justification is linked to public health considerations. Private enterprise cannot be expected to give adequate weight to the health benefits accruing to the whole community through a supply of pure water. In addition, large cities in growing areas may have to reach quite far to secure

12. *Principles of Political Economy,* ed. W. G. Ashley (London: Longmans, Green, 1920), pp. 143–44.

an adequate water supply and this may require the use of extraordinary powers not readily available to a private concern.

Public ownership of electric power companies is much less common and is usually confined to distribution rather than generating systems. Gas is supplied in the United States by both public and private enterprises. As far as transportation systems are concerned, public ownership is the norm for major mass transit systems while bus lines are generally privately owned.

It is commonly held that public service enterprises should be self-supporting. The generalization, however, hides ambiguities. Sometimes it means merely that the enterprises should cover operating costs, or operating costs plus depreciation and interest. But since the enterprises do not pay taxes, a sum equivalent to the taxes that would be paid by a private concern should also be included as a cost. Unless this is done, consumers of the services are subsidized in kind, the amount of the subsidy depending on the amount of their consumption.

And many public enterprises do operate at a deficit. As can be seen in appendix table A-15, local transit expenditures have traditionally been larger than revenues—and the gap has increased over time. Local gas and electric utilities and water supply systems continue to have operating surpluses, but the differences between revenues and expenditures are shrinking, as these figures on local water supply systems show:[13]

Year	*Revenue (millions of dollars)*	*Expenditure (millions of dollars)*	*Expenditure as a percent of revenue*
1953	939	631	67.2
1963	1,865	1,273	68.3
1973	3,463	2,650	76.5
1984	10,467	9,141	87.3

A local government may make a deliberate decision to operate a public enterprise at a deficit. Such a plan may be thought desirable if it promotes some collective goal, or if it brings about a redistribution of income from richer to poorer persons. Thus a deficit in a water supply enterprise may be thought desirable on the ground that some portion of the benefits from water consumption accrues to citizens collectively rather than to them as individuals. Similarly a deficit in a public transit system may be accepted

13. Appendix table A-15.

on the ground that consumption is largely by low-income users, and that the amount of consumption varies inversely with income.

The question relevant to this case is: Who are the recipients of the subsidy when the price is less than cost? Obviously the users, and they receive a subsidy in kind rather than in money. If all users have low incomes, or indeed if the percent of consumption to income falls as income rises, the subsidy would seem to be properly directed. Actual measurement of use in relation to income status is difficult. But the common situation is that some users of the services of a transit system have low incomes, and some do not; some low-income users are large users, some are small, and some are nonusers. Subsidization in kind (through a deficit) has the built-in defect that it is specific rather than general. A low-income person who does not use the service gains no subsidy. Therefore government, when subsidizing for welfare reasons, should be wary of pricing commercial services below unit cost as a method of subsidization.

Still another awkward question arises when the incidence of the deficit is examined. The annual deficit of, for example, a transit system has to be met by taxes. The taxes may offset—wipe out—the subsidy. If the incidence of these taxes is regressive, their burden, as a percentage of income, falls more heavily on low- than on high-income persons. The likelihood—almost the certainty—is, however, that individual low-income persons who are steady users of the transit system will retain a substantial subsidy. Local tax systems, while regressive, do collect much larger absolute amounts from persons as their income rises. Thus, a sales tax with an effective rate of 4 percent for a person with an income of $10,000 and 2 percent for a person with an income of $40,000 collects $400 and $800 from each, respectively. A flat subsidy worth $500 yearly per steady user would, therefore, be cut into but not wiped out for a low-income user by a regressive tax; it would be negative for a higher-income user.

In view of the imperfections of subsidization through public enterprises, one may wonder why it is so extensive. Part of the explanation seems to be inflexibility in the face of changing circumstances, part the familiar intrusion of "political" decisions. Rising money costs, coupled with a rising price level, have prevailed since the end of World War II; increases of prices of the products of public enterprises have lagged. The visibility of unit increases in transit fares is great; the effectiveness of protest in checking action has been demonstrated; the certainty that repeated deficits will not bring a decrease in supply of the service—all these factors encourage irrational pricing by municipal enterprises despite the desperate need of local governments for additional revenue.

Other User Charges

Beyond fees for publicly provided utilities, user-based charges apply to a wide range of goods and services that are provided by localities. Swimming pools, parks, museums, and hospitals are, in part, financed with user charges. Often, however, the charge does not cover all of the costs so that an element of subsidy continues to exist. It can also be argued that revenues from licensing fees, such as building inspection fees, exist to cover the locality's cost of regulating the particular activity.

A form of benefit-based charge that has been growing in absolute and relative importance is the special assessment. These are mandatory charges levied on property to pay for specific investments that will be of benefit to the property owner. Special assessments to provide for sidewalks, street paving, fire protection, and other municipal services have become increasingly common.[14] Localities are assessing fees on developers so that newcomers, rather than existing residents, absorb the costs of development.

Under what conditions are user charges to be preferred to free distribution of services financed by general taxation? Of necessity, the benefit must accrue to a well-defined subset of individuals rather than spilling over to the public in general. If it is impossible to keep nonpayers from enjoying the benefits of the service, then both efficiency and equity demand that public provision of the service be financed by general taxation. But even if these basic conditions exist, user charges may be inappropriate if they would impose hardship on some potential users or if the administrative costs of collection are too high.

On the other hand, there are strong arguments to support a system of user charges. By charging prices that reflect the cost of providing public service, the efficiency properties of the market place can be tapped. If the public good or service were provided at no charge, more of the service would be produced and consumed than is socially optimal, with the result

14. Between 1957 and 1977, funds generated by special assessments grew at a 5.7 percent annual rate. The annual rate of increase jumped to 10.5 percent between 1977 and 1983.

being a distortion in the allocation of resources both between the public and private sectors and across public expenditure categories.

Recent Trends in Local User Charges

Since the late 1970s, local user charges have been the fastest-growing component of local government revenues. In the period from 1977 to 1983, user-based charges grew at an annual rate of 11.4 percent, an increase from the 9.3 percent annual growth rate in the previous twenty years (see table 8-7). The increase in the use of fees has taken place at the same time as and perhaps as a result of the pressure for state and local governments to limit tax rate increases. The growing desire for property tax relief was the driving force behind many states' adoption of tax and expenditure limitations. However, given the continuing demand for local government services along with the decline in inflation-adjusted federal assistance to localities, it is not surprising to find local governments financing their operations more with user charges and relatively less with general tax revenues.

Taxpayers seem reasonably happy with the increased emphasis on user charges—55 percent of those who responded to a 1981 ACIR survey felt that user charges were the best way to raise revenue.[15] The idea of "paying for what you get" had a strong appeal to many of them.

Revenues from user charges have been growing quite rapidly in the financing of utilities and of hospitals, sewer systems, and sanitation programs. Their overall importance is apparent in their relation to local tax collections. In 1957, user charges provided 40 percent as much revenue as local taxes; in 1977, they provided 45 percent as much; and by 1983, the ratio had risen to 64 percent.[16]

There is a great diversity among states in the use of fees and charges. The reasons for this diversity include tradition, limitations of state law, and the fiscal conditions of individual states. User charges are relied on most heavily in the Southeast, Southwest, and Far West. The Northeast makes least use of this source of financing.[17]

15. User charges were twice as popular as the next preferred alternative—sales taxes. ACIR, *Changing Public Attitudes on Government and Taxes* (GPO, 1981), p. 38.

16. Robert Cline, "User Charges" (Washington: ACIR, October 1984), table 6-1.

17. Cline, "User Charges," p. 11, table 6-2.

Table 8-7. *Local Government User Charges, 1957, 1977, and 1983*

	Millions of dollars			*Average annual rate of growth (percent)*	
Revenue source	*1957*	*1977*	*1983*	*1957–77*	*1977–83*
Current charges	2,536	18,977	39,443	10.6	13.0
Education	665	3,492	5,703	5.7	8.5
Hospitals	459	5,722	13,935	13.4	16.0
Sewerage	219	2,488	5,809	12.9	15.2
Sanitation	76	662	1,644	11.4	16.4
Parks and recreation[a]	131	756	1,308	9.2	9.6
Housing and urban renewal	280	916	1,496	6.1	8.5
Other	706	4,941	9,548	10.2	11.6
Special assessments	284	862	1,569	5.7	10.5
Water	1,235	4,994	9,498	7.2	11.3
Other utilities and transit	1,709	9,197	22,145	8.8	15.8
Total	5,764	34,030	72,655	9.3	11.4

Source: Robert Cline, "User Charges" (Washington: ACIR, October 1984), table 6-1.
a. Includes natural resources.

State Service Revenues

The purposes for which state governments collect user charges are more concentrated (table 8-8). In 1984 education is the largest item; user charges amount to more than half of total state user charges. They furnish, however, only 30 percent of state expenditures on education (exclusive of local school costs). Eight-tenths of this state expenditure (again exclusive of local school costs) is for state institutions of higher education. A controversy of long standing over the financing of these institutions has, in recent years, become much more acute. This controversy relates to the low level of charges (fees) of state, compared to private, institutions. Private institutions complain of unfair competition, and certainly the subsidy here has a peculiar bias, since it goes to some institutions in a state and not to others that nonetheless are providing similar or identical services.

Of the other types of state user charges, the steady rise in highway charges stems from toll facilities, and state user charges from hospitals come largely from mental institutions. The two classes of state user charges that approach the category of commercial charges are housing and nonhighway transportation (including air transport, and water transport and terminals). Subsidization of these two classes of charges raises again familiar questions.

Table 8-8. *State Government User Charges, 1973 and 1984*

	Millions of dollars		*As a percent of direct expenditures for service*	
Government services	*1973*	*1984*	*1973*	*1984*
Nonhighway transportation	178	578	43.2	73.3
Natural resources, parks, and recreation	275	1,152	10.5	16.3
Hospitals	1,306	5,731	24.3	37.6
Housing	19	204	7.2	24.9
Education	4,891	14,593	26.8	30.0
Highways	975	1,683	8.1	7.2
Other	965	1,797	...	...
Total	8,609	25,738	12.8	19.9

Sources: Appendix table A-16; Census Bureau, *State Government Finances in 1984* (GPO, 1984), tables 1, 2.

Lotteries

The fiscal pressures of the 1960s brought renewed interest in the public lottery as a source of revenue for state and local governments. In 1964 and 1967, state lotteries were introduced in New Hampshire and New York, respectively. The results were disappointing because in both cases actual revenues were far less than anticipated.[18] New Jersey's experience was somewhat different. Its lottery, established in 1971, offered more prizes more frequently and charged a lower price for tickets than the others. The New Jersey experiment led to modifications in both the New Hampshire and New York games. By 1983, seventeen state governments operated public lottery systems.

In general, none of the lotteries provides a very good buy for the gambling consumer. Prizes as a percent of gross receipts are much lower for state-run lotteries than for casino gambling or the illegal numbers game. Moreover, the lottery is continuously attacked as being regressive and immoral. In 1983, lotteries produced only 1.6 percent of the seventeen states' overall revenue per capita. Moreover, the costs of operating the systems are extremely high—reaching 12.6 percent of net revenue in 1983. This compares unfavorably with the cost of administering the

18. See Tax Foundation, *Nontax Revenues* (New York: Tax Foundation, 1968), p. 41; J. Richard Aronson, Andrew Weintraub, and Cornelius Walsh, "Revenue Potential of State and Local Public Lotteries," *Growth and Change,* vol. 3 (April 1972), p. 208; Sam Rosen, "New England's State Operated Lotteries," *New England Journal of Business and Economics,* vol. 1 (Spring 1975), pp. 1–10.

remainder of the states' revenue system which was only 2.5 percent of revenue in 1983.[19]

Conclusion

Is further growth in the use of fees and charges to be expected? Maybe not. Much of the increase in utility fees has been aimed at reaching full-cost pricing. Thus, further large increases may be unnecessary and unrealistic. On the other hand, revenue from special assessments may continue its rapid growth. More municipalities are adopting these charges, and fees on residences in new developments are on the upswing.

Even if user fees were to continue to grow at current rates, it is questionable whether this would lead to a significant increase in governments' total revenue. Over the last several years, user charges have substituted for, rather than augmented, local taxes. Their further growth is limited by the fact that user charges are not deductible from federal taxes. Without the advantage of this partial offset, fees are less attractive than alternative revenue sources that qualify for the federal tax deduction.

A final drawback of fees is that they may lead to "unbundling." As a greater portion of local expenditures is funded on a benefit basis and resistance to funding government programs via taxes grows, the result may be that tax-financed activities, which often are directed to the needs of the poor, will lose favor.

19. Allen D. Manvel, "State Lotteries—A Source of High-Cost Revenue," *Tax Notes* (January 7, 1985), pp. 97–98.

CHAPTER NINE

State and Local Debt

So foul a sky clears not without a storm.

King John

HISTORICALLY, the volume of state and local borrowing has proceeded in waves, usually being heaviest when the volume of federal borrowing is lightest. The first wave of state borrowing developed in the 1820s and 1830s when many states engaged in "internal improvements"—canals, highways, railways, and so on. This effort was feasible not only because the nation was prosperous and had begun to accumulate savings, but also because the federal debt was being retired with great celerity. Holders of this debt, forced to seek new outlets for their capital, were attracted to state issues. Unfortunately, many of the internal improvements turned out to be unprofitable; the debt issued for them proved to be deadweight. When, in 1837, severe depression struck and continued for several years, the burden of this deadweight debt was aggravated. Nine states and one territory defaulted.[1] All state credit was impaired, and borrowing by state governments came to an abrupt halt. Most of the states resumed interest payments before 1850, although four states repudiated some debt.[2] In a spirit of reaction against the mistakes that had been made, many state constitutions were framed to restrict future state borrowing.

The Civil War brought a new wave of state borrowing. Defense had not, at this time, become wholly a federal function, and the state governments borrowed to finance military operations. But at the close of the war the debts of the northern states were retired, usually through federal financial assistance. In the Reconstruction period, after 1865, carpetbag governments in the southern states issued considerable amounts of bonds, the

1. Default is a broad term, meaning that a government, for whatever reasons, is failing to pay interest, or installments of principal, when due. The default may be temporary or long contained. No satisfactory method of weighting the seriousness of a default is available.

2. B. U. Ratchford, *American State Debts* (Duke University Press, 1941), pp. 98–99, 105–14.

proceeds of which were often wasted. After ejection of the carpetbaggers, nine southern states made extensive adjustments. Most of the debt was repudiated; the remainder was scaled down and, in the process, a few states reduced pre-Civil War debts.[3]

In the last two decades of the nineteenth century, borrowing by state governments declined sharply. State debt less sinking funds was $9.15 per capita in 1870 and only $3.10 in 1900. Bitter experience, coupled with a conservative philosophy, had led voters in most states to endorse severe constitutional or statutory limitations on state borrowing.[4]

It turned out, however, that some local governments in the 1870s had become creditworthy; they stepped into the vacuum and began to borrow extensively to finance internal improvements, notably railways. Their experience paralleled the earlier experience of the states. Borrowing was overdone; much of the capital was wasted; the annual carrying charges were beyond what local governments were prepared to finance. During the depression of 1873, defaults were widespread—perhaps 20 percent of the total.[5] State governments nearly everywhere imposed limitations on local borrowing, usually in the form of a debt-to-property ratio.

For two decades these limitations were restrictive, but in the twentieth century they proved to be elastic. Local governments, especially large cities, borrowed at an accelerating pace for the construction of schools and streets. In 1902, as table 9-1 shows, local debt was eight times larger than state debt.

The onset of the depression in the 1930s did not at first slacken state and local borrowing. But as the depression continued and deepened, the reaction was very severe; after 1932, net borrowing was extremely low and during a few years repayments actually exceeded new borrowing. The rate of interest paid by state and local governments rose sharply, despite a marked drop in flotations (in 1932, 52.5 percent of the issues bore a rate of 5 percent or more, and many offerings could not be marketed at all); interest remained high, compared with the rate on federal debt. Table 9-2 shows state and local interest payments per $1,000 of personal income for selected years from 1902 to 1984.

3. Ibid., pp. 191–96.

4. A. James Heins, *Constitutional Restrictions Against State Debt* (University of Wisconsin Press, 1963), pp. 7–9, gives a brief history of state action.

5. A. M. Hillhouse, *Municipal Bonds: A Century of Experience* (Prentice-Hall, 1936), p. 17. Defaults amounted to about $100 million to $150 million during the 1870s out of outstanding bonds that ranged from $516 million in 1870 to $821 million in 1880 (ibid., pp. 36, 39).

Table 9-1. *State and Local Debt Outstanding, Selected Years, 1902–84*
Millions of dollars

Year	*Local debt*	*State debt*	*Total*
1902	1,877	230	2,107
1913	4,035	379	4,414
1927	12,910	1,971	14,881
1932	16,373	2,832	19,205
1938	16,093	3,343	19,436
1946	13,564	2,353	15,917
1948	14,980	3,676	18,656
1960	51,412	18,543	69,955
1964	67,181	25,041	92,222
1966	77,487	29,564	107,051
1970	101,563	42,008	143,570
1973	129,110	59,375	188,485
1978	177,864	102,569	280,433
1982	251,820	147,470	399,290
1984	318,653	186,377	505,030

Sources: U.S. Census Bureau, *Historical Statistics of the United States: Colonial Times to 1957* (U.S. Government Printing Office, 1960), pp. 728, 730; Census Bureau, *Governmental Finances in 1983–84* (GPO, 1985), table 16, and earlier issues. In all tables years are fiscal unless otherwise noted and figures are rounded.

Equally startling was the rise in defaults. By the mid-1930s, perhaps 10 percent of municipal bonds—$1.5 billion out of more than $15.0 billion—were in default. Some rough indication of the impact of the depression is provided by the growth in the number of defaults. In the five years before March 1932, about 226 defaults took place—an average of 45 yearly. On November 1, 1932, 678 local units were listed as in default; two years later the figure was 2,654, and on November 1, 1935, it was 3,251.[6] Default was not confined to bonds of inferior quality, since 90 percent were, in 1929, rated as Aa or higher.[7]

What lay behind the traumatic record? State and local debt had doubled in the 1920s, while the gross national product had risen by only 40 percent. Much more significant in impact was the fall in the price level, incomes, and employment, each of which added to the burden of debt. Despite increases in rates, local tax revenues declined by 17 percent in the

6. Ibid., pp. 17–21. One-quarter of the defaulting governmental units were reclamation, irrigation, and special assessment districts. Only one state, Arkansas, defaulted on its debt. During the 1920s Arkansas borrowed heavily for highways and Confederate pensions. Spending of the borrowed money was both wasteful and corrupt. Default came in 1932–33, followed by a bitter struggle over refunding. See Ratchford, *American State Debts*, chap. 15.

7. The quality ratings range from Aaa (the best rating) down to C.

Table 9-2. *Interest Expenditure of State and Local Governments per $1,000 of Personal Income, Selected Years, 1902–84*

Year	Millions of dollars	Dollars per $1,000 of personal income[a]	Year	Millions of dollars	Dollars per $1,000 of personal income[a]
1902	68	3.37	1962	2,008	4.57
1913	147	4.36	1964	2,826	6.12
1927	584	7.34	1966	3,268	6.14
1932	741	14.79	1970	5,123	6.88
1934	739	13.79	1973	7,828	8.37
1948	399	1.89	1978	14,044	9.20
1957	1,106	3.18	1982	24,088	10.00
1960	1,670	4.17	1984	34,439	12.59

Sources: Census Bureau, *Historical Statistics*, pp. 139, 728, 730; Census Bureau, *Governmental Finances in 1983–84*, tables 3, 27, and earlier issues.
a. Personal income data are for calendar years, and beginning in 1964 for the preceding calendar year.

years from 1930 to 1934. Tax delinquency in 1934 was more than 23 percent in 150 cities with populations over 50,000.

During World War II state and local net borrowing remained low. Public construction for civilian purposes was at a standstill and, as revenues picked up with full employment, state and local governments had large surpluses which they used to retire debt. At the end of 1946 their gross debt was 18 percent less than in 1938. And this was not the only favorable financial circumstance. Yields on state and local bonds were low beyond all precedent, with the result that new borrowing cost less and old debt could be refunded on a favorable basis.

The contrast between the market reception of state and local bonds in 1946 and the mid-1930s was marked. In 1937 the average yield of high-grade long-term state and local bonds was 3.10 percent, compared to a yield of 3.26 percent for Aaa corporation bonds—the differential as a percentage of the corporate yield was 5 percent. In 1946 this differential was 36 percent (yields of 1.64 percent on state and local bonds and 2.53 percent on corporation bonds). The main force behind this widening spread was the exemption of interest on state and local bonds from federal income tax. The value of this exemption had risen because of the marked wartime increase in the level and progression of federal income tax rates, coupled with the decrease in volume of exempt bonds and pessimistic market expectations concerning future increase in their volume.

This overview of state and local debt should call attention to differences between the growth of state debt and local debt in recent decades. Begin-

Table 9-3. *Indexes of State and Local Debt, Selected Years, 1938–84*

Base year 1938 = 100.0

Year	*Local debt*	*State debt*	*Total*
1938	100.0	100.0	100.0
1948	93.1	110.0	96.0
1960	319.5	554.7	360.0
1962	367.1	657.2	417.0
1964	417.5	749.1	474.5
1966	481.5	884.4	550.8
1970	631.1	1,256.6	738.7
1973	802.3	1,776.1	969.8
1978	1,105.2	3,068.2	1,442.9
1982	1,564.8	4,411.3	2,054.4
1984	1,980.1	5,575.1	2,598.4

Sources: Table 9-1; Census Bureau, *Governmental Finances in 1961–62*, p. 26.

ning in the 1930s, state debt grew at a faster rate than did local debt (table 9-3). The severity of the depression forced states to assume governmental tasks that, in ordinary circumstances, were local. But it also led them to assume new governmental responsibilities, a factor that has, since World War II, grown in importance. Nonetheless, the actual amount of local debt outstanding in 1973 and again in 1984 was still much larger than state debt (see table 9-1).

Table 9-3 shows the remarkable overall increase in state and local debt since World War II. The increase, however, has not been uniform among governmental units. For example, between 1966 and 1984, state outstanding debt per capita increased by $639, from $152 to $791. But table 9-4 shows the considerable interstate variation in the amount of growth. In one state the increase amounted to less than $100 per capita; and fourteen states experienced an increase of more than $1,000 per capita. Table 9-4 also shows the uneven increase in per capita debt among large cities over the period 1966 to 1984. In sixteen of the largest forty-eight cities, per capita debt increased by $1,000 or more. At the same time, however, per capita debt in two cities actually fell.

The Advisory Commission on Intergovernmental Relations (ACIR) in 1973 focused its attention on the ability of cities to meet their debt obligations. In a report that attempted to pinpoint warning signs of financial trouble, the following were identified as important:

> an operating fund . . . imbalance in which current expenditures significantly [exceed] current revenues in one fiscal period; a consistent pattern of current expenditures exceeding current revenues by small amounts for several years;

Table 9-4. *Change in Per Capita Total Debt of State Governments and Forty-eight Largest Cities, 1966–84*

Change in debt per capita (dollars)	*Number of state governments*	*Number of large city governments*
Decrease, all magnitudes	0	2
Increase		
0–99	1	1
100–199	5	1
200–299	4	4
300–399	5	3
400–499	2	5
500–599	5	2
600–699	7	2
700–799	3	4
800–899	3	6
900–999	1	2
1,000–1,099	0	2
1,100–1,199	1	1
1,200–1,299	2	1
1,300–1,399	4	0
1,400 and over	7	12

Sources: Census Bureau, *State Government Finances in 1984* (GPO, 1984), table 28, and *1966* issue; Census Bureau, *City Government Finances in 1983–84,* table 7, and *1965–66* issue.

> an excess of current operating liabilities over current assets (a fund deficit); short-term operating loans outstanding at the conclusion of a fiscal year (or in some instances the borrowing of cash from restricted funds or an increase in unpaid bills in lieu of short-term operating loans); a high and rising rate of property tax delinquency; a sudden substantial decrease in assessed values for unexpected reasons.

The study concluded that "in general, the present fiscal problems facing cities need not cause a financial emergency in the technical sense, provided there is no major national economic depression."[8]

In general, in the period 1966–73 the debt burden of state and local governments in relation to their ability to pay remained constant. Table 9-5 shows that although per capita debt of state and local governments increased from $547 in 1966 to $898 in 1973, debt service payment in relation to general revenue remained at about the 20 percent level. An alternative measure of debt burden—the ratio of total debt outstanding to total personal income—also remained at about 20 percent during this period.

However, fiscal concern did grow in the mid-1970s. The problem cen-

8. Advisory Commission on Intergovernmental Relations, *City Financial Emergencies: The Intergovernmental Dimension* (U.S. Government Printing Office, 1973), p. 4.

Table 9-5. *Debt Service Estimates of State and Local Governments, 1966, 1973, and 1984*

Item	*1966*	*1973*	*1984*
Debt (billions of dollars)			
Long-term, outstanding	101.0	172.6	485.1
Long-term, retired	5.6	9.0	33.9
Short-term, outstanding	6.1	15.9	19.9
Interest	3.3	7.8	34.4
Revenue (billions of dollars)[a]	75.0	159.5	483.2
Debt service as a percent of revenue[b]	20.0	20.5	18.3
Personal income (billions of dollars)[c]	532.1	935.4	2,734.1
Debt outstanding as a percent of personal income[d]	20.1	20.2	18.5
Debt per capita (dollars)	547	898	2,144.0

Source: Census Bureau, *Governmental Finances in 1983–84,* tables 5, 18, and earlier issues.
a. General revenue of state and local governments from own sources plus utility revenue.
b. Long-term debt retired, short-term debt outstanding, and interest on debt.
c. U.S. total, for calendar years 1965, 1972, and 1983, respectively.
d. Long- and short-term debt outstanding.

tered on the finances of several large cities, especially New York. Rough estimates of debt service payments as a percent of general revenue following the formula of table 9-5 showed, for New York City, an increase from 35 percent in 1966 to 44 percent in 1973. The situation deteriorated. In late 1975 banks refused to continue to lend to the city and in order to avoid outright default, the state found it necessary to create the Municipal Assistance Corporation (Big Mac) to buy and manage the city's debt obligations. In addition, the federal government authorized the Treasury to lend to the city up to $2.3 billion to finance seasonal short-term borrowing.[9]

The fiscal crisis in New York and a later scare in Cleveland led to a more general fear that there was a growing fiscal weakness throughout the country. By 1978, however, the debt service ratio and the ratio of debt outstanding to personal income had fallen from their 1973 levels. Moreover, by 1984 (as table 9-5 shows) both ratios stood at 18 percent rather than the pre-1978 levels of 20 percent.[10]

The ACIR in a 1984 updating of its 1973 study, *City Financial Emergencies,* emphasized that "a searching review finds no evidence that local

9. For a comprehensive analysis, see Attiat F. Ott and Jang H. Yoo, *New York City's Financial Crisis: Can the Trend Be Reversed?* (Washington: American Enterprise Institute, 1975).

10. See J. Richard Aronson and Arthur E. King, "Is There a Fiscal Crisis Outside of New York?" *National Tax Journal,* vol. 31 (June 1978), pp. 153–63.

Table 9-6. *State Long-Term Debt, by Function, 1941, 1973, and 1984*
Millions of dollars and, in parentheses, percent of total

Function	*1941*	*1973*	*1984*
Highways	1,373 (45.8)	16,088 (29.0)[a]	14,857 (8.1)
Education	123 (4.1)	14,304 (25.8)	29,474 (16.1)
Hospitals	50 (1.7)	1,200 (2.2)	16,113 (8.8)
Water transportation and terminals	151 (5.0)	563 (1.0)	1,195 (0.6)
Public welfare	449 (15.0)	n.a. ...	n.a. ...
Other[b]	855 (28.5)	23,242 (42.0)	121,569 (66.5)
Total	3,001 (100.0)	55,397 (100.0)	183,208 (100.0)

Sources: Census Bureau, *Financial Statistics of States, 1941*, vol. 3: *Statistical Compendium* (GPO, 1943), p. 66; Census Bureau, *State Government Finances in 1984*, table 17, and earlier issues.

n.a. = not available.

a. Includes $6.9 billion for toll facilities.

b. Includes general control, natural resources, public welfare, parks and recreation, veterans' aid, and housing and community development.

governments generally are experiencing increased financial emergencies or that they are likely to do so in the future."[11]

Types of Debt

There are two basic types of state and local debt—guaranteed debt, secured by the full faith and credit of the issuing unit, and nonguaranteed debt. Until quite recently most debt was guaranteed. This is no longer true. State and local governments have issued so much nonguaranteed debt that it now represents about two-thirds of total state and local debt outstanding.

State and local debt is generally issued in serial form. When the debt is incurred, a percentage of the issue comes due every year. The annual service charge for a twenty-year issue includes the repayment of, say, one-twentieth of the principal, as well as the required interest. This method of repayment is superior to the older device of sinking funds which required the accumulation of large sums for the final redemption of the whole issue at maturity. The temptation to raid such funds, or to alter the terms, was often irresistible to hard-pressed state and local governments.[12]

11. ACIR, *Bankruptcies, Defaults, and Other Local Government Financial Emergencies* (Washington: ACIR, 1985), p. i.

12. The old-fashioned sinking fund, however, did provide state and local governments with assets that could be invested in U.S. government securities which, because they are not

Table 9-7. *Long-Term Debt of Forty-three Largest Cities, by Function, 1941, 1973, and 1984*

Millions of dollars and, in parentheses, percent of total

Function	*1941*	*1973*	*1984*
General debt[a]	3,210 (50.6)	16,853 (71.5)	36,779 (75.6)
Education	589 (9.3)	1,865 (7.9)	1,550 (3.2)
Highways	653 (10.3)	1,684 (7.1)	2,172 (4.5)
Sewerage	373 (5.9)	1,928 (8.2)	3,723 (7.6)
Housing and urban renewal	n.a. . . .	2,780 (11.8)	3,812 (7.8)
Other and unallocable	1,595 (25.1)	8,596 (36.5)	25,522 (52.4)
Utility debt	3,136 (49.4)	6.723 (28.5)	11,890 (24.4)
Water supply systems	1,148 (18.1)	2,892 (12.3)	4,987 (10.2)
Other	1,988 (31.3)	3,831 (16.2)	6,903 (14.2)
Total debt	6,346 (100.0)	23,576 (100.0)	48,669 (100.0)

Sources: Census Bureau, *Financial Statistics of Cities Having Populations over 100,000, 1941*, vol. 3: *Statistical Compendium* (GPO, 1943), pp. 101–05; Census Bureau, *City Government Finances in 1983–84*, table 7, and *1972–73* issue.

n.a. = not available.

a. The Census Bureau cautions that because the scope of municipal government operations differs, debt figures are not fully comparable. In particular, if public schools are operated by independent school districts, municipal debt figures do not include all debt of the cities as geographic units.

Most state and local borrowing is for capital expenditure for roads, buildings, and public service enterprises. As table 9-6 shows, there was a sixty-one-fold increase in the total amount of state long-term debt between 1941 and 1984. There were also significant relative shifts in particular items. Highway debt, which was dominant in 1941 and 1973, has become less important. And borrowing for water transportation has, over time, fallen to insignificant levels. The proportion of debt devoted to hospitals has, on the other hand, been increasing. The single most important use of debt remains education. Since 1973, however, it has declined in relative importance, accounting for 16 percent of total state borrowing in 1984.

Table 9-7 shows the purposes of the long-term debt of the forty-three largest cities in 1941, 1973, and 1984 (figures for all local debt are not available). General debt had risen from 50.6 percent of the total in 1941 to 75.6 percent in 1984. One new function, housing and urban renewal, had emerged and, in 1984, accounted for 7.8 percent of total debt. Also, the relative importance of education in local borrowing has been falling. Education accounted for 9.3 percent of local debt in 1941, and in 1984 it stood at 3.2 percent.

tax exempt, generally carry a higher yield to maturity than do municipal bonds of the same maturity. See Roland I. Robinson, "Debt Management," in J. Richard Aronson and Eli Schwartz, eds., *Management Policies in Local Government Finance* (Washington: International City Management Association, 1975), p. 233.

The life of most state and local debt is geared to the expected life of the asset provided by the debt, or to an estimate of the revenue to be derived from the asset, but the gearing is loose. The life of water and sewer issues is usually twenty years, a maturity that readily assures receipts covering interest and annual maturities.[13]

Borrowing and capital spending of state and local governments is influenced by the business cycle. Since 1948 there has been a tendency for bond sales to reach higher levels during years of recession trough than during the year in which the previous peak was attained. What explains this general pattern? State and local governments try to avoid the high interest rates on long-term bonds during expansion by using short-term debt as temporary financing, drawing down liquid assets, or cutting some current expenditures. Sometimes they succeed but sometimes they do not. During the 1980–81 recession, long-term borrowing was higher at the peak than it was in the trough that followed.[14]

The capital spending of state and local governments has not displayed as much cyclical variation as has their borrowing. A survey conducted in 1966 by the Federal Reserve showed that although the high interest rates of that year had a great effect on the borrowing plans of large governments, the effect on capital spending was marginal.[15] And a similar study of state and local government finances in 1970 came to a similar conclusion; borrowing was reduced much more than was capital spending.[16] Starting in 1975, however, the situation began to change, as it became more difficult and more expensive to maintain capital expenditures with short-term financing techniques. The combination of high interest rates and low liquidity levels forced state and local governments to cut back on capital spending. The significant cuts made in the two recessions of the early 1980s led one group of analysts to conclude that "reduced capital spending during recessions now appears to be an action state and local

13. Roland I. Robinson, *Postwar Market for State and Local Government Securities* (Princeton University Press for National Bureau of Economic Research, 1960), pp. 46–47.

14. Roy Bahl, Larry DeBoer, and Dana Weist, *Inflation, the Business Cycle and State and Local Government Finances*, Metropolitan Studies Program, Occasional Paper 90 (Maxwell School, Syracuse University, 1985), pp. 78–85.

15. Paul F. McGouldrick and John E. Petersen, "Monetary Restraint and Borrowing and Capital Spending by Large State and Local Governments in 1966," and "Monetary Restraint, Borrowing, and Capital Spending by Small Local Governments and State Colleges in 1966," *Federal Reserve Bulletin*, vol. 54 (July and December 1968), pp. 552–81, 953–71.

16. John E. Petersen, "Response of State and Local Governments to Varying Credit Conditions," *Federal Reserve Bulletin*, vol. 57 (March 1971), pp. 209–32.

Table 9-8. *Outstanding Long-Term and Short-Term State and Local Debt, 1966, 1973, and 1984*[a]

Billions of dollars and, in parentheses, percent of year's total

Type of debt	*State debt*	*Local debt*	*Total*
1966 total	29.6 (100.0)	77.5 (100.0)	107.1 (100.0)
Long-term	28.5 (96.3)	72.5 (93.5)	101.0 (94.3)
Short-term	1.1 (3.7)	5.0 (6.5)	6.1 (5.7)
1973 total	59.4 (100.0)	129.1 (100.0)	188.5 (100.0)
Long-term	55.7 (93.8)	116.9 (90.5)	172.6 (91.6)
Short-term	3.7 (6.2)	12.2 (9.5)	15.9 (8.4)
1984 total	186.4 (100.0)	318.7 (100.0)	505.0 (100.0)
Long-term	183.2 (98.3)	301.9 (94.7)	485.1 (96.0)
Short-term	3.2 (1.7)	16.8 (5.3)	20.0 (4.0)

Source: Census Bureau, *Governmental Finances in 1983-84,* p. 40, and earlier issues.
a. Debt at end of fiscal year. Short-term debt is repayable within one year.

governments will continue to take, especially in light of continued reductions in Federal aid."[17]

In 1984, 96 percent of state and local debt was long term (table 9-8). This is in distinct contrast to federal practice—43 percent of federal marketable interest-bearing debt matures within one year. The federal Treasury also issues a variety of intermediate-term debt that has no parallel in state and local practice. State and local governments use short-term debt mostly in anticipation of tax receipts; they seldom use it to finance the start of capital projects. They have less flexibility and discretion in the use of short-term debt since refunding is subject to constitutional or statutory limitations and is, moreover, frowned on by local banks.[18] Nevertheless, as table 9-8 shows, short-term debt has gone through a cycle in recent years. Between 1966 and 1973 it increased from 5.7 percent to 8.4 percent of the total of all state and local debt; but by 1984 the proportion of total debt that was short term had come down to 4.0 percent.

Tax Exemption

The most important and distinctive characteristic of state and local issues is their freedom from federal taxation.[19] The federal government

17. Bahl, DeBoer, and Weist, *Inflation*, p. 85.

18. A characteristic of New York City's financial crisis was the abuse of short-term debt. See Aronson and King, "Is There a Fiscal Crisis?"

19. Interest on arbitrage bonds and large industrial aid bonds is taxable. Realized capital gains on municipal bond transactions are also taxable. However, the implicit interest embodied in a bond originally issued at discount is not taxable.

does not tax the interest on state and local securities through the income tax, and state and local governments cannot tax federal securities. State and local governments may tax their own securities, although most do not exercise this right; they may, and generally do, tax each other's securities.

The failure of the federal government to tax income from state and local securities rests on the specific statutory exclusion of such income by Congress. When the Sixteenth Amendment to the Constitution was in process, assurance was given to some state governors that the amendment merely was to remove the constitutional requirement that a federal income tax, as a direct tax, be apportioned among the states according to population. And when Congress passed the individual income tax of 1913, it implicitly accepted this position by providing that interest on state and local securities be excluded from income. This statutory exclusion has been retained.

The Supreme Court has never decided the question of the constitutional right of Congress to delete the exclusion and to tax interest on state and local securities as income. For some years after 1913, the inference of many decisions seemed to be that the amendment had not altered the taxable status of state and local securities. But in the late 1930s several decisions that curtailed the immunity of governmental instrumentalities raised doubts anew.

These decisions seemed to depend on the theory that nondiscriminatory taxation, federal or state, was permissible and tolerable. The epigram of Chief Justice Marshall in *McCulloch* v. *Maryland,* that "the power to tax involves the power to destroy," had been capped by the epigram of Justice Holmes that "the power to tax is not the power to destroy while this Court sits." The courts, as the referees of a federal system with a dual sovereignty, would protect the states even if, as Justice Butler believed, the doctrine of reciprocal immunity was "presently marked for destruction."[20]

The federal Treasury has made several attempts to abolish the exemption, at first only for future issues, but in 1942 for outstanding issues as well. All efforts have failed, in the face of sharp resistance by state and local governments and the unwillingness of Congress to impair the financial powers of these governments at a time when their financial responsibilities were large and expanding.

The benefits derived by state and local governments from the issuance

20. *McCulloch* v. *Maryland,* 4 Wheat. 316, 431 (1819); Holmes, dissenting, in *Panhandle Oil Co.* v. *Mississippi,* 277 U.S. 218, 223 (1928); Butler, dissenting, in *Graves* v. *New York ex. rel. O'Keefe,* 306 U.S. 466, 493 (1939).

of tax-exempt bonds are by no measure evenly distributed. Governmental units in high-income areas gain greater benefits than those in low-income areas because they issue more debt. High-income states have a high state-local debt per capita, low-income states a low debt (see appendix table A-17). Therefore, exemption if regarded as a subsidy is inefficient. And even though the exemption may not be more valuable to governmental units with high credit ratings than to those with low ratings, the exemption is not distributed according to need.[21]

Yield Differentials

Tax-exempt bonds have always sold at a lower yield than taxable bonds of similar quality and maturity. The yield differential depends chiefly on the relative expected supply of the two kinds of bonds and on the anticipated amount of tax that can be avoided. The holder of tax-exempt bonds does not pay income tax on the interest. The provision for tax-free interest on bonds brings an increase in their price equal to the present value of the exemption to the marginal buyer. When income is taxed progressively, as under the federal income tax, the value of the exemption becomes worth more to buyers as the size of their taxable income increases.

For example, a taxpayer in the top (50 percent) bracket who buys a taxable bond yielding $120 annually can keep only $60. To him, the exemption from income tax is worth 50 percent of the yield. He would be as well off to purchase at par a tax-exempt bond yielding 6 percent as a taxable one yielding 12 percent. A taxpayer in the 20 percent bracket keeps $96 out of $120, and to him exemption is worth less than it is to the richer person. Thus, to a taxpayer in the 20 percent bracket an exempted yield of 9.6 percent is equivalent to 12 percent from a taxable bond.

If it is assumed that the actual supply of tax-exempt bonds is relatively small, then perhaps all could profitably be bought by persons in the top bracket, and the market yield would be 6 percent. But if the supply is so large that buyers in the lower brackets must be tapped, the yield for those in the 20 percent bracket would have to rise to 9.6 percent. These are the marginal buyers, whose income after taxes is the same whether they buy tax-exempt or taxable securities. Since the market is undifferentiated, all

21. See Carolyn V. Kent, "The Subsidy to State and Local Governments Implicit in the Exemption of Municipal Bond Interest from Federal Tax" (Ph.D. dissertation, Lehigh University, 1975).

Table 9-9. *Yields on High-grade Long-term Municipal and Corporate Bonds, Selected Years, 1928–84*

Year	*Yield (percent)* Municipal bonds[a]	Corporate bonds[b]	Differential	Differential in yield as a percent of corporate yield
1928	4.02	4.55	0.53	12
1938	3.01	3.19	0.18	6
1946	1.64	2.53	0.89	35
1963	3.23	4.26	1.03	24
1966	3.82	5.13	1.31	26
1973	5.18	7.44	2.26	30
1976	6.49	8.43	1.94	23
1984	10.15	12.71	2.56	20

Sources: *The Bond Buyer's Municipal Finance Statistics, 1974,* vol. 13 (June 1975), p. 19; *1983 Statistical Supplement,* p. 5. Board of Governors of the Federal Reserve System, *Banking and Monetary Statistics* (The Board, 1943), p. 468; *Economic Report of the President, February 1986,* p. 332.

a. Average of high and low yields for the year on twenty municipal bonds.

b. Aaa.

buyers get the same yield as the marginal buyers and the high-income buyers secure a sort of surplus of tax saving.

Over the decades the differential between the yield of taxable and tax-exempt securities has widened or narrowed in response to pressure from various forces. In the 1920s, when the rates and progression of the federal individual income tax were sharply decreased and these trends were widely expected to continue, the differential was narrow (see table 9-9). Thus, the advantage to high-income persons from holding tax-exempt bonds was modest, and so was the loss to the federal Treasury from its inability to tax the income from exempted bonds. During World War II the differential widened; by 1946 the yield of high-quality tax-exempt bonds was about 65 percent that of similar taxable bonds. Behind this lay the marked increase in the level and progression of federal income taxes, as well as the decrease in the volume of exempted bonds. The differential has since narrowed, partly because of a decrease in federal income tax rates and partly because of the rise in the volume of exempted bonds. The gross proceeds from issues of state and local securities, which in 1946 amounted to 6.2 percent of all new issues, rose in the mid-1960s to about 28 percent and by the early 1970s was averaging about 23 percent. As a result, the advantage to state and local governments from the exemption privilege diminished and the advantage to high-income buyers increased.

Can the trend toward a lower percentage differential be expected to continue? Two forces suggest that it will. The move toward lower and less progressive taxes appears strong. The Economic Recovery Tax Act of

Table 9-10. *Estimated Holdings of State and Local Securities, by Type of Owner, 1966, 1973, and 1984*

Billions of dollars and, in parentheses, percent of total

Type of owner	*1966*	*1973*	*1984*
Households	40.0 (37.8)	50.5 (26.6)	201.4 (37.6)
Commercial banks	41.2 (38.9)	95.7 (50.4)	172.1 (32.2)
Insurance companies	15.7 (14.8)	33.8 (17.8)	96.7 (18.1)
State and local governments[a]	4.6 (4.3)	3.9 (2.1)	11.2 (2.1)
Other	4.4 (4.2)	6.0 (3.2)	53.9 (10.1)
Total	105.9 (100.0)	190.0 (100.0)	535.3 (100.0)

Sources: *Bond Buyer's Municipal Finance Statistics, 1974*, p. 17 (estimated on December 31), and *1984* issue.
a. General fund and retirement fund holdings.

1981 lowered tax rates significantly and advocates of a flat tax may convince Congress to adopt lower and more proportional tax rates in the future. Another reason to expect a declining yield differential is the increased borrowing that is likely if state and local governments go about maintaining and rebuilding their infrastructure.[22]

Holders of Tax-Exempt Securities

As table 9-10 indicates, only a small portion of state and local interest-bearing securities is held in investment funds of state and local governments themselves (2.1 percent in 1984).[23] The three groups that hold the bulk of these securities are commercial banks, high-income individuals, and insurance companies. A significant change in the distribution of ownership took place between 1966 and 1973. In 1966, commercial banks and households owned 39 percent and 38 percent of the securities, respectively, but by 1973, commercial banks held half of total debt and households about a quarter. A possible explanation for this shift is the reduction in tax rates on individual income relative to the rate on corporate income that took place after 1964. But between 1973 and 1984 the relative amount

22. ACIR, *Financing Public Physical Infrastructure* (GPO, 1984), pp. 3–4; Joint Economic Committee, *Hard Choices: A Report on the Increasing Gap Between America's Infrastructure Needs and Our Ability To Pay for Them,* prepared for the Subcommittee on Economic Goals and Intergovernmental Policy, 98 Cong. 2 sess. (GPO, 1984), p. 5. The Joint Committee estimates that $1.1 trillion will have to be spent on infrastructure needs over the period 1983–2000.

23. Since state and local governments are not taxed by the federal government, it makes little sense for them to hold tax-exempt bonds yielding less than taxable U.S. government securities.

held by households rose once again to parity with that held by commercial banks. Inflation and taxpayers' consequent move to higher tax brackets no doubt would explain renewed popularity of municipal debt as an investment for individuals.

Debt Limitations

Most states impose limitations on the authority of the state legislature to borrow. The limitations have often reflected impulsive reactions to misdirected overborrowing; their objective is to protect taxpayers, and the credit of the governments, against recurrences of past mistakes. There are different types of restrictions. In some states a constitutional amendment is required for authorization of debt. Or the restrictions may be in the form of referendum requirements or monetary limits placed on debt authorizations. There are also legal provisions for exceeding debt limits.[24]

Besides limiting their own borrowing power, states also impose constitutional or statutory limitations on the borrowing power of their local governments. A common practice is to set a ceiling on debt as a percentage of the property tax base of the local government.[25] Another device, mandated by constitution or statute in most states, is a requirement that the issuance of debt be approved by referendum.

State limitations on local government borrowing are designed to protect the solvency of local governments (as well as that of the state), and to protect bondholders. The ACIR has rephrased the purposes as follows: "To empower local governments to make use of borrowing, prudently and in a responsible and locally responsive manner, as one means for financing their requirements."[26]

The limitation that sets a ceiling on local borrowing in terms of the

24. For a convenient listing of these restrictions, see ACIR, *Significant Features of Fiscal Federalism, 1976–77 Edition* (GPO, 1977), table 63. Also see National Association of State Budget Officers, *Limitations on State Deficits* (Lexington, Ky.: Council of State Governments, 1976); New York State Legislative Commission on State-Local Relations, *New York's Limits on Local Taxing and Borrowing Powers—A Time for Change?* (Albany, N.Y.: The Commission, 1983), pp. 109–55.

25. For a summary of these restrictions, see ACIR, *Significant Features, 1976–77,* table 61.

26. ACIR, *State Constitutional and Statutory Restrictions on Local Government Debt* (Washington: ACIR, 1961), p. 39.

property tax base has often been criticized. Some critics declare that it is technically deficient. It focuses on the property tax base of the individual local government, even though that same base may be shared by several overlapping local governments. Summation of the ratios of debt to assessed value of property for all the governmental units in a geographic area might produce an aggregate ratio that would seem alarming to voters. If consolidation of the units in order to achieve a simpler and more efficient governmental structure were under consideration, some officials would oppose this step simply because of their fear that, in the process, the aggregate borrowing power of the area would be curtailed.

Conversely, the creation of new governmental units has been induced and stimulated by a desire to gain new borrowing power. Fragmentation of governmental functions through proliferation of special districts and authorities destroys the unity of governmental budgets and deprives citizens of understandable information concerning government finances. A basic premise of responsible state and local government is thereby impaired.

Limitations tied to the property tax base are less relevant now than in the past. Fifty years ago the property tax supplied 95 percent of the tax revenue of local governments; in 1984 it supplied 75 percent. The debt-carrying capacity of local governments is, therefore, not measured by their property tax base alone. This is the more so because state-imposed limits usually relate to assessed value, which, in most cases, is less than full value.

Perhaps the most important defect of such attempts at debt limitation is that the limit usually applies only to full faith and credit debt, secured by the general revenues of the government, and not to nonguaranteed debt, secured only by the revenues of the enterprise or activity for which this debt is contracted. Studies continue to show that state restrictions on local debt issuance appear to be ineffective in limiting the total amount of local debt issued.[27] In recent years there has been dramatic growth in the volume of nonguaranteed debt, which has severely reduced the significance of traditional techniques for limiting debt.

27. See William E. Mitchell, "The Effectiveness of Debt Limits on State and Local Government Borrowing," *The Bulletin* (New York University, Graduate School of Business Administration, 1967); Commission on State-Local Relations, *New York's Limits,* p. 133.

The Nonguaranteed Bond

The most important device used to avoid debt limitations has been the revenue bond, a form of nonguaranteed debt. Strictly defined, revenue bonds are those for which interest and principal are payable exclusively from the earnings of a specific enterprise. In such case they are not serviced from the general revenues of a local or state government; they are not, therefore, subject to the constitutional or statutory limitations imposed on the issuance of full faith and credit bonds.

In their original use, revenue bonds were mostly issued to finance revenue-producing enterprises—public utilities, toll facilities, and so on. This use of nonguaranteed debt was greatly enlarged during the 1930s when the Public Works Administration was attempting to stimulate state and local construction of public works. State and local limitations on borrowing stood in the way. The legal division of the PWA decided that nonguaranteed bonds were a device that would circumvent the limitations, and it offered to help state and local governments in drafting bills authorizing the issuance of such bonds. The help was widely accepted. In 1931 only fifteen states permitted local governments to use nonguaranteed bonds; by 1936 the number had risen to forty; and now nonguaranteed bonds are used in every state. Even more surprising than the growth in the volume of such bonds was the expansion in the types of projects financed by them. In addition to the usual public utilities, local governments have constructed swimming pools, golf courses, college dormitories, and so on.

Since World War II the nonguaranteed bond has been widely utilized by both state and local governments. As figure 9-1 shows, in 1949 full faith and credit debt accounted for 87.6 percent of all state and local long-term debt; in 1984 it had fallen to 34.4 percent. While the relative use of full faith and credit debt diminished at both the state and local levels, the decline was greater at the state level where, in 1984, full faith and credit debt was only 31.3 percent of the total. Similarly, the figures show that the postwar growth of nonguaranteed debt was greater at the state level.

The annual publication *State Government Finances* supplies debt figures for individual states. In 1941 thirty-four states had more than half of their net long-term debt in the form of full faith and credit bonds; in 1973 and in 1984 the number was twenty-two (see appendix table A-19). Though the relative importance of full faith and credit bonds has been

Figure 9-1. *Percent of State and Local Debt in Full Faith and Credit and Nonguaranteed Form, 1949, 1957, 1968, 1978, and 1984*

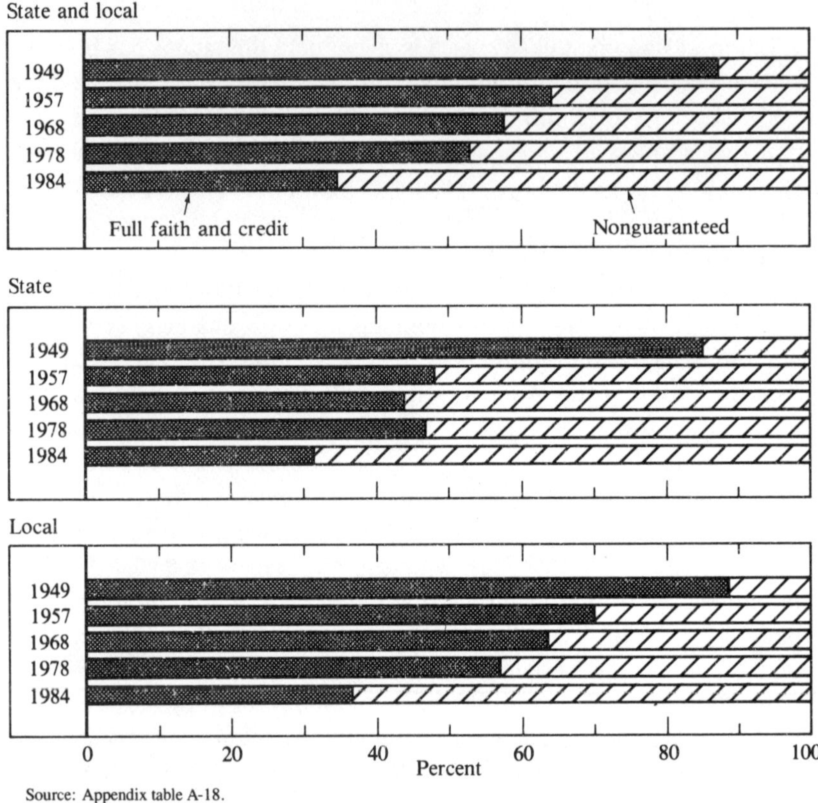

Source: Appendix table A-18.

fairly constant, the number of states with less than half the total of their long-term debt financed in this manner has been increasing—from only fourteen states in 1941 to twenty-eight in 1984.

Among the disadvantages of nonguaranteed bonds is the long time period for which they are issued, usually in order to provide "a safe margin for coverage of costs and debt charges."[28] Extension of maturity tends to increase the rate of interest that must be paid. Another of their faults is their tendency to bias the use of government resources toward purposes for which the device is readily applicable.

A serious danger of nonguaranteed bonds arises from their use for purposes that are not self-financing and that therefore burden the budgets

28. ACIR, *State Constitutional and Statutory Restrictions*, p. 55.

of state and local governments. If these purposes are public, and if they should be financed by borrowing, issuance of full faith and credit debt is superior in all respects to the issuance of revenue bonds. By concealing or obscuring what state and local governments are doing, the use of nonguaranteed bonds stimulates imprudent practices. And if governments should default on even a modest number of these bonds, all state and local credit would be adversely affected.

The rapid growth of nonguaranteed debt is ironical. In some measure, the use of nonguaranteed debt aims at avoiding constitutional or statutory limitations on borrowing. Thus an effort to protect state and local governments against the dangers of borrowing has induced growth of a type of debt that is more dangerous than the debt that was restricted.[29]

Bonds for Industrial Development and Other Nontraditional Purposes

Nonguaranteed bonds have been used to aid private industry. In almost all states, local governmental units have been authorized to issue revenue bonds in order to acquire land, buildings, and equipment that are leased to private firms. The firms pay a rental to cover servicing of the debt.

This practice is objectionable for several reasons. It exploits the interest exemption of state and local bonds from federal income taxation for purposes that are proprietary and private rather than public; it enables recipient firms to derive a cost advantage over other private firms; it induces firms to move from one state to another when market forces by themselves are not favorable. Of course, once the use of these bonds has been established, individual states have little choice but to join in the competition. Those who abstain may suffer a decline in their industrial base.

Often, such nonguaranteed bonds are not the obligations of local government. A governmental unit issuing revenue bonds to finance an industrial aid project incurs no legal obligation to pay interest or redeem the debt out of its own resources. The bonds are secured through the earnings of the firm occupying the facility, and the market judges quality of the bond issue on the basis of the firm's credit. Since investors, in effect, lend their credit to the private firm, the governmental unit merely serves as the

29. Some bonds do fail. In June 1982, the Washington Public Supply System (Whoops) defaulted on $2.3 billion in bonds. *Business Week* (July 11, 1983), pp. 80–87.

Table 9-11. *New Long-Term, Tax-Exempt Bonds by Traditional and Nontraditional Purposes, Selected Years, 1970–82*

Type of bond	*1970*	*1972*	*1974*	*1976*	*1978*	*1980*	*1982*
				Billions of dollars			
Traditional public purposes[a]	17.2	18.4	17.5	24.1	27.4	22.5	39.8
Nontraditional purposes	0.8	3.6	5.4	9.2	14.6	31.4	43.4
Housing	0.7	2.2	1.9	3.4	6.1	15.8	14.3
Industrial development	0.1	0.3	0.5	1.5	3.4	9.2	12.7
Pollution control	n.a.	0.6	2.2	1.9	2.7	2.3	5.3
Hospitals	n.a.	0.5	0.8	2.3	2.1	3.6	9.5
Student loans	n.a.	n.a.	n.a.	0.1	0.3	0.5	1.6
Refundings	0.1	1.7	0.7	3.2	8.7	2.0	4.3
Total	18.1	23.7	23.6	36.5	50.7	55.9	87.5
				Percent			
Nontraditional as share of total	4.4	15.2	22.9	25.2	28.8	56.2	49.6

Source: Advisory Commission on Intergovernmental Relations, *Strengthening the Federal Reserve System: Implications for State and Local Taxing and Borrowing* (Washington: ACIR, 1984), p. 117.

a. Includes education, transportation, water and sewerage, public power.

n.a. = not available.

organ through which the firm borrows. Nonguaranteed industrial aid bonds, therefore, effectively convert the debt of private companies into tax-exempt obligations.

Table 9-11 shows trends in the use of bonds for industrial development and other nontraditional purposes. First, compare trends in the volume of new long-term debt for traditional and nontraditional purposes. Bonds have traditionally been used to finance education, transportation, water and sewerage, and public power. In addition to industrial development, nontraditional purposes include housing, pollution control, hospitals, and student loans.

In 1970 the $800 million of new long-term bonds issued for nontraditional purposes was insignificant in relation to the $17.2 billion of bonds floated for traditional purposes. But by 1980 the tables were turned. In 1982 the volume of industrial development bonds had risen dramatically to $12.7 billion, while bonds to finance private housing, pollution control, hospitals, and student loans brought the volume of bonds for nontraditional purposes almost equal with those for traditional purposes. What has caused this explosive growth in the volume of private-purpose tax-exempt bonds? The ACIR offers as reasons state and local governments' expanded perception of their roles, and their need to finance facilities for federally mandated functions such as pollution control or to compensate for cutbacks in federal programs such as student loans.[30] Tax exemption is a convenient way of offering small business people and potential homeowners a reduction in interest rates. The bonds are an important tool in governments' competition for jobs and industry and they are outside the debt limitations placed on general obligation bonds.

Can the volume of these private-purpose bonds be expected to continue to increase? The answer is a qualified no. The federal government would like to limit the use of these bonds. In 1968 Congress passed legislation to restrict the use of industrial development bonds, and for a few years the bonds almost disappeared. But the law was not tight. Small issues of industrial development bonds and bonds to finance the purchase of equipment to control air and water pollution were not restricted. As a result, the use of tax-exempt bonds began to grow again and spread to finance enterprises such as race tracks, racquet clubs, and even massage parlors. Congress reacted to this abuse by prohibiting, in the Tax Equity and Fiscal Responsibility Act of 1982 (TEFRA), the use of tax-exempt bonds to finance certain recreational, auto service, food, and sports facilities and massage parlors. In addition, a sunset provision was enacted to remove by 1987 the tax exemption for small issue industrial development bonds.

Further restrictions, incorporated in the Deficit Reduction Act of 1984, placed a cap on the volume of industrial development bonds and student loan bonds issued. The state cap was $150 per person, or a total of $200 million, whichever was greater, until 1986, and after that $100 per person. The restrictions will retard the issuance of private-purpose bonds, but for most states the caps are not particularly low, and not all bonds are included in the sunset legislation.[31]

Reform of Borrowing Limitations

The ACIR in 1961 recommended a complete revision of the maze of debt restrictions on local government borrowing. Authority to issue bonds

30. ACIR, *Strengthening the Federal Revenue System: Implications for State and Local Taxing and Borrowing* (Washington: ACIR, 1984), pp. 117, 120.

31. For detailed description and analysis of industrial development bonds and bonds used to finance other private projects, see Stacey Kean, "Industrial Development Bonds: Action in the 98th Congress to Restrict Their Growth," Issue Brief 1B84088 (Library of Congress, Congressional Research Service, 1984); Congressional Budget Office, *The Federal Role in State Industrial Development Programs* (GPO, 1984); Federal Reserve Bank of Cleveland, *Economic Commentary* (August 13, 1984).

"should be legally vested in the governing bodies of local governments, subject to a permissive referendum only, on petition, and with participation in any such referendum available to all eligible local voters and the results determined—except under unusual circumstances—by a simple majority vote on the question."[32] This is still good advice. Existing state restrictions have not limited the total amount of debt issued by local units but may have induced them to use nonguaranteed bonds where general obligation bonds would have been appropriate. States might also consider increasing the technical assistance in debt management that they offer their local units. Among the types of oversight that state governments now provide are review of legal and fiscal aspects of local bond sales, state assistance in preparing bond documents, and mandatory state approval of local bond sales.[33]

32. ACIR, *State Constitutional and Statutory Restrictions*, pp. 4–5.
33. Commission on State-Local Relations, *New York's Limits*, p. 109.

CHAPTER TEN

Earmarked Revenues, Retirement Systems, and Capital Budgets

If to do were as easy as to know what were good to do, chapels had been churches, and poor men's cottages princes' palaces.

The Merchant of Venice

IN MAKING fiscal decisions, executive officers and legislative bodies of state and local governments are concerned with satisfying the public desires that fall within their jurisdiction. The task of spending, taxing, and borrowing to meet these demands is one of efficient allocation of resources, and a budgetary process has evolved that is designed to provide the necessary funds and to establish priorities of need.

This state-local job differs from the federal budgetary process in two major respects; it is concerned only minimally with problems of economic stabilization and with alterations in the distribution of income and wealth. Stabilization is a national objective for which responsibility must rest chiefly with Congress and the federal executive. While state-local budgeting may perhaps be arranged to assist federal action, such efforts are supplementary. That alterations in the distribution of income are a federal responsibility may be more controversial and, in practice, state and local governments have played an important role in determining the welfare programs now in existence. Nonetheless, it is quite important to recognize that the possibility of interstate movement of people and resources limits the force of state activity in this area.

The Budgetary Process

State and local budgeting aims at an accurate determination of governmental needs and an efficient appraisal of how these needs can be met. Competing needs must be weighed, and revenues must be raised and allotted to them. After formulation and enactment, budget programs must be executed according to plan.

The time period of a budget depends on the timing of legislative sessions. In about a third of the states, sessions are biennial and therefore budgets must be planned for a two-year period. Local budgets are for a one-year period. A fiscal year may, but usually does not, coincide with the calendar year. The most common opening and closing dates are July 1 and June 30, respectively.

A standard textbook rule is that a budget should be comprehensive—all expenditures and receipts should be reported in it. Only in this way can proper allocations be made. In practice comprehensiveness is seldom achieved, and for understandable reasons. Some types of spending seem to require different and special treatment. For example, government enterprises are excluded from the budgetary process in an effort to secure nonpolitical and efficient business-type operation. What of capital expenditures, which are irregular and often provided by borrowing? And what of special funds, with earmarked tax revenues? Have they features that justify their exclusion from the budgetary process?

The first step in governmental budgeting is preparation of the budget. This should be the job of the executive and, in almost all states and a growing number of cities, this is the case. An executive budget is constructed and presented. But the force of executive recommendations may be strong or weak. It is weak when important agencies, or departments, or activities are exempt from executive control. In some states, departments headed by elective officers are exempt on the ground that they receive a direct mandate from the electorate. Activities financed by earmarked revenues, and those of business-type enterprises, are usually free from executive control since they depend on assigned or earned revenues and do not compete in the budgetary process with other programs. Budgets of the judiciary and the legislature are exempt in conformity with the theory of separation of governmental powers. Similarly, the budgets of institutions of higher learning—the "fourth branch" of government—are frequently quite free from executive control.

Most—perhaps all—states require the state government, and local governments as well, to present a balanced budget. This does not mean that current expenditures and revenues must equate, but merely that any excess of expenditures be covered by borrowing. Authorized receipts from loans serve to balance the budget. The balance is often tricky. Estimates of revenue are frequently higher, and those of expenditure lower, than a candid appraisal would provide. At the local level, fudging of this sort may be curbed by requiring that local estimates be reviewed by a state authority; it is less easy to curb at the state level.

The form in which the state budget should be presented to the legislature has been much debated. A line-item budget shows estimates of the sums needed to provide specific objects—salaries for so many clerks, sums for purchase of office supplies, and so on. It leans heavily on prior expenditures, and it does not indicate what the clerks are to do or what the supplies will be used for. When a government is small, this method is useful both to the executive and to the legislature. But when the government is large, a line-item budget becomes bulky and incomprehensible; it conceals any view of functions or programs. Executives, legislatures, and citizens should be concerned with what government is trying to do, and with reckoning the cost of a program in comparison with what it provides. It is, therefore, wise to present budgets not only in line-item fashion but in functional form as well.

After the budget has been framed, the next step is its transmittal to the legislative body. The primary job of the legislative branch is to examine, modify, and approve the budget. In a state where the budgetary powers of the executive are large, agencies are expected to support the budget as presented.

The most common legislative organization at the state level for review of the budget is an appropriations and revenue committee in each house. The drawback of this procedure is that there are two separate considerations of expenditure and revenue and that they demand repetitive presentation, appraisal, and recommendation. Modifications exist in some states—one appropriations committee and one revenue committee, or a combined appropriations and revenue committee. The efficiency of legislative examination depends heavily on proper staffing, since members of the legislature often cannot find time to analyze budgetary programs in detail. In a few states the power of the legislature to alter the budget—especially the power to add items—is restricted. In New York, for example, the legislature may eliminate or reduce items; it may add items only if they are "stated separately and distinctly from the original items of the bill and refer each to a single object or purpose."[1] Moreover, legislative alteration of state budgets has been curbed by giving governors the right of item veto; the curb is even more effective when the governor has the power not only to veto, but also to reduce, items.

1. New York Constitution, art. 7, sec. 4.

Execution of the budget is the step in the budgetary process that follows legislative approval. Expenditure must not only go to the proper purposes, it must also be properly timed. Usually a schedule is set up by which a flow of money will be made available to be spent. This ensures a pattern of spending that fits appropriations, and the executive may be empowered to modify the pattern in the light of changed conditions. The legislature in providing appropriations recognizes that flexibility must be allowed in execution of the budget, usually by permitting the transfer of items within broad categories. Flexibility at different phases of the business cycle has also received some recognition in state budgets. New York, for example, has enacted a simple and logical scheme. Two tax reserves were set up in 1946, one for local assistance and the other for the remainder of the state budget. An operating surplus can be transferred to, or a deficit withdrawn from, these reserves. By this device state spending in recession can be maintained or expanded, and, at the same time, the budget kept in balance as the law requires. Many other states have also established "rainy day" funds to improve their budget flexibility.[2]

In the years since World War II, as governmental activities have grown, new managerial techniques have been applied to the budgetary process. Program and performance budgets, zero-based budgeting, accrual accounting, integrated purchasing—these and other techniques have been applied by some state and local governments. The old objective of checking irregularities, which inspired the early advocates of formal budgeting, has been supplemented by the objective of making the budget a positive tool in the appraisal of competing uses for government money. Before performance budgeting was brought to public attention by the Hoover Commission, some state and local governments had utilized functional or program budgeting, which separated the budget items into program areas. Legislative bodies have a limited amount of time they can devote to separate items and therefore need to focus on programs. The new budgeting techniques offer them a variety of means for comparing programs.

The first of the new planning techniques, developed in the early 1960s in the Department of Defense and extended by President Johnson to most federal departments, was the planning-programming-budgeting (PPB) system. The distinctive characteristics of the system are its identification of

2. Advisory Commission on Intergovernmental Relations, *Significant Features of Fiscal Federalism, 1984 Edition* (Washington: ACIR, 1985), pp. 160–61.

governmental objectives; explicit consideration of future implications; consideration of all pertinent costs; and systematic analysis of alternatives. The process of program analysis is, of course, complicated by difficulties in obtaining quantitative measures for many economic and social aspects of programs, especially when those programs serve various objectives.

The strong interest in the PPB system among state and local officials led to an intergovernmental, pilot demonstration of planning, programming, and budgeting in five cities, five counties, and five states.[3] Six years later, however, an investigator could find "few success stories to emulate, few examples of what works, and no solid evidence of the benefits to be derived from PPB. The traditions established in earlier years continue to dominate the budget process, while PPB stands on the outside, a fashionable but peripheral feature of state administration."[4]

A more recent managerial technique designed, like program budgeting, to help control expenditures is zero-based budgeting (ZBB). The objective of zero-based budgeting is to continuously scrutinize the entire budget. Items are not to be included in this year's budget simply because they appeared in last year's. The approach generally involves preparing budget proposals with alternative levels of spending grouped into what are called decision packages. The decision packages are ranked in order of preference into what are called budget choice units. The decisionmakers are then in a position to choose, for each program, the level of spending they wish.

Zero-based budgeting has not provided a managerial panacea. If done properly, it requires a tremendous amount of paper work and the construction of thousands of decision packages. Experience has shown that busy executives and legislators have neither the time nor interest in participating in such a process.[5] They are more likely to take an incremental approach. That is, budget-makers are likely to accept last year's budget as legitimate and concentrate their attention for the current budget on marginal or incremental changes from the earlier one. The weakness of such incremental budgeting is that it may make adding new programs easier than removing old ones.

3. State-Local Finances Project, George Washington University, directed by Selma J. Mushkin. See Harry P. Hatry and John F. Cotton, *Program Planning for State, County, City* (George Washington University, State-Local Finances Project, 1967).

4. Allen Schick, *Budget Innovation in the States* (Brookings, 1971), p. 103.

5. Thomas D. Lynch, *Public Budgeting in America* (Prentice-Hall, 1979), p. 34.

Earmarked Revenues

Earmarking may be defined as a restriction imposed on the use to which a governmental revenue may be put. The legislative body is required by statute or by constitutional provision to channel certain revenues to specified purposes. Quite commonly earmarking is accomplished by providing special funds, which are not included in the budget. But sometimes revenue that flows into the general fund may have its use restricted.

Earmarking is used in varying degrees at the state, federal, and local levels of government. Local budgets earmark the revenue from special assessments and use it to pay the cost of improvements, such as construction of a boulevard; revenue from fees collected for hunting and fishing licenses is earmarked and used to support related governmental activities; revenue or contributions collected for employee retirement funds are earmarked for benefit payments. More important, and more questionable on logical grounds, is the financing of local education almost everywhere by earmarked revenues, especially property tax collections. Although there are but a few purposes for which revenues are earmarked at the federal level, the dollar amount is large. Table 10-1 shows that in 1984 federal insurance trust revenue was $223 billion. Earmarking for these purposes is sound practice. But earmarking by state governments goes far beyond these purposes; indeed it is remarkable for its diversity.

Rationale

Many writers in the field of public finance have been critical of earmarking, and certainly the actual practice offers scope for legitimate criticism. But a rationale can be offered, resting on the link between benefits received by particular users of governmental service and taxes collected from those users. A level of government will spend appropriately for some purpose such as provision of highways, and this expenditure will render particular and measurable benefits to highway users. Taxes may reasonably be imposed, and limited to highway users, in an amount that will roughly equate benefits and payments for each user. This is an example of indirect pricing. The government should not collect less in annual revenues than the cost of these services because, in such a case, it would have to meet the deficiency by general taxes, levied according to ability or sacrifice. The government should not collect and use more because this

Table 10-1. *Governmental Insurance Trust Revenue, by Purpose and by Level of Government, 1984*
Billions of dollars

Purpose	*Federal*	*State*	*Local*	*Total*
Unemployment compensation	0.2	16.7	0.1	17.0
Employee retirement	4.4	38.6	7.6	50.6
Old-age, survivors, disability, and health insurance benefits	213.5	...	...	213.5
Railroad retirement	4.1	...	...	4.1
Other	0.7	5.7	...	6.4
Total	222.9	61.0	7.7	291.6

Source: U.S. Census Bureau, *Governmental Finances in 1983–84* (Government Printing Office, 1985), table 21. In all tables years are fiscal unless otherwise noted and figures are rounded.

would finance collective benefits through taxes raised from particular groups of taxpayers.[6] On what ground could collection of more be justified? If this method seemed to be better than any other by which to finance expenditures that yielded collective benefits. On what ground could collection of less be justified? If a legislature estimated that the collective benefits from the excess expenditure justified the levy of general taxes equal to the deficiency.

Quite frequently, pragmatic reasons lie behind the desire to employ earmarking. Pressure groups have sought to ensure that a type of government expenditure will be provided by revenues outside of the appropriation process. They wish to avoid the annual legislative scrutiny, evaluation, and vote of money. Assignment of all, or some part, of the revenue from a well-established tax fulfills their aim. The more socially significant the expenditure, or the more powerful the pressure group, the more persuasive will be the appeal to the legislature. The incidence of the allocated tax on individuals may be wholly unrelated to the benefits that individuals receive. Indeed, a tax based on ability or sacrifice has no tie to any particular governmental expenditure. The amount paid by an individual as income, sales, or property tax is largely unrelated to the benefits he

6. The argument is sometimes made, erroneously, that persons who are forced to pay particular levies should receive particular governmental services in return—that, for example, there should be a link between the collections of liquor and tobacco taxes and expenditure of the collections for the benefit of consumers of liquor and tobacco. This inverts the relationship. Government does not try to discover what benefits are received by users of liquor and tobacco. Its decision to tax them grows chiefly out of the sumptuary purpose of limiting and controlling consumption. Taxation raises the price of the taxed product. In itself, this may not be an effective curb on consumption. But it is the only power of a sumptuary tax, and if government is not satisfied, other steps are available.

receives either from aggregate or from particular government expenditures.[7]

Another pragmatic reason for earmarking has been the association of a needed and widely approved expenditure with new and unpalatable methods of finance. When the city of New York, in 1934, introduced its retail sales tax, the proceeds were earmarked for welfare expenditures; when New Hampshire, in 1963, introduced a state lottery, it earmarked the expected receipts for education. After the new revenue measure has been enacted, inertia—and the obstacles in the way of statutory or constitutional alteration—leads to the continuance of artificial earmarking.

Defects

Even when earmarking meets the test of a direct link between cost and benefit, it has the fault that it removes certain governmental revenues and expenditures from regular and periodic legislative control. For activities that are similar to those provided by government enterprise, this has recognized advantages. Government enterprises will ordinarily be run more efficiently if they are somewhat outside the budgetary process and if the legislature, when it wishes to act with respect to them, must do so by altering existing legislation. A parallel infringement of the budgetary process may be sensible when pricing for the service is indirect. But earmarking does impair the unity of the governmental budget. The total impact of government finance can be judged only when the spending and receipts of all special funds (or at least the algebraic sum of their surpluses and deficits) are added to those of the legislative budget.

7. To public choice theorists, earmarking prompted by the desire to tie the hands of the legislature may have desirable economic and financial results. They point out that if all people are assumed to have perfectly uniform preferences or if there exists an enlightened, benevolent dictator, then general fund financing is appropriate. Tying the dictator's hands through earmarking can prevent him from providing the optimal distribution of services. But, what if citizen-voters are assumed to have diverse preferences and there is no benevolent dictator? General funding then amounts to a tie-in sale; there is a single distribution of public services to accept or reject. Earmarking, on the other hand, allows the citizen-voter to express his preferences or vote for several public services separately rather than together. Greater choice should increase individual welfare. For detailed analysis, see James M. Buchanan, "The Economics of Earmarked Taxes," *Journal of Political Economy,* vol. 71 (October 1963), pp. 457–69; Charles J. Goetz, "Earmarked Taxes and Majority Rule Budgetary Processes," *American Economic Review,* vol. 58 (March 1968), pp. 128–36; Walter W. McMahon and Case M. Sprenkle, "A Theory of Earmarking," *National Tax Journal,* vol. 23 (September 1970), pp. 255–61.

Another practical and related defect is that numerous earmarking formulas, some quite intricate, complicate administration. Although this may seem to be a legislative aberration, subject to legislative remedy, it often arises because of attempts to make precise and exclusive tie-ins between particular services and tax collections.

When earmarking does not meet the test of direct linkage of cost and benefit—when finance of a general or collective function of government is segregated from other functions—its faults are more serious. In such cases the legislature is abdicating an essential duty. It should, through the budgetary process, determine the appropriate expenditure for each collective function and also indicate how the annual revenues are to be naturally linked. Failure to make such decisions will allow the levels of particular expenditures and revenues to become too large or too small in relation to current needs.

Status

Earmarking is provided for either constitutionally or by statute. Only by laborious scrutiny of state budget reports, accounting practices, and tax classifications can the status of earmarking be gleaned. The practice of earmarking, however, is not insignificant and it has been widely applied to highway finance, debt service, and education.

HIGHWAY USER TAXES. For many years federal policy encouraged the states to earmark all revenue from motor fuel taxes for highway purposes. Diversion to other purposes was frowned upon. When the depression of the 1930s pushed a number of states into using some of this revenue for relief and education, Congress responded in 1934 by passing the Hayden-Cartwright Act which penalized such diversion by cutting federal grants for highway construction. Though a federal motor fuel tax was first imposed in 1931, revenue from the tax was not earmarked until twenty-five years later, under the Highway Revenue Act of 1956. Thereafter, a large slice of the revenue from the motor fuel tax and from the manufacturers' excises on automobiles, trucks, parts, tires, and so on, was assigned to the Highway Trust Fund. In 1982, Congress passed the Surface Transportation Assistance Act, raising motor fuel taxes and providing increased revenue for the trust fund.

Earmarking of a large portion of highway user revenues for the purposes of highway construction and maintenance is now given widespread approval. These taxes provide indirect pricing of the benefits of highway use. To be sure, some collective benefits accrue (although how much is a matter of controversy) and therefore some part of the cost of highways may be placed on revenues from other sources. Moreover, it is clear that, over time, assignment of revenues by type of highway has been inaccurate, notably by favoring nonurban roads. Part of the explanation is that allocation formulas get out of date and yet are too inflexible to be altered. And until recently rural areas were overrepresented in state legislatures and in Congress. At any rate, the amount of motor fuel tax and of other user charges paid by an individual can only be a rough measure of the benefits received by that individual. These are important flaws in the application of indirect pricing, and they admit of no sure remedy.

In the mid-1980s the interstate highway system was nearly complete but much of the existing system was seriously in need of repair. Projected expenditures outstripped the amounts the federal and state highway trust funds could be expected to gather.[8]

DEBT SERVICE. State governments have very often assigned specific taxes, or some segments of them, to service specific security issues. This practice complicates the debt structure and builds up a confusing system of prior and subordinate liens on state revenues for different issues. The correct technique is to declare by statute (or even constitutional provision) that debt obligations are to be secured by a preferred and equal claim on the general fund. The state credit would thereby be enhanced and the cost of borrowing reduced. Borrowing would have an immediate and direct impact on general fund revenues; such a straightforward practice might encourage more responsible borrowing decisions.

EDUCATION. State governments have been very eclectic in their choice of taxes earmarked for education, since no major type is unutilized. Indeed, in many states part of the revenue from several taxes is pledged. The broad-based and productive taxes on retail sales and income are most utilized. In all of this there is no link of cost with benefit. The benefits that flow from governmental expenditure for primary and secondary education are mainly collective, and the costs should, therefore, be provided through general taxes. In this sense the practice of many states is correct. But earmarking all or part of the revenues from particular taxes is questionable

8. Congressional Budget Office, *Public Works Infrastructure: Policy Considerations for the 1980s* (U.S. Government Printing Office, 1983), p. 30, estimated that $23 billion per year of highway expenditure would be needed for the remainder of the decade.

since there is no provision for recurrent legislative appraisal of what the state government spends in aid to education.

PUBLIC WELFARE. Earmarking revenues for public welfare was a phenomenon of the 1930s. Many states, in order to finance the great expansion of welfare payments, introduced sales taxes and pledged all or part of the receipts. The same period witnessed the repeal of prohibition and, as states secured new revenues from taxation or sale of alcoholic beverages, some chose to assign them to welfare expenditure. However, in recent years state reliance on earmarked taxes to finance welfare has lessened.

MISCELLANEOUS EARMARKED REVENUES. The justification of earmarking for such purposes as retirement funds, unemployment insurance, and workmen's compensation is rooted in their origins. At the outset all of these schemes leaned heavily on the analogy of private insurance. Contributors made payments that earned them the right to benefits; they were thus insured against the danger of legislative cuts in their subsequent receipts. General taxpayers were assured that benefits, being linked to contributions, would not be liberalized for political reasons. With the growth and acceptance of these systems, the social aspects of social insurance have become more important, especially in the federal systems.

Conclusion

The popularity of earmarking is an illustration of the wariness shown by voters in the wisdom and steadfastness of state legislatures. A group of citizens, deeply interested in state performance of a particular activity, will try to free that activity from legislative control by having earmarked funds provided for it. Legislatures often acquiesce, thus debarring periodic exercise of legislative judgment concerning those segments of the state budget. This practice also hampers the state's chief executive, who should frame a budget with full knowledge of how all state governmental resources are utilized and with freedom to recommend changes. Earmarking limits the powers of the executive. When the limitation has a logical rationale—when benefits are linked to costs—the advantages can outweigh the disadvantages.

What is required is effective compromise between independent operation and periodic legislative scrutiny. Just as governmental enterprises need to be free from legislative heckling, so do those activities for which earmarking is legitimate. And yet some periodic legislative scrutiny is necessary in order to weigh performance of the governmental activities.

State and Local Retirement Systems

The retirement system of a state or local government is a complex financial arrangement.[9] A package of benefits must be agreed on and a financing scheme must be adopted. Eligibility rules for membership must be established. A variety of matters must be carefully weighed: whether employees should be accepted into the plan immediately or should serve a probationary period; what kinds of benefits should be provided (should disability, death, and survivor benefits be included, or should the plan be limited to providing pensions to retirees?); whether benefits should be set as a fraction of the employee's average salary or be determined by the future value of the periodic contributions made by the employee and his government employer; how rights to the government's contribution become vested in the employee before retirement; what the retirement age will be; and whether early retirement should be permitted.

Retirement systems contain so many features that it is not surprising to find wide variations in the plans adopted by state and local governments. There are certain essential features, however, that characterize most plans.[10] A common benefit formula bases the employee's annual pension on the number of years he has worked multiplied by 2 percent of his average salary in the five highest-paid of his last ten years of service. Thus an individual who has worked for twenty-five years will retire with a pension equal to 50 percent of his final average salary. Often, a cost-of-living adjustment guarantees that pension benefits will increase with the consumer price index up to a maximum of 3 percent a year. Most plans offer an early retirement option.

The right of an employee to a proportionate share of the pension fund is called vesting. Usually five years of employment is required before vest-

9. See David J. Ott, Attiat F. Ott, James A. Maxwell, and J. Richard Aronson, *State-Local Finances in the Last Half of the 1970s* (Washington: American Enterprise Institute, 1975), chaps. 3, 4; E. Schwartz, V. Munley, and J. R. Aronson, "Reforming Public Pension Plans to Avoid Unfunded Liability," in International City Management Association, *Management Information Service Report* (Washington: ICMA, May 1983).

10. See Robert Tilove, *Public Employee Pension Funds* (Columbia University Press, 1976), chap. 2; Schwartz, Munley, and Aronson, "Reforming Public Pension Plans."

ing occurs. Employees who leave their jobs before vesting occurs can get back their own contributions to the pension fund plus interest, but not the amount contributed by the employer. Those who leave after vesting has occurred are entitled to all that has been promised. Benefits are usually deferred, however, until those individuals reach retirement age.[11]

Disability pensions and a variety of death benefits are other common features included in state and local pension plans. If an employee dies after at least one year of employment, his beneficiary is often entitled to a half year's salary and if he has been employed for ten years, the benefit is usually a full year's salary. If the employee dies at a time he is eligible to retire, the surviving spouse is entitled to an annuity equal to what would have been received if retirement had occurred just before death.

Methods of Funding and Intergeneration Equity

Alternative schemes for financing pension systems range between pay-as-you-go financing and full funding. From a narrow point of view, the cost of a pension plan to the community as a whole is the same in terms of present value no matter which financing scheme is adopted. Assume that a governmental unit enters into a pension arrangement with some of its employees, that it agrees to pay the full costs of the plan, and that its expected payments to pensioners will be zero in the first three years of the plan, $100 in the fourth and fifth years, and zero thereafter.[12] If the plan is financed on a pay-as-you-go basis, the $100 payments in the fourth and fifth years will, with a 10 percent rate of discount, cost the government (in present value terms) $130.39.

If the government decides to have a fully funded plan, it might consider making a single lump-sum contribution at the time the pension plan is initiated; the amount needed to cover all of the obligations of the plan—again, $130.39—will be paid in the first year. It might instead wish to finance the benefits by equal annual contributions of $41.13 over four years. Assuming a 10 percent rate of interest, both types of full funding will grow to $190.90 by the end of the fourth year. At that time $100 must

11. See Munley, Schwartz, and Aronson, "Reforming Public Pension Plans," p. 2; Joseph J. Melone and Everett T. Allen, *Pension Planning: Pensions, Profit Sharing, and Other Deferred Compensation Plans* (Irwin, 1966), p. 53; *Bulletin of the Commission on Insurance Terminology of the American Risk and Insurance Association,* vol. 1, no. 4.

12. This example is drawn from J. Richard Aronson, *Public Finance* (McGraw-Hill, 1985), pp. 536–39.

be paid to pensioners. The $90.90 left in the trust fund will grow to $100 by the end of the fifth year, providing exactly the amount needed for pensioners.

The fact that the present value of future obligations is the same under all three methods of finance does not mean that the schemes are equally satisfactory. A pay as-you-go system has some undesirable features. In the pension plan of a private firm, for example, it would offer no assurance against reductions in the level of pension benefits (or even total loss if the firm were to go bankrupt). Under a trust fund (the fully funded approach), on the other hand, the assets of a retirement system would be segregated from other assets and the claims of pensioners would thus be protected.[13] These distinctions are not of great consequence for public employees because the chance of a state or city ceasing operations is slight. Moreover, their rights to their pensions are protected by law. In public employee retirement systems the trust fund approach is preferable to a pay-as-you-go approach because it assures some degree of equity between present and future taxpayers and because the governmental unit is protected from potential fiscal strain.

Under a pay-as-you-go plan, pension benefits due in each year are financed by general taxation in that year. Tax rates to finance pension benefits need not rise over time as long as the tax base (income and wealth of the community) rises at least as quickly as pension benefits rise. However, if the population and the tax base of a governmental unit should decrease, the level of pension benefits would not decrease as quickly; then a pay-as-you-go pension plan would require higher tax rates. Assuming that any existing employee contribution rate is held constant and that there is no trust fund, the burden of the pension plan, in the form of higher tax rates, would be felt by future residents rather than the generation of taxpayers who incurred the retirement obligations. Moreover, the necessary increase in tax rates, at a time when the tax base was shrinking, would aggravate the fiscal problems of the community and for smaller governmental units could even lead to further reductions in the tax base.[14]

The fully funded approach avoids these problems. Since the employee

13. Of course, it is impossible to protect trust fund assets against mismanagement or the failure of private insurance companies.

14. For an analysis of how changes in tax rates can induce changes in the tax base of a community, see J. Richard Aronson and Eli Schwartz, "Financing Public Goods and the Distribution of Population in a System of Local Governments," *National Tax Journal*, vol. 26 (June 1973), pp. 137–60.

and the government (taxpayers) would contribute to the fund while pension liabilities were accruing rather than when payments were made, intergeneration equity would be preserved.[15] Moreover, higher future tax rates to finance benefits would not be inevitable if the tax base of the governmental unit should decline. The trust fund and its interest earnings, along with a constant rate of government contributions based on covered payroll, would provide the funds to meet benefit payments. As long as the community tax base did not decrease at a faster rate than covered payroll, tax rates would not have to rise.

In 1978 a study of public employee retirement systems found that the propensity to use actuarial funding techniques rather than the pay-as-you-go method varied by size of the plan. Large public systems were most likely to be actuarily funded (over 70 percent). For medium-sized plans 60 percent used actuarial methods, but only about 45 percent of the many smaller plans used procedures that were actuarily sound.[16]

Trends and Future Outlook

Membership in state and local government retirement systems is very high and is likely to remain so. Almost all full-time employees belong to some state or local pension system; in 1982 no less than 2,564 different state and local retirement systems were in operation. Although these plans have a common form and pattern, the variation among them in size and composition of membership, amount of assets, and financial structure of payments and benefits is great. In 1982 the 116 largest systems contained 91 percent of total membership. Nonetheless, small systems persist; 1,709 of the systems had fewer than 100 members in 1982.[17]

The diversity of the systems means that it is impossible to make generalizations about their finances. Those that are new and expanding in membership have few current beneficiaries and a rising annual ratio of

15. When a plan is initiated or benefit provisions liberalized, current employees are given credits for past service. This financial obligation, usually referred to as a supplemental unfunded balance, generally is amortized over a lengthy period. These credits interfere with intergeneration equity because their costs must be spread over future generations.

16. ACIR, *State and Local Pension Systems* (Washington: ACIR, 1980), p. 23; *Pension Task Force Report on Public Employee Retirement Systems,* prepared for the House Committee on Education and Labor, 95 Cong. 2 sess. (GPO, 1978), pp. 292–93.

17. Census Bureau, *Finances of Employee Retirement Systems of State and Local Governments in 1982–83* (GPO, 1984), p. 11.

Table 10-2. *Number of Beneficiaries and Ratio of Beneficiaries to Membership in State and Local Retirement Systems, 1957, 1962, 1967, 1972, and 1982*[a]

Item	*1957*	*1962*	*1967*	*1972*	*1982*
			Thousands of beneficiaries		
Benefit base	522.4	739.1	1,029.8	1,463.4	2,897.4
Normal retirement	424.2	600.2	844.5	1,241.0	2,404.0
Disability	43.4	60.7	77.2	92.3	249.9
Survivors	54.8	78.1	108.2	130.1	243.6
			Percent of total membership		
Beneficiaries in system					
All systems	13.0	13.8	14.6	16.1	25.0
State administered	9.3	10.5	11.7	13.9	22.3
Locally administered	24.2	26.3	27.5	26.7	43.3

Sources: Census Bureau, *Census of Governments, 1982,* vol. 6, no. 1: *Employee-Retirement Systems of State and Local Governments* (GPO, 1983), table 4, and earlier issues.
a. Last month of fiscal year.

payments to receipts. Some systems, even when new, pursue a full-funding policy, while others operate on a pay-as-you-go basis, and still others on a combination of the two.

Because of their diversity, trends in the systems' functioning are obscured. And the time lag in the impact of most changes in pension systems further complicates judging their soundness. Lowering the retirement age, for example, affects immediately only the annual trickle of members who retire. Higher benefit payments affect existing retirees, and they are only a fraction of membership. In short, the cash effect of financial liberalization (or retrenchment) of a retirement system is lagged rather than immediate.

One significant change in retirement systems is the rise in the ratio of beneficiaries to membership between 1957 and 1982 from 13 percent to 25 percent (see table 10-2). In 1982, the ratio of beneficiaries to membership in locally administered systems in thirty states was 30.1 percent or more, while this ratio was reached in only eight state-administered plans. Receipts of all systems grew remarkably, both because of growth in membership and because the rate of earnings on investments rose from 2.78 percent in 1957 to 7.76 percent in 1982.[18] This growth was marked by a shift in the composition of assets. In 1957 two-thirds of the $12.8 billion in assets was held in government securities. As table 10-3 shows, however, the systems have turned sharply to nongovernmental securities, including

18. U.S. Census Bureau, *Census of Governments, 1982,* vol. 6, no. 1: *Employee-Retirement Systems of State and Local Governments* (GPO, 1983), p. 2, and *1967* issue.

Table 10-3. *Assets of State and Local Retirement Systems, 1957, 1962, 1967, 1972, and 1982*

Billions of dollars and, in parentheses, percent of total

Type of asset	*1957*	*1962*	*1967*	*1972*	*1982*
Government securities	8.4 (65.7)	10.2 (43.6)	9.1 (23.1)	6.1 (8.9)	58.8 (24.0)
Nongovernment securities	4.2 (32.7)	12.8 (55.2)	29.7 (75.7)	61.8 (89.9)	181.1 (73.8)
Corporate bonds	3.4 (26.3)	9.5 (40.9)	20.3 (51.6)	37.9 (55.1)	84.2 (34.3)
Corporate stocks	0.2 (1.4)	0.7 (3.0)	2.4 (6.1)	12.6 (18.3)	54.3 (22.1)
Mortgages	0.5 (3.5)	2.1 (8.8)	4.8 (12.3)	7.0 (10.2)	18.8 (7.7)
Other	0.2 (1.4)	0.6 (2.5)	2.2 (5.7)	4.3 (6.2)	23.8 (9.7)
Cash	0.2 (1.7)	0.3 (1.2)	0.4 (1.1)	0.8 (1.1)	5.4 (2.2)
Total	12.8 (100.0)	23.3 (100.0)	39.3 (100.0)	68.8 (100.0)	245.3 (100.0)

Source: Census Bureau, *Census of Governments, 1982,* vol. 6, no. 1, table 2, and earlier issues.

corporate stocks. By 1972 the proportion of pension fund assets held in government securities had fallen as low as 9 percent, but it had risen to about one-fourth of pension fund assets in 1982.

The responsibility for providing future payments to beneficiaries depends heavily on employee and government contributions, mostly the latter. Governmental contributions have already risen substantially—from $5.8 billion in 1972 to $21.8 billion in 1982—but they will continue to grow as systems mature and attempts are made to bring the plans closer to full-funding status. Some of the funds recently have strengthened their finances, and as indicated in table 10-4 the ratio of payments to receipts of funds in the aggregate fell from 40.8 percent in 1967 to 39.0 percent in 1972 and 37.3 percent in 1982.

Projecting the financial position of state and local retirement systems through examination of the past record has a serious fault. Most of the current disbursements of a retirement system are the result of costs that accrued a generation earlier; they do not reflect costs that will accrue in the future. Prospective disbursements arising out of wage and salary adjustments or benefit improvements in the form of earlier retirement or larger payments need to be reckoned with. The best way to project costs is to apply actuarial methods that estimate the accrual of future costs and translate these costs into present values.

The Financial Volatility of Defined-Benefit Pension Plans

Most of the 2,564 state and local retirement systems are partially funded. Because there are so many individual differences in the systems and so few actuarial reports on them, it is difficult to project their potential

Table 10-4. *Receipts and Payments of State and Local Retirement Systems, 1957, 1962, 1967, 1972, and 1982*

Retirement system	*1957*	*1962*	*1967*	*1972*	*1982*
All systems					
Receipts (millions of dollars)	2,455	3,997	6,580	12,620	48,961
Payments (millions of dollars)	958	1,589	2,684	4,920	18,267
Payments as a percent of receipts	39.0	39.8	40.8	39.0	37.3
State administered					
Receipts (millions of dollars)	1,504	2,695	4,656	9,285	37,944
Payments (millions of dollars)	522	948	1,654	3,279	13,469
Payments as a percent of receipts	34.7	35.2	35.5	35.3	35.5
Locally administered					
Receipts (millions of dollars)	951	1,302	1,924	3,336	11,017
Payments (millions of dollars)	437	641	1,030	1,641	4,799
Payments as a percent of receipts	46.0	49.2	53.5	49.2	43.6

Sources: Census Bureau, *Census of Governments, 1982,* vol. 6, no. 1, table 2, and earlier issues.

future fiscal impact on state and local governments. Estimates of unfunded liability derived from an elementary present-value model of pension-fund financing reveal that they depend heavily on the assumed values of payroll growth, interest rates, and other financial variables.[19] In the early 1970s, when the rate of increases in wages was higher than prevailing interest rates, the financial condition of many pension funds appeared particularly weak. On the other hand, in the early 1980s the level of interest rose above the growth rate in wages and the financial condition of many pension plans showed dramatic improvement.

A pension plan is fully funded when it contains sufficient assets and earnings on those assets to pay each retiree an annual life annuity corresponding to the level of benefits as defined or promised by the plan. Determining the level of contributions needed to keep the plan fully funded depends on many factors—the projected value of the employee's life annuity based on life expectancies and on the length of his working-life contributions, and forecasts of the increase in salaries over time and of the projected interest-rate earnings on the fund's assets. The final pension is determined, at retirement, by length of service times a fixed percentage times some average of final years' salaries. Financial planning must anticipate adjustments in benefit levels to compensate people for inflation after their pensions have started.

19. Ott and others, *State-Local Finances,* chap. 4; it includes a detailed description of the model. Also see Schwartz, Munley, and Aronson, "Reforming Public Pension Plans," pp. 5–8.

Table 10-5. *Pension Fund Estimates and Annual Benefit Levels under Various Assumptions Concerning Wage Growth and Interest Rates*

	Assumed wage growth w *and interest rate* i				
Item	w = *3%* i = *4%*	w = *5%* i = *9%*	w = *6%* i = *4%*	w = *7%* i = *10%*	w = *8%* i = *12%*
Final pension fund, after 30 years of service (dollars)	81,600	223,700	125,000	328,000	497,400
Annual pension, for expected 15 years (dollars)	7,300	27,800	11,200	43,100	73,000
Salary level, final year (dollars)	23,600	41,200	54,200	71,100	93,200
Pension as a percent of final salary	30.9	67.6	20.7	60.6	78.3
Percent contribution required to generate pension of 50 percent of final salary	16.2	7.4	24.2	8.3	6.4

Source: E. Schwartz, V. Munley, and J. R. Aronson, "Reforming Public Pension Plans to Avoid Unfunded Liability," in International City Management Association, *Management Information Service Report* (Washington: ICMA, May 1983), p. 5.

Table 10-5 illustrates how difficult it is to estimate what level of contribution is needed to fund a pension plan. The examples are based on the assumptions that the employee's initial salary is $10,000 and that the annual contribution to retirement is 10 percent of salary, beginning at thirty-five years of age and lasting thirty years; the retirement period is assumed to last fifteen years.[20] The objective of the plan is to offer a pension of 50 percent of final salary. The problem of fiscal management is to determine what part of current payroll must be put into the fund each year to make the 50 percent pensions feasible. The contribution necessary to sustain the pension varies widely according to the relationship between the rate of future salary growth and the available market interest rates.

When the rate of wage growth *w* is 3 percent and the rate of interest *i* is 4 percent, and 10 percent of each year's salary is placed in the fund, the total accumulation at the end of thirty years is $81,600. Over a period of fifteen years the employee can expect to collect an annual pension of $7,300. That amounts to only 30.9 percent of the $23,600 salary in the employee's thirtieth year of service. To provide a pension of 50 percent of final salary, the annual contribution to retirement would have to have been 16.2 percent rather than 10 percent.

If the worker's wage growth *w* is 6 percent rather than 3 percent and the interest rate *i* remains at 4 percent, his annual pension should be $11,200

20. Actuarial life expectancies are more complex mathematically, but the average life expectancy of males and females in the United States in the early 1980s was about eighty.

over the fifteen-year retirement period. But that is only 20.7 percent of his final salary. To reach 50 percent of final salary, his rate of contribution should have been 24.2 percent. Clearly, financing requirements are quite difficult when the wage growth rate outpaces the interest rate.

When the interest rate is significantly above the rate at which salaries are expected to grow, the opposite is true. To provide a pension equal to 50 percent of final salary when wages grow at 8 percent a year while the interest rate is 12 percent would require a 6.4 percent annual contribution to the employee's pension fund.

State Role in Monitoring Pension Plans

In recent years, the fiscal condition of many state and local pension plans has improved. Not only have market conditions been favorable, but state and local officials have recognized the need to increase the funding of their plans.[21] Pennsylvania's Municipal Pension Plan Funding Standard and Recovery Act, passed in 1984, is a particularly good example of the actions states can take to maintain the integrity of municipal plans. That act requires regular evaluations of pension funds using acceptable actuarial cost methods and established actuarial assumptions, and annual pension contributions sufficient to meet normal costs and administrative expenses and to amortize any unfunded liabilities that the actuarial reports reveal. It provides for distribution of state aid for municipal pension plans on a rational and regular basis. State authorities are responsible for establishing an objective procedure to determine the degree of financial distress of pension plans in trouble and for setting up recovery programs for those in distress.

Conclusion

Of course, most of the problems associated with the financing of pension systems occur because the plans are based on defined benefits. Financing would be more manageable if pensions were based on defined contributions. Under a defined contribution plan, employer and employee agree on a portion of annual compensation to be set aside to provide funds for retirement. The contributions are invested in income-earning assets and the employee's pension at retirement is based on what has been accumulated on his behalf.

21. ACIR, *State and Local Pension Systems*, pp. 7–8.

The employee bears some risk under a pension system based on defined contributions. The amount of the pension depends on the investment climate and the skill of those entrusted with managing the funds. On the other hand, there will be no unfunded liability, and the problems associated with the vesting and portability of pension benefits are easily handled. Unfortunately, defined contribution plans are not likely to become popular. Employees prefer the certainty of defined benefits and employers appear to value the ability to leave to future administrations the responsibility of funding the pension promises they have made.

Capital Budgets

At state and local levels some kinds of expenditures raise special difficulties, notably those that are large and irregularly timed. Most commonly, these involve construction of new facilities with a long life.

Simply as a matter of procedure, it makes sense to separate those items in the budget that create special difficulties in planning and execution. School buildings, streets, sewage facilities, and so on, demand long-range planning, and their annual provision must be regularized in order to minimize the problems of financial support. Priorities have to be arranged in advance. In short, state and local governments find it sensible to bundle certain items into a capital budget in order to facilitate financial planning and decisions. Nonetheless, the capital budget is properly a section of the total comprehensive budget. The total budget is a device for handling one-year segments of longer-range operating and capital programs; comprehensiveness is a vital feature.

A capital budget in this sense should be distinguished from the budgets of government enterprises.[22] A government enterprise spends annually for capital and for current items, but none of its expenditures is appropriated by a vote of the legislature. All of its budget should, ordinarily, be removed from the budgetary process (although the general budget should show any subsidy granted to or revenue received from a government

22. A descriptive account of state organizations for central capital budgeting—including the preparation, legislative review, and execution of capital budgets—is provided in A. M. Hillhouse and S. K. Howard, *State Capital Budgeting* (Lexington, Ky.: Council of State Governments, 1963). For an analysis of capital budgeting techniques, see J. Richard Aronson and Eli Schwartz, "Capital Budgeting," in J. Richard Aronson and Eli Schwartz, eds., *Management Policies in Local Government Finance* (Washington: International City Management Association, 1981).

enterprise). Similarly, trust funds as a whole are outside the budgetary process.

Pay-As-You-Go versus Pay-As-You-Use

What is the character of the items to be placed in a capital budget? Their distinctive feature is a stream of returns that stretches into the future. Such budget items, it is argued, should be financed by borrowing. Ordinary items that are consumed currently should be financed by annual taxes, on a pay-as-you-go basis, but items that are used over a considerable period of time should be financed on a pay-as-you-use basis. The term of the borrowing should coincide with the life of the capital item, and the current budget should merely carry charges equal to interest and amortization paying off the principal of the debt as the benefits from the initial outlay are secured. Only through financing public durable goods by loans will intergenerational equity be provided. A project that yields services over many years should be paid for by people according to their use, so that an older person pays less of the cost of a new project than a younger one. This principle, so Richard A. Musgrave states, is particularly important in municipal finance "where the composition of the resident group is subject to more or less frequent change."[23] An elderly person who became resident in a locality that, soon thereafter, made large expenditures on durable items that were financed on a pay-as-you-go basis would be treated inequitably.

Another justification of loan finance relates to items of expenditure that are irregular in time and large in amount. Assume a small district is in need of a new school. If the whole cost were provided by raising tax rates for one or two years, the effects would be unnecessarily disturbing. One alternative would be to establish reserves that could be drawn on to meet such episodic expenditures; and still another would be to borrow to construct the school, raising annual taxes only enough to cover interest and amortization. The irregularity argument for loan finance, however, can be overemphasized. The expenditure of a large, or even a moderate-sized, unit of government on each particular type of public works will be irregular, but the yearly aggregate expenditure is, or can be made, approximately constant.

Table 10-6 illustrates the effects of a shift from pay-as-you-go to pay-

23. *The Theory of Public Finance: A Study in Public Economy* (McGraw-Hill, 1959), p. 563.

Table 10-6. *Illustrative Effect of Capital Budgeting on Total Annual Spending and Taxing*

Thousands of dollars

	Expenditures				Tax collections		
		Capital projects			Budgeting method		
Year	*Current*	*Interest*	*Amortization*	*Total*	*Pay-as-you-go*	*Pay-as-you-use*	*Decrease or increase under pay-as-you-use*
1	4,000.0	45.0	100.0	4,145.0	5,000.0	4,145.0	−855.0
2	4,000.0	85.5	200.0	4,285.5	5,000.0	4,285.5	−714.5
3	4,000.0	121.5	300.0	4,421.5	5,000.0	4,421.5	−578.5
4	4,000.0	153.0	400.0	4,553.0	5,000.0	4,553.0	−447.0
5	4,000.0	180.0	500.0	4,680.0	5,000.0	4,680.0	−320.0
6	4,000.0	202.5	600.0	4,802.5	5,000.0	4,802.5	−197.5
7	4,000.0	220.5	700.0	4,920.5	5,000.0	4,920.5	−79.5
8	4,000.0	234.0	800.0	5,034.0	5,000.0	5,034.0	+34.0
9	4,000.0	243.0	900.0	5,143.0	5,000.0	5,143.0	+143.0
10	4,000.0	247.5	1,000.0	5,247.5	5,000.0	5,247.5	+247.5
11	4,000.0	247.5	1,000.0	5,247.5	5,000.0	5,247.5	+247.5
12	a	a	a	a	a	a	a

a. Same as for eleventh year.

as-you-use financing.[24] Assume that a government has a stream of capital projects yearly amounting to $1 million, and that its other expenditures are $4 million. If they were financed on a pay-as-you-go basis and if the budget were balanced, the tax levy would be $5 million. But suppose the government shifts to a two-budget system, providing $1 million yearly by borrowing at 4.5 percent with amortization on a ten-year basis. Table 10-6 and figure 10-1 indicate the financial effects of the shift. Tax collections under pay-as-you-use financing—always assuming a balanced budget—would go down by $1 million in the first year minus annual amortization and interest. Thereafter, expenditures would gradually rise as interest and amortization rose. In the eighth year, the total collected in taxes to balance the current budget would be $5,034,000, exceeding the amount of yearly collections ($5 million) under pay-as-you-go financing. In the tenth year, tax collections would be $5,247,500, and would remain at that figure.

What would be the financial gain and loss by adoption of the capital budget? In the first year, tax collections would decrease by $855,000 ($1 million minus amortization of $100,000 and interest of $45,000).

24. For a more detailed analysis of the differences between pay-as-you-go and pay-as-you-use financing, see James A. Maxwell and J. Richard Aronson, "The State and Local Capital Budget in Theory and Practice," *National Tax Journal,* vol. 20 (June 1967), pp. 165–70; Earl R. Rolph, "'Pay-As-You-Use Finance': A Comment," and Maxwell and Aronson, "The State and Local Capital Budget in Theory and Practice: Reply," *National Tax Journal,* vol. 21 (June 1968), pp. 210–12, 213–14.

Figure 10-1. *Illustrative Effect of Capital Budgeting on Total Annual Spending and Taxing*

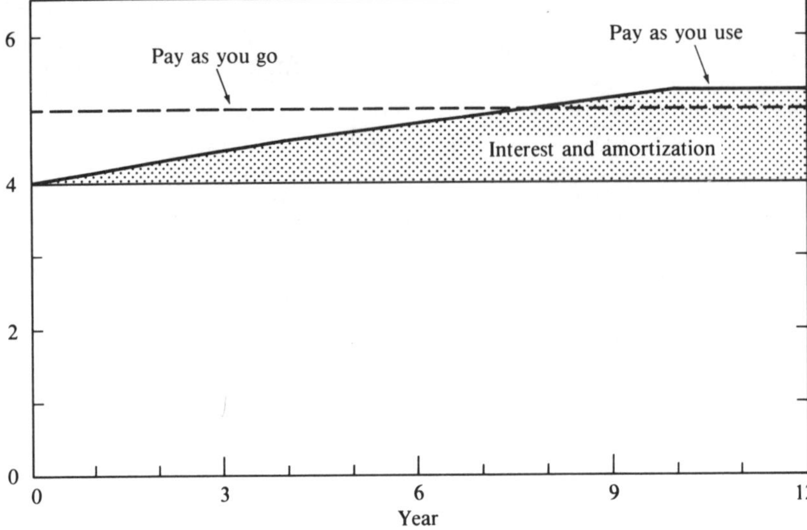

Source: Table 10-6.

Thereafter, the tax levy would rise steadily until the tenth year, when it would stabilize. However, neither the decreases in tax collections of the first seven years nor the increases afterwards should be regarded as financial gains or losses to the community. The net present value (at 4.5 percent) of the tax savings minus the tax increase is zero.[25] Therefore the choice between a pay-as-you-go and a pay-as-you-use system must revert to the question of intergenerational equity or other considerations.[26]

Practical Difficulties

There are some practical difficulties involved in capital budgeting. Accurate depreciation of public durable consumer goods is hard to calculate, and borrowing has often been abused. Expenditure must be assumed to represent the value of an asset; estimates must be made of the time period of benefits from an outlay. In short, the apparatus of asset account-

25. The interest and debt repayment changes do, however, bring transfer costs and distributive effects that may be considered unfortunate.

26. Pay-as-you-use financing has a tax-induced advantage over pay-as-you-go financing because interest on municipal bonds is exempt from federal tax and citizens of any given community are thus better off borrowing through their government rather than individually.

ing should be applied. Depreciation rates for durable goods must be either quite subjective or quite routine. In Massachusetts the state law specifies the purposes for which local governments may borrow, and the duration of the loans. The categories of purposes are broad: "stone, block, brick . . . or other permanent pavement of similar lasting character," "extension of water mains and for water departmental equipment," "remodeling [or] reconstructing . . . private buildings owned by the city or town," and so on. The investment value and the period of depreciation of each project in such categories should not be uniform; yet to determine an appropriate period for each would be difficult. For commercial outlays, public or private, such calculations rest on market factors that are moderately objective; for noncommercial public outlays, they rest on social appraisals, the nature of which defies analysis.

Should a capital budget be formulated to include only tangible assets? The argument has been made that this procedure rests on the business concept of net worth which is inappropriate for social accounting. Educational training, for instance, brings future benefits; it adds to the productivity of the economy over a period of years. But if such expenditure is accepted as an investment, what should be the time period of borrowing? What should be the depreciation rates?

The purport of these questions is that many unsolved operational issues prevent logical development of full-fledged capital budgets. The merit of capital budgets as a procedural device has been perceived by many state and local governments. But controversy over pay-as-you-go versus pay-as-you-use financing remains unresolved. As a practical compromise, a considerable slice of public consumer durable goods has been loan-financed without formal depreciation through the techniques of asset accounting. But state and local governments have utilized a rough and ready financial equivalent in the form of serial bonds, which mature in installments throughout the life of the issue. They have, moreover, sometimes indicated an intuitive awareness that social appraisals, unless restrained, are likely to lead to overborrowing with unfortunate long-run results. The financing of some capital items through the ordinary budget has, therefore, been customary. And state and local governments have failed to place "investment in human resources" in capital budgets, not so much because of a "prejudice in favor of expenditures on hardware"[27] as because of a complete inability to measure the effects of such investment on that part of the economy they can reach by taxes.

27. Musgrave, *Theory of Public Finance*, p. 562.

CHAPTER ELEVEN

Education Finance

Human history becomes more and more a race between education and catastrophe.

H.G. Wells, *The Outline of History*

DURING the past century there has been a remarkable growth in the amount of resources devoted to education. In 1930, total public and private expenditures for education accounted for only 3 percent of the gross national product (see table 11-1). By 1975, this figure rose toward 8 percent before falling below 7 percent in the early 1980s. The bulk of the increase came after World War II, even as real per capita GNP was rising at previously unattained rates. With education claiming a rising share of a rapidly expanding economy, real per pupil expenditures had more than quadrupled thirty-five years after the war.

By 1982, education was the primary activity of 60.8 million of America's 232 million people. Counting 57.2 million students and 3.6 million teachers and administrators, more than one out of four of the American population was involved in education.[1]

Perhaps the major force underlying the increased importance of education is the expanded role played by governments. At the beginning of the century, education was primarily a private and local responsibility. Over the years, however, the states have become the major source of education funds. The federal government has also expanded its role in financing education. By 1982, states provided over 38 percent of funding for educational institutions and local governments about 25 percent. Private support amounted to another 26 percent of expenditures, and the federal government provided the remaining 10 percent (see table 11-2).

1. National Center for Education Statistics, *Digest of Education Statistics, 1983–84* (U.S. Government Printing Office, 1983), p. 1.

Table 11-1. *Expenditure for Education, Selected Years, 1930–84*

Year	*Expenditure (billions of dollars)*	*Percent of GNP*
1930	3.2	3.1
1939	3.2	3.5
1945	4.2	2.0
1959	23.8	4.9
1970	75.7	7.6
1975	118.7	7.7
1980	182.8	6.9
1984	244.4	6.7

Source: National Center for Education Statistics, unpublished data. In all tables years are academic and figures are rounded.

Table 11-2. *Expenditures of Educational Institutions, by Source of Funds, 1970, 1976, and 1982*

Billions of dollars and, in parentheses, percent of total

Educational level and source of funds	*1970*	*1976*	*1982*
All levels, public and private	70.4 (100.0)	121.6 (100.0)	199.8 (100.0)
Federal	7.5 (10.7)	12.8 (10.5)	20.0 (10.0)
State	22.2 (31.5)	44.4 (36.5)	76.3 (38.2)
Local	22.6 (32.1)	34.6 (28.5)	50.7 (25.4)
Private	18.1 (25.7)	29.8 (24.5)	52.8 (26.4)
Elementary and secondary, public and private	45.7 (. . .)	78.9 (. . .)	126.7 (. . .)
Total public	41.0 (100.0)	70.9 (100.0)	112.4 (100.0)
Federal	3.4 (8.2)	6.3 (8.9)	9.7 (8.6)
State	15.8 (38.6)	31.6 (44.6)	53.6 (47.7)
Local	21.7 (52.9)	32.9 (46.4)	48.8 (43.4)
Other	0.1 (0.3)	0.1 (0.1)	0.3 (0.3)
Total private	4.7 (100.0)	8.0 (100.0)	14.3 (100.0)
Institutions of higher learning, public and private	24.7 (. . .)	42.7 (. . .)	73.1 (. . .)
Total public	15.8 (100.0)	29.1 (100.0)	48.8 (100.0)
Federal	2.4 (14.9)	4.0 (13.8)	5.8 (11.9)
State	6.3 (39.7)	12.5 (43.0)	22.2 (45.5)
Local	0.8 (5.1)	1.6 (5.4)	1.7 (3.5)
Other	6.3 (40.3)	11.0 (37.8)	19.1 (39.1)
Total private	8.9 (100.0)	13.6 (100.0)	24.3 (100.0)
Federal	1.7 (18.8)	2.5 (18.1)	4.5 (18.5)
State	0.1 (1.6)	0.3 (2.3)	0.5 (2.1)
Local	0.1 (0.7)	0.1 (0.8)	0.2 (0.7)
Other	7.0 (78.9)	10.7 (78.8)	19.1 (78.7)

Source: National Center, *Digest of Education Statistics, 1982* (GPO, 1982), table 14.

Table 11-3. *School Enrollment, 1900, 1940, 1960, 1970, and 1984*

Millions of full-time students

Level	*1900*	*1940*	*1960*	*1970*	*1984*
All levels	17.2	29.8	45.2	58.6	57.5
Public	15.7	26.5	38.1	51.1	49.0
Private	1.5	3.3	7.1	7.5	8.5
Elementary and secondary	17.0	28.3	42.0	51.4	45.0
Public	15.6	25.7	36.3	45.9	39.3
Private	1.4	2.6	5.7	5.5	5.7
Higher education	0.24	1.5	3.2	7.1	12.5
Public	0.09	0.8	1.8	5.1	9.7
Private	0.15	0.7	1.4	2.0	2.8

Source: National Center, unpublished data.

Trends in Enrollments and Expenditures

Enrollments in educational institutions have more than tripled in this century (see table 11-3). From a level of 17 million students in 1900, enrollments reached an all-time high of 61.3 million students in 1975 before declining to 57.5 million in 1984.[2] The growth of enrollments in the first three decades of the century was disrupted by the depression and World War II but enrollments surged after the war.

The number of students enrolled in institutions of higher learning has shown remarkable growth. In 1900 there were only 238,000 students at colleges and universities; in 1984 there were 12.5 million. Unlike elementary and secondary education, where enrollment peaked in the 1970s, higher education enrollment continued to increase into the 1980s.

The financing of public schools by the three levels of government has undergone dramatic change (see table 11-4). In the 1920s, localities provided over 80 percent of the funds to support public elementary and secondary schools; the states provided almost all of the remainder. In 1984 the local share had fallen to 45 percent and the state share had risen to 48 percent. Federal funding, which amounted to less than 1 percent in 1920, stood near 7 percent.

With regard to government support of public higher education the historical division of governmental responsibility has been more stable over time. The states and the federal government have played the major role. In

2. Ibid.

Table 11-4. *Support for Public Elementary and Secondary Education, Selected Years, 1920–84*

Millions of dollars and, in parentheses, percent of total

Year	*Federal*	*State*	*Local*	*Total*
1920	* (0.3)	0.16 (16.5)	0.81 (83.2)	0.97 (100.0)
1940	0.04 (1.8)	0.68 (30.3)	1.54 (68.0)	2.26 (100.0)
1950	0.16 (2.9)	2.17 (39.8)	3.12 (57.3)	5.44 (100.0)
1960	0.65 (4.4)	5.80 (39.1)	8.33 (56.5)	14.75 (100.0)
1970	3.22 (8.0)	16.06 (39.9)	20.98 (52.1)	40.27 (100.0)
1980	9.50 (9.8)	45.35 (46.8)	42.03 (43.4)	96.88 (100.0)
1984	8.70 (6.9)	60.70 (47.9)	57.30 (45.2)	126.70 (100.0)

Source: National Center, *Digest of Education Statistics, 1982,* table 27, p. 35; National Center, unpublished data.
* Less than $50,000.

1982, states provided 45.5 percent of support and the federal government almost 12 percent; local units of government provided 3.5 percent. The remaining 39 percent of expenditures was funded by tuition payments and other means (table 11-2). Government support also flows to private institutions of higher learning. The federal government provides over 18 percent of their expenditures while the state and local shares sum to only 3 percent.

These national averages tend to conceal the great diversity of financing arrangements among the states. At one extreme is Hawaii where a highly centralized system depends exclusively on state and federal revenues. On the other hand, New Hampshire, without either a state income tax or a sales tax, relies on localities to provide 88 percent of expenditures (appendix table A–21). Not only do the shares of support show great variability among states, but there are also marked differences in the levels of per pupil expenditures. In 1984, New York spent $4,364 per pupil for elementary and secondary education while Alabama spent only $1,978 per pupil (see table 11-5).

Although wealthier states tend to spend more per pupil than poor states, the differences in the state levels of per pupil expenditure cannot be explained entirely by differences in underlying fiscal capacities. Regression studies find a positive relation between per pupil expenditure and fiscal capacity, but price, socioeconomic status, and preferences can also be important.[3]

3. Martin Feldstein, "Wealthy Neutrality and Local Choice in Public Education," *American Economic Review,* vol. 65 (March 1975), pp. 75–89.

Table 11-5. *Highest and Lowest Expenditures for Public Elementary and Secondary Schools, by State, 1984*[a]

Expenditure level and state	*Expenditure per pupil (dollars)*	*Source of revenue receipts (percent)*		
		Federal	*State*	*Local and other*
Highest expenditures				
Alaska	6,002	1.8	75.5	22.7
New York	4,364	3.8	41.4	54.9
New Jersey	4,337	3.4	40.0	56.6
Wyoming	4,243	3.3	28.7	67.9
District of Columbia	4,033	11.8	. . .	88.2
Lowest expenditures				
Arkansas	2,094	11.4	57.6	31.1
Tennessee	2,030	11.2	45.8	43.0
Mississippi	1,998	17.8	56.7	25.5
Alabama	1,978	12.7	70.7	16.6
Utah	1,937	5.8	53.2	41.0

Source: Appendix table A-21. Figures based on average daily attendance.
a. Figures not available for West Virginia, Michigan, Missouri, Idaho, and California.

The Federal Role in Financing Education

In 1982, the federal government spent $20 billion in support of education. Approximately half went to elementary and secondary schools and half to institutions of higher learning (table 11-2). Three-quarters of the federal monies went to public schools, with the $4.5 billion for private schools going exclusively to institutions of higher learning.

The federal role in financing education has not always been so large. Before World War II, the federal government's initiatives in support of education were largely by-products of efforts to achieve other priorities such as a strong national defense. The establishment of military and merchant marine academies, education benefits for veterans, and distribution of surplus goods to schools are all examples of this.

But following the war a number of forces combined to increase the federal role in financing education. In a booming postwar economy the importance of an educated citizenry was generally recognized. Moreover, millions of Americans were determined that greater educational opportunities would be available to their children. And national defense factors also gave momentum to an expanded federal role in education. A large number of veterans took advantage of the GI Bill to further their education, and the government increased its support of advanced research.

However, the most dramatic shift in federal policy, with regard to both scope and financial commitment, occurred in the 1960s. Moved by the growing concern to achieve equity among racial and income groups, the federal government launched several programs aimed at increasing educational opportunity.[4] The Elementary and Secondary Education Act of 1965 gave grants to school districts to provide programs for children of low-income families. In 1964 and again in 1968, the government provided funds to assist economically disadvantaged college students.

The federal government also turned its attention to groups such as the handicapped in the 1960s and 1970s. Vocational and adult education became a matter of federal concern. The Manpower Development and Training Act of 1962 and the Economic Opportunity Act of 1964 funded programs designed to train and upgrade the skills of the unemployed while the Comprehensive Employment and Training Act (CETA) of 1973 directly funded jobs where training was provided. The federal government has also funded training programs aimed at specific groups, including those displaced by import competition (1963, 1974, 1979), the long-term or structurally unemployed (1983), and unemployed youths (1964, 1977, 1983).

By the beginning of the 1980s, a clear-cut federal role in education had been established. The federal government had taken the lead in protecting the rights of the disadvantaged and special groups of students, led research and training efforts aimed at meeting national priorities, and acted as a catalyst to the reform of states' education systems. And, of course, along with these increased responsibilities had come a larger financial commitment.

The Reagan administration, however, sought to reduce the role of the federal government in financing education. It believed that more responsibility should be shifted back to state and local governments and it continually proposed spending levels lower than Congress was willing to approve. Yet the administration was successful in halting real increases in education funding. Over the period from 1980 to 1985, federal inflation-adjusted outlays for education decreased by 14 percent (even as total federal inflation-adjusted outlays grew by 21 percent).[5]

The administration also proposed giving greater autonomy to states and localities in spending federal funds. The Education and Consolidation and Improvement Act of 1981 consolidated several categorical grants into

4. National Center, *Digest of Education Statistics, 1983–84,* pp. 165–72.

5. "Education Funding Issues: FY1985 and FY1986" (Library of Congress, Congressional Research Service, June 4, 1985), p. 1.

block grants, giving states and localities wide leeway in the allocation of funds. As part of his New Federalism initiative, the president proposed that the federal government turn back numerous education programs to the states.[6] And the administration made several legislative proposals that emphasized individual and private sector activity in education.[7] It suggested that the funds the government provides to public schools to assist in the education of economically disadvantaged students be paid directly to qualifying individuals in the form of vouchers to purchase education services at public or private schools. And it proposed that tuition tax credits be offered to offset a portion of a taxpayer's private school expenses. It also favored allowing taxpayers to create education savings accounts, with interest and dividends exempt from federal taxation, which would provide savings of as much as $1,000 per student per year.

Equity in Education

In the 1950s attention was focused on the problem of unequal opportunity in education. The civil rights movement provided a powerful impetus in the attack since denial of equal educational opportunity was most apparent along racial lines. In 1954 the Supreme Court issued its landmark decision in *Brown* v. *Board of Education,* demanding the desegregation of public school systems and laying the legal foundation for a process that continues today.[8]

At the same time that racial inequality was coming under attack, concern about the problem of poverty was increasing. Congress responded to both problems with the Elementary and Secondary Education Act, authorizing grants for elementary and secondary school programs for children of low-income families. Other education programs designed to help the disadvantaged were the Head Start program for children and funds to assist economically disadvantaged college students that were part of the Economic Opportunity Act of 1964, as well as funds authorized in the Higher Education Amendments of 1968 to provide assistance to disadvantaged

6. *Major Legislation of the 98th Congress,* MLC-022 (Library of Congress, Legislative Reference Service, October 1984).

7. Ibid.

8. *Brown* v. *Board of Education of Topeka,* 247 U.S. 483 (1954).

college students through counseling and tutorials. These were followed in 1972 by the creation of basic education opportunity grants (Pell grants) targeted to aid low-income students.

Despite the federal government's major education initiatives and focus on the issue of equity in education, resolution of the issue rests on the actions of state and local governments.[9] The major source of inequity in school finance is the disparity in the fiscal capacities of school districts. Simply put, the education provided by a poor district is not likely to be as easily financed as that of a wealthier district.

School Finance Litigation

Between 1960 and 1982, cases were filed in twenty-seven states challenging the constitutionality of existing systems for financing education.[10] This route to reform was induced by the U.S. Supreme Court's 1973 decision in *San Antonio Independent School District* v. *Rodriguez.*[11] In that case, the court held that education is not a fundamental right under the U.S. Constitution and thus the inequities inherent in the Texas education finance system did not make it unconstitutional. The Court also refused to accept the argument that the Texas system should be overturned because it violated the equal protection clause of the Fourteenth Amendment; clearly, judicial redress of inequities related to states' systems of school finance would have to come from state courts.[12]

9. The federal government passed legislation in 1970 designed to assist states in assessing needs of their education systems and planning for possible change (Elementary and Secondary Education Assistance Programs, Extension). In addition, the Education Amendments of 1974 established a national center to gather and disseminate education statistics.

10. Education Commission of the States, *School Finance Reform in the States: 1983* (Denver: The Commission, 1983), p. 31. By 1982, state courts in seventeen states had ruled on school finance reform cases. In nine of these cases, the existing school finance system was found to be unconstitutional.

11. 411 U.S. 1 (1973).

12. The Court refused to demand "strict scrutiny" of the Texas system which would have required that Texas demonstrate both a compelling state interest in the design of the school finance system *and* that it had chosen reasonable ways to achieve that interest. It ruled that poor students or poor school districts do not represent a "suspect class" to which such a strict standard must be applied. Instead, the Court held the system up to a weaker "rational basis" test. While recognizing inequities in the system, the Court agreed that the system rationally achieved the goal of local control and therefore passed constitutional muster.

State Education Finance Systems

States employ three basic kinds of school finance systems. The oldest and most commonly used is the foundation plan. Under this plan, the state establishes a dollar level of per pupil expenditure which it guarantees to all districts that tax at a rate greater than or equal to some fixed rate. In terms of equity, problems arise with the plan if the foundation level of support is set too low. Districts wishing to spend above the foundation level of support must raise the revenue from their own tax bases but this puts poor districts at a disadvantage.

Several states have sought to avoid the problems inherent in the foundation plan by adopting district power equalizing plans.[13] Under these plans, the states use matching grants to ensure that a poor district can spend for education as if it had a tax base equal to that of a wealthier (key) district.[14] By relating the state matching rate to the fiscal capacity of school districts, the plan guarantees that 1 percent of tax rate levied in a poor district will yield the same level of per pupil expenditure as 1 percent of tax rate levied in the key district. For example, a district that is half as wealthy as the key district will have half of its school budget paid by the state. Since the state matches local revenues, the district has the power to spend for education as if it had the tax base of the key district.

The third form of school finance is a hybrid of the district power equalizing and foundation plans. In essence, this system applies power equalization to levels of expenditure above the foundation level. Maine, Minnesota, Missouri, Montana, Texas, and Utah have adopted this two-tier approach.

Gains from Reform?

Have states made progress in their attempts to achieve equity among students? A study that undertook to determine whether states that had reformed their finance systems had been successful in eliminating student

13. Colorado, Connecticut, Kansas, Michigan, New Jersey, and Wisconsin use a district power equalizing system.

14. John E. Coons, William H. Clune III, and Stephen D. Sugarman, *Private Wealth and Public Education* (Belknap Press of Harvard University Press, 1970), pp. 200–42. Also see J. R. Aronson and J. L. Hilley, "Taxpayer Equity in the Financing of Public Education," in Esther Tron, ed., *Selected Papers in School Finance* (Department of Health and Human Services, 1981).

inequities reported that several had shown improvement in one or more measures of horizontal equity, but several others had either shown no improvement or had regressed.[15] Moreover, comparison of reform and nonreform states does not allow the conclusion that reform yields superior improvement in horizontal equity.

Other studies corroborate the view that while reform states gained in equity in the early and mid-1970s, factors such as economic recession and other priorities in education (excellence, efficiency, special needs) permitted some back-sliding on equity in the late 1970s and early 1980s. And in several states (California, Colorado, Illinois, Michigan, and New Mexico, for example) there were clear gains in eliminating the dependence of per pupil expenditure levels on fiscal capacity, even though the other measures of equity gave more ambiguous results.[16]

These early evaluations indicate that the achievement of equity must be an ongoing pursuit. When the fiscal capacities of wealthy districts grow relative to those of poor districts, and school finance systems do not have a recapture provision, steady increases in state aid are necessary to maintain equity.[17]

The biggest source of inequity in the provision of education has not yet been approached. Discussions of equity are routinely couched in terms of intrastate disparities, but this narrow focus ignores interstate disparities in fiscal capacity. Without strong federal leadership or a federal judicial mandate, this issue is unlikely to be addressed.

Equity versus Excellence

As the issue of "educational excellence" has gained the national spotlight, concern has been expressed that the pursuit of this goal might hamper the achievement of equity. At one level there is a fear that within an existing education budget, an increase in expenditures to improve quality might leave less available for fiscal equalization. At another level there is a concern that as more funds are allocated to instruction in mathematics,

15. Robert Berne and Leanna Stiefel, "Changes in School Finance Equity: A National Perspective," *Journal of Education Finance*, vol. 8 (Spring 1983), pp. 419–35. The authors looked for improvement in four measures of horizontal equity based on core per pupil expenditures: the federal range ratio (ratio of ninety-fifth percentile to fifth percentile), coefficient of variation, Gini coefficient, Theil's measure.

16. Ibid, p. 433.

17. Recapture provisions redistribute funds from wealthy to poor school districts.

science, and technology, the disadvantaged will not share equally. The problem is that attention might be drawn away from basic skills and vocational training.

Care must be taken in the allocation of state funds if such conflicts are to be avoided. If, for example, funds are targeted to districts to match local expenditures aimed at improving the quality of education, then any existing effects of disparities in local fiscal capacity could be amplified. As a solution, funds to improve the quality of education should be allocated in line with fiscal equalization formulas, so that state aid offsets, in some degree, the advantages enjoyed by wealthy school districts.

The eight states that had enacted reforms aimed at quality improvement by 1984 had also increased the level of per pupil funding for less wealthy school districts.[18] Much of the money available for education reform was being allocated through school finance formulas. Questions remain about whether new curriculum and graduation standards established in the 1980s create greater problems for some groups of children than others, and whether programs might be needed to assure that all students have access to the use of computers and other learning devices and to the select core of master teachers.

Expanding Parental Choice in Education

In 1984, 87 percent of elementary and secondary school students attended public schools (table 11-3). The dominant position of public schools in American education belies the importance of private schools. These schools offer wide-ranging alternatives to public education and enable many parents to exercise freedom of educational choice.

Private schools must be able to offer an education that satisfies their users or they will be unable to attract and retain students. While the mechanisms may not be as direct, public schools must also respond to the constituents they serve. The voters ultimately control the school board and the education infrastructure, and they can make their wishes felt. Many public schools directly involve parents in the planning and decisionmaking process, responding quickly and effectively to citizens' desires. For many parents and students, however, this democratization of the public school

18. Allan Odden, *Education Finance in the States, 1984* (Denver: Education Commission of the States, 1984), pp. 18–19.

system does not go far enough to guarantee that the product they desire is the one that is offered.

Two approaches have been put forward that would expand educational alternatives and allow parents greater control over their children's schooling. The first aims at reducing the financial burden of attending a private school. Currently, parents have the right to choose private schools, but often they cannot afford to exercise their right because they must pay tuition in addition to the taxes that support public education. In numerous states and in Congress, proposals have been put forward to allow the use of tax credits, tax deductions, tax deferrals, grants, or other forms of support for private education.

A second set of initiatives is more radical. Their implementation would change the fundamental structure of the American education system by eliminating the distinction between public and private schools and allowing all schools to compete for enrollments on an equal basis.

Government Support of Private Schools

Since the 1960s many proposals have been offered at both the state and the federal level to reduce the cost to families of private schooling. In Congress, tuition tax credits have been the most popular. Typically, such bills would permit about half of private tuition to be used as a credit against the federal personal income tax. The credits would be capped (limited, for example, to $300) and not available to high-income families (those with $60,000 incomes, for example). None of these bills has been acted on favorably by Congress.

Tuition tax credits and other forms of government aid to private schools have proven to be controversial for a number of reasons. They raise the fear that government assistance to private schools would weaken the public school system. Government support also raises the constitutional question of the separation of church and state, since in 1982, 83 percent of private schools were affiliated with religious institutions.[19] Tuition tax credits would be useless to poor people who pay no federal income taxes. And because private schools have a higher proportion of white and wealthy students than public schools, government support of private schools would enhance the position of those groups.

Proponents of tax credits do not view the proposal as an attempt to

19. U.S. Census Bureau, *Statistical Abstract of the United States, 1986* (GPO, 1985), p. 145.

undermine the public school system but see it as an effort to partially offset a substantial advantage currently enjoyed by public schools. In fact, proponents argue that the competition from a strong private school sector would help to improve public school performance. In response, opponents of tax credits argue that the public schools' financial advantage is justified by the special responsibilities and burdens associated with their mandate to admit and educate all students, and not just those deemed to be acceptable by a particular set of criteria.

The Free Choice Challenge

In the 1960s, Milton Friedman outlined the structure of a radically different approach to education finance.[20] Rather than relying on a government monopoly to provide education, he advocated a market-based system that would place the purchasing power for education in the hands of consumers. Under Friedman's proposal, the government would, each year, award each student a voucher for a year's schooling at the school of the voucher-holder's choice. There would be no distinction between public and private schools and a school's revenue would be derived solely from its enrollment of students and their tuition payments. Just as in the purchase of most commodities, consumers would evaluate the competing products and spend their funds at the school whose offerings were most in line with their preferences.

This market-based approach attempts to capture the efficiency properties of a market system—the gains from lower costs and greater choice. Whether the resulting system would be considered equitable and whether or not it would overlook the external benefits generated by public education is another question.

The Constitutionality Issue

Any initiative that would result in government funds flowing to private schools would raise problems because so many private schools in America have a religious affiliation. The Supreme Court has ruled that aid to private school users breaches the high wall separating church from state and therefore violates the establishment clause of the First Amendment.[21]

20. *Capitalism and Freedom* (University of Chicago Press, 1962), pp. 85–98.

21. *Committee for Public Education and Religious Liberty* v. *Nyquist,* 413 U.S. 756 (1973). The Court did affirm a federal district court decision upholding a Minnesota statute that allowed the deduction of school expenses (public and private) from state taxes; see *Mueller* v. *Allen*, 463 U.S. 388 (1983).

Generally, if the essential or "primary effect" of government action is to positively influence the pursuit of a religious tradition, or the expression of a religious belief, it will be struck down as violating the establishment clause. This aspect of the clause has not been insurmountable, however. Religious schools may be substantially benefited by state-directed aid programs. As long as the "essential effect" of such aid is not to promote religious interest, the programs will not fail the "primary effect" test.

With regard to the tax credit proposals that have appeared before the Congress, aid would flow primarily to private, sectarian schools. It is, therefore, difficult to see how these proposals could pass the primary effect test. However, the more radical plans for altering the structure of the education finance system may actually be better suited to gain constitutional favor. Free choice would allow those who desire religiously affiliated schools to send their children to such schools. But since public *plus* private schools are predominantly secular in character, government aid would fall heavily to the nonreligious schools, which comprised 87 percent of elementary and secondary enrollments in 1985.[22] Thus the primary effect of government support would not be to aid religious schools.

22. National Center for Education Statistics, unpublished data.

CHAPTER TWELVE

Whither State and Local Finance?

IN THE MID-1980s, state and local governments found themselves at a financial crossroads. A number of forces were moving them toward an expanded role in providing civilian services. Not only were states and localities being asked to fill some of the gap in resources left by reductions in federal support, but they were also being called on to provide an improved, and in some cases, expanded range of services. The willingness of many states to launch new programs, while simultaneously adjusting to smaller amounts of federal aid, testifies to the initiative of state and local leaders as well as to the improved condition of their governments' finances. The financial condition of most state and local governments was good. During 1985, more states cut taxes than raised them and those taxes that were raised were often dedicated to particular spending programs such as education. But even though there seemed to be no mismatch between resources and responsibilities, there was more than the usual uneasiness about what the future might hold.

The two recessions in the early 1980s were a fresh reminder that the health of state and local finances depends largely on the performance of the American economy. And the movement to limit taxes showed that even during periods of economic growth, taxpayers will limit the increase of state and local expenditures and revenues when their perception of the benefits versus the costs of government activity is unfavorable. Behind states' tax-cutting initiatives lurked the spirit of the tax limitation movement, sending the message that surpluses should be refunded rather than spent or saved.

Awareness that the federal system of finance may undergo fundamental change prompted concern not only about how responsibilities would be assigned to the different levels of government but also about what revenue sources would support them. Some states might be willing to play a larger role in funding and providing services such as education and transportation under a New Federalism. But those responsible for state and local administration were not in favor of reducing federal support in the areas of health, welfare, and social services.

Perhaps the federal initiative that would have the most significant consequences for state and local governments was the Reagan administration's tax reform proposal. The deductibility of state and local taxes would be eliminated from the federal income tax. Repeal of tax deductibility would have a significant impact on the price and quantity of state and local services. Coupled with a reduction of federal grants, the curtailment of these tax expenditures would force many states and localities to choose between higher taxes and providing a lower level of services.

Revenue and Expenditure Limitations

Revenue and expenditure limitations are a set of constitutional and statutory laws aimed at controlling and constraining the fiscal activities of state and local governments. Restrictions come in many forms. They have been placed on the size of tax bases and on tax rates and made contingent on the growth of population or of personal income or on the level of the previous year's spending. California's Proposition 13 enacted in 1978 and Massachusetts's Proposition 2½ of 1980 are perhaps the best-known restrictive measures, but fiscal limits have existed in most states for years.

The emergence of the modern fiscal limitation movement in the late 1970s can be seen as part of a broader movement aimed at limiting the size of the public sector. The initiatives were initially bolstered by the large surpluses in state and (in some cases) local budgets that were generated by the economic expansion and inflation of the late 1970s. Budget and revenue cutters were presented with a sitting target to aid their case.

Limitations on State Governments

Table 12-1 shows that between 1976 and 1982 nineteen states, starting with New Jersey, adopted constitutional or statutory limitations on their own revenues or expenditures. Fifteen set restrictions on expenditures and four set guidelines for revenues. Since states are, in general, required to plan balanced budgets, a limitation on revenues that is effective amounts to a limitation on expenditures as well. And it is also important to note that as spending has been constrained by expenditure limitations and budget

Table 12-1. *Measures Limiting State Expenditures or Collection of Revenue, 1976–82*

State	*Year adopted*	*Measure*	*Limit on*	*Limit tied to*
Alaska	1982	Statutory	Expenditures	Inflation and population growth
Arizona	1978	Constitutional	Expenditures	Level of personal income
California	1979	Constitutional	Expenditures	Inflation and population growth
Colorado	1979	Statutory	Expenditures	Previous year's expenditures
Hawaii	1978	Constitutional	Expenditures	Growth of personal income
Idaho	1980	Statutory	Expenditures	Level of personal income
Louisiana	1979	Statutory	Revenues	Growth of personal income
Michigan	1978	Constitutional	Revenues	Ratio of revenue to personal income in base year
Missouri	1980	Constitutional	Revenues	Ratio of revenue to personal income in base year
Montana	1981	Statutory	Expenditures	Growth of personal income
Nevada	1979	Statutory	Expenditures	Inflation and population growth
New Jersey	1976	Statutory	Expenditures	Growth of personal income per capita
Oregon	1979	Statutory	Expenditures	Growth of personal income
Rhode Island	1977	Statutory	Expenditures	Previous year's expenditures
South Carolina	1980	Statutory	Expenditures	Growth of personal income
Tennessee	1978	Constitutional	Expenditures	Growth of personal income
Texas	1978	Constitutional	Expenditures	Growth of personal income
Utah	1979	Statutory	Expenditures	Growth of personal income
Washington	1979	Statutory	Revenues	Growth of personal income

Source: Steven D. Gold, *State Tax and Spending Limitations: Paper Tigers or Slumbering Giants?* Legislative Finance Paper 33 (Denver; National Conference of State Legislatures, 1983), pp. 5–10.

surpluses have arisen, there has been a tendency for states to distribute the surplus through rebates to taxpayers.[1]

Yet fiscal limitations have not always been completely effective. There are means of avoiding their severest impacts.[2] Because the limitations, in general, were not adopted to roll back existing revenue or expenditure levels but to set guidelines for future magnitudes, the base to which they apply often was set above existing levels, leaving some initial breathing room. Often the limitations do not apply to important expenditure components. Earmarked funds for highways, special projects, pensions, debt service, or aid to localities are exempt from limitation in many instances.

1. Steven D. Gold, *State Tax and Spending Limitations: Paper Tigers or Slumbering Giants?* Legislative Finance Paper 33 (Denver: National Conference of State Legislatures, 1983), pp. 5–10.

2. Ibid., pp. 3–4.

Most states also exempt self-supporting enterprises (utilities) from the limits and have been careful not to restrict expenditures that are required to qualify for matching federal funds.

In some states, the maximum permissible levels of revenue and expenditures are increased each year by the allowable limit regardless of actual tax or expenditure levels. The increases in allowable ceilings that occurred in many states during the two recessions of 1980–82 while expenditures and revenues fell have created considerable leeway for states to increase both their taxes and expenditures. Where the gap is narrow, limitations can in most states be overridden either through the normal legislative process or through a two-thirds vote of both houses, voter referenda, or the governor's declaration of an emergency.

TYPES OF STATE LIMITATIONS. There are several different types of state expenditure and revenue limitations. Allowable rates of increase in expenditures may be tied to personal income, inflation, or previous year's spending levels—all with potentially different effects on real per capita state expenditure levels.

Most states allow expenditures to grow at the state's rate of growth of personal income. To the extent that personal income growth exceeds the sum of the inflation and population growth rates, real per capita public expenditure is permitted to rise.

Under California law, the rate of increase is limited to the rate of inflation plus the rate of population growth. In effect, this means that the real per capita expenditure level may not increase. Colorado limits the increase in general fund expenditures to 7 percent of the preceding year's level. This restriction may be more or less severe than those related to the growth of personal income, depending on whether the sum of the inflation and population growth rates is greater or less than 7 percent.

PROBLEMS OF DESIGN. Several conceptual issues must be confronted in designing a provision that limits fiscal activity. Not all expenditures and revenues can be placed under limitations. Certain expenditures are mandated obligations of the governmental unit. For example, consider unemployment outlays. When recession comes, unemployment claims and other public welfare expenditures will rise. These obligations must be honored. It is a formidable problem to design limitations that control total spending but that also allow states the flexibility to carry out mandated programs.

Indexes such as personal income, inflation, and population growth typically are used to establish permissible rises in revenue and expenditure. Thought must be given to the impact of adopting any one of these indexes; the hazards are particularly great when the relation between the index and the states' revenue and expenditure programs is not clear.

The choice of a base year must be made with care. It must be representative of the state's fiscal situation and performance. A bad choice can hinder fiscal decisions in the years to come.

LIMITATIONS AND BUSINESS CYCLES. In the late 1970s, many states reduced tax rates. In terms of discretionary tax changes, thirty-two states lowered their income or sales taxes between 1978 and 1980.[3] Unfortunately, these reductions began to take hold just as the U.S. economy entered a period marked by two recessions. The combined effects of tax reduction, recession, and reduced federal aid were to create severe pressure on state budgets.

Reluctant to raise tax rates during a recession, states adopted several other fiscal measures that would serve as stopgaps until the economy recovered. Outlays and capital projects were delayed or trimmed back and the real wages of many public employees were not allowed to rise. But these measures proved inadequate and many states were eventually forced to raise tax rates. In 1983, sixteen states increased their personal income tax while twelve increased revenue through the general sales tax. Business taxes were raised in fifteen states while most states raised cigarette, alcohol, or fuel taxes.[4]

These tax increases coincided with the economic recovery that began in 1983. The combined effect of previous austerity measures, tax increases, and economic recovery was to restore the health of state treasuries. Some of the surplus was immediately used to lower tax rates. But many of the increased taxes had been earmarked for education and long-neglected capital projects that state and local governments are reluctant to give up.

Limitations on Local Governments

Restrictions on local governments' revenues and expenditures have existed for decades. Most of the limitations set ceilings on property tax rates but several states have restricted either the total tax levies or the expenditures of local governments.

3. These tax reductions were achieved either by offering rebates, lowering rates, or expanding exemptions and deductions.

4. Steven D. Gold and Karen M. Benker, *State Budget Actions in 1983,* Legislative Finance Paper 38 (Denver: National Conference of State Legislatures, 1983), p. iv.

In the 1970s many states placed new and further restrictions on local governments. By 1981, thirty states had enacted limitations on revenues or expenditures. Many states restrict local governments in more than one way. Thirty-six have limits on local property rates while nineteen restrict property tax levies. Five states set limits on localities' general revenue and six restrict expenditures.

Why the need for this new round of restrictions? Certainly part of the reason is rooted in a desire to restrain the growth of the public sector. But the main reason is simply recognition that earlier constraints were ineffective. Both econometric and case studies point to the conclusion that the limitations enacted before the 1970s had not served their intended purpose.[5] In many cases, such as California, increases in assessments were used to bolster local revenues, even as property tax rates held constant.

Have the new restrictions been effective? California's Proposition 13 limitations were severe and comprehensive enough to have had a major immediate impact on local government revenues and expenditures. Similarly, strict property tax controls adopted by Indiana probably curbed the growth of local revenues. And there are indications that limitations on local property tax levies have probably been effective in Arizona, Colorado, Iowa, and New Jersey. For other states, there is not enough evidence to indicate whether the constraints have been binding.

It is not surprising, of course, to find that as restrictions began to pinch, governmental units found ways to sidestep them.[6] Local governments have turned increasingly toward income, sales, and business taxes and to user charges to compensate for property tax restrictions. Special districts have been created to take up local functions that have been restricted by the state-imposed limits. And localities have increased their dependence on state aid. In many states, voter referenda have been used to allow spending at levels in excess of the limitations. And certain expenditure categories (medical, retirement) have been removed from the limitations as expenditure limits have become effective. Where limitations pertain to subsets of expenditures, funds have been shuffled between restricted and unrestricted uses.

5. See, for example, Robert P. Inman, "Subsidies, Regulations and the Taxation of Property in Large U.S. Cities," *National Tax Journal*, vol. 32 (*Supplement*, June 1979), pp. 159s–68s.

6. Steven D. Gold, *Results of Local Spending and Revenue Limitations: A Survey*, Legislative Finance Paper 5 (Denver: National Conference of State Legislatures, 1981), p. 52.

The Future Strength of Fiscal Limitations

In 1984 it seemed that the tax and expenditure limitation movement was gaining momentum. Major signature-gathering campaigns aimed at placing initiatives on the November ballot were conducted in eight states, with sufficient signatures being gathered in four states to place the initiative before the voters. In four other states, actions by state legislatures resulted in tax and expenditure referenda appearing on the November ballot.

The strongest initiative was Michigan's Proposition C. It called for rolling back state and local taxes to the levels that existed in 1981 and would have required future tax increases to be approved by a majority of voters in a popular election. In California, Proposition 36 was designed to achieve further reductions in property taxes (via retroactive rebates on increases that had been implemented before Proposition 13) and would have made future tax increases more difficult. Initiatives in both Nevada and Oregon were designed to limit the annual rate of property tax increases.[7]

Two of the state referenda were aimed at containing the growth of state spending. Louisiana would have limited the growth in general fund spending to 85 percent of the increase in state personal income while Arizona would have been forced to hold state spending to 6.5 percent of personal income. A South Carolina initiative proposed to limit the increase in state spending to the growth of state personal income, restrict the growth in state employment, and limit the debt service on general obligation bonds. Finally, Hawaiian voters were asked to repeal a requirement mandating taxpayer refunds when the state runs budget surpluses. In the November balloting, voters rejected all of the initiatives except South Carolina's.[8]

Although the harsher forms of limitation seem to have run their course, voters have clearly demonstrated their power to act when the burden of taxation no longer coincides with their perception of the services being delivered by state and local governments. And, limitations may once again gain in popularity if tax reform legislation succeeds in repealing the deductibility of state and local taxes from the federal income tax. States and localities would be under pressure to either raise taxes or reduce expenditures and depending on the approach taken, demands for limitations could once again be revived.

7. The Nevada initiative would have limited property tax increases to 5 percent annually while in Oregon they would have been limited to 2 percent.

8. See *Tax Notes* (November 12, 1984), pp. 592–94.

Deductibility of State and Local Taxes from Federal Income Taxes

State and local taxes have been deductible from the federal income tax base since the tax was first established in 1913. President Reagan, however, in his tax reform proposal asked that this feature of the tax code be repealed.[9] Such a change would have a significant impact on state and local governments.

From the viewpoint of the taxpayer, the argument in favor of deducting state and local taxes emphasizes that these taxes are compulsory payments and are used to provide services yielding general benefits to the community as a whole. Under this view, the income that is "spent" on state and local taxes brings no direct personal benefit and therefore should not be considered part of an individual's spendable income to be taxed. Thus, if the taxpayer's ability to pay federal taxes is to be properly gauged, the federal base should not include taxes paid to state and local governments.

However, to the extent the taxes are substitutes for fees and user charges and that the funds raised are used to provide goods that have the characteristics of private goods, the case for deductibility is diminished. In short, if state and local taxes are viewed as prices paid for goods yielding only private benefits, there is no reason to provide a tax preference for state and local government expenditures over other consumption or investment items.

From the viewpoint of state and local governments, the major effect of deductibility is the inducement to increase and improve the level of services they provide. In essence, deductibility provides an implicit grant-in-aid to state and local governments by lowering the price of state and local public services. For the taxpayer in the 30 percent marginal tax bracket an extra $100 worth of services will cost $70 and for the itemizing taxpayer in the 50 percent marginal tax bracket they will cost but $50.[10] Presumably the lower price encourages people to demand a greater amount of services

9. *The President's Tax Proposals to the Congress for Fairness, Growth, and Simplicity* (GPO, 1985), p. 3. Under current law not all state and local taxes are deductible. Some are deductible by individuals only if they are incurred in carrying on an income-producing activity. This category is mainly made up of excise and other miscellaneous taxes. Taxpayers who itemize their deductions are permitted to deduct state and local taxes on real and personal property, general sales, and income.

10. For taxpayers who do not itemize deductions there is no price reduction associated with acquiring state and local public services.

from their state and local governments. Obviously, it encourages states to finance their services with deductible taxes rather than nondeductible fees and user charges.

The need to stimulate the provision of state and local public services rests on two points. One is that there is significant spillover from these services and that without the implicit grant-in-aid, the level of activity provided by state and local governments would be less than optimal. The other argument is that with the implicit grant-in-aid the federal government induces state and local governments to provide services that the federal government would otherwise have to provide.

Effects of Repeal

Repealing the deductibility of state and local taxes would have redistributive effects among individuals and states. It would also affect the level of services provided, the mix of revenue sources used by state and local governments, and the progressivity of the overall tax structure.

REDISTRIBUTION. The benefits of deductibility are not spread evenly over individuals or states. High-income taxpayers in high-tax states take most advantage of this tax provision. Lower-income taxpayers in states that tax at average or low rates gain a smaller advantage from the provision. Repeal of deductibility would therefore work to the relative advantage of those who are currently less favored. The dollar amount of the impact, of course, would depend on whether reductions in tax rates accompanied the base broadening achieved by the repeal of deductibility.

The U.S. Treasury estimated in 1985 that on a per capita basis deductibility favors citizens in New York, Maryland, and New Jersey while the losers live in South Dakota, Louisiana, and Wyoming.[11] Supporters of reform suggest that it is unfair to promote a system in which the residents of low-tax states subsidize those of high-tax states. But, it should be noted that redistribution is a by-product rather than an explicit goal of deductibility. And redistribution can be justified as a means of encouraging all state and local governments to increase and improve their services.

Moreover, the redistribution among states that results from the federal tax and expenditure system should not be measured solely in terms of the impact of one particular provision such as state and local deductibility. The other side of the deductibility coin is that high-income states pay more taxes and generally receive smaller direct transfers from the federal gov-

11. See *The President's Tax Proposals*, p. 68.

ernment than do low-income states. One analysis suggests that the high-income states that would lose most from the repeal of state and local deductibility are generally those whose net benefits (grants minus taxes) from the federal government are already negative.[12]

LEVEL OF SERVICES. The repeal of deductibility would raise the price of state and local services. What impact would the price rise have on the demand for these services? The answer depends on several factors. Which voters have the most influence in political decisionmaking? Would those taxpayers who face a significantly higher tax-price for state and local services be able to express their desires through the bureaucratic and political process? Would business and residential location decisions be affected by the loss of deductibility? The Advisory Commission on Intergovernmental Relations estimates that if deductibility were eliminated, state and local spending across the United States could be expected to fall by about 7 percent relative to the spending level anticipated before the elimination of deductibility.[13]

MIX OF REVENUE SOURCES. Under current law there is a bias against the use of fees and user charges. Even where fees and charges would be appropriate, there exists an incentive to use general fund financing to take advantage of deductibility. Repeal of deductibility would eliminate this bias, perhaps accelerating the trend toward reliance on user fees.

PROGRESSIVITY OF THE OVERALL TAX STRUCTURE. The overall tax structure can be divided into two parts—the tax structure of the federal government which is mildly progressive and the tax structure of state and local governments which is roughly proportional.[14] Deductibility of state and local taxes, by itself, acts to make the federal tax system less progressive than it otherwise might be. It also increases the size of the state and local sector relative to that of the federal government, thus reducing the progressivity of the overall structure. Repeal of deductibility, by eliminating these factors, would be likely to result in a more progressive tax system.[15]

12. "JEC's Obey Blasts Plan to End State and Local Deductions," *Tax Notes* (June 10, 1985), pp. 1282–83.

13. Advisory Commission on Intergovernmental Relations, *Strengthening the Federal Revenue System: Implications for State and Local Taxing and Borrowing*, A-97 (Washington: ACIR, 1984), p. 48. Later unpublished estimates by the ACIR show a smaller impact on spending from eliminating deductibility.

14. See Joseph A. Pechman, *Who Paid the Taxes, 1966–85?* (Brookings, 1985), p. 60.

15. This conclusion might not follow if the repeal of deductibility were part of a tax reform that lowered federal income tax rates.

Alternative Approaches

In the debate over tax reform, suggestions representing the middle ground between complete retention and complete repeal of deductibility have been offered. One approach recognizes that some state and local services provide public benefits while others are more in the nature of private goods. It has been proposed that taxpayers be allowed to deduct only those state and local taxes in excess of 1 percent of their adjusted gross income.[16] The rationale is that some amount of state and local taxes provides consumption for the taxpayer and that taxes in excess of this amount support state and local governments' other responsibilities. Thus, only amounts above the threshold would be subsidized through the deductibility provision. Tying deductions to adjusted gross income sets the threshold for deductibility at a lower level for lower-income taxpayers than for others. Implicit in this approach is the view that the benefits of state and local services rise with the level of income.

Yet another approach would calculate the allowable federal tax savings as the amount of state and local taxes paid times a set federal tax rate. This rate could be set significantly lower than the rate faced by the taxpayer on his last dollar of income. The result would be to reduce the value of deductibility to taxpayers in higher-income brackets. By allowing the deduction at a common tax rate, the tax-price for state and local services would be equalized across most income classes.

Conclusion

In the early 1980s, the stage has been set for state and local governments to play an expanded role in the financing and provision of civilian services. Their own improved financial condition, coinciding with a diminished federal presence, has created a momentum toward state and local assumption of responsibility. Thus far, economic recovery has paid the way. But in the longer run, the government that pays the bills must have access to revenue sources that can cover them.

Looking to the end of this century, the infrastructure needs of the states are great. The other major areas where state and local activity is important also point to a need for increased resources. Several states have taken

16. Senate bill 315; House Resolution 2825, introduced in the Ninety-ninth Congress.

education initiatives aimed at increasing the quality and the equity of the public school system. Spending on health and hospitals can be expected to rise as costly medical advances and longer life spans drive public and private health expenditures up. In the area of welfare, the debate over federal versus state responsibility creates a reasonable presumption that, here too, the state role may grow.

How will these expenditures be financed? Governments must cope with reduced federal aid by turning to alternative sources. For local governments, the natural appeal to the property tax has been blunted by the tax limitation movement. Greater use will have to be made of nonproperty taxes and user fees. Devices such as the special assessment are likely to gain greater acceptance as a way to pay for local services.

Most states rely on both a sales and an income tax. The high income elasticity of the income tax makes it a boon in good times but not in bad. The sales tax is more stable but has its own well-known drawbacks. States, like localities, will turn increasingly to user fees and charges. Since 1970, states have improved the productivity of their revenue systems by diversifying their tax base while improving administration. Yet much can still be done. The states' corporate income taxes must be brought into greater uniformity with each other and should be harmonized with federal tax law. States should work with the federal government to clarify and codify state and federal use of death taxes.

In the next several years state and local governments could assume an even more important role than they now have in performing civilian functions. Perhaps it will be at the state and local levels that the greater imagination and initiative are applied in the solution of the nation's problems. However the responsibilities may be sorted out, there is likely to be a continuation of the "cooperative federalism" that has provided the flexibility for state, local, and federal governments to work with each other in the provision and financing of important public services.

APPENDIX

Statistical Tables

Table A-1. *General Expenditure for Civil Functions, by Classification of Intergovernmental Payments and Level of Government, Selected Years, 1902–84*[a]

Millions of dollars and, in parentheses, percent of total

Classification of payments and year	Level of government: Federal	Level of government: State and local	Total
Intergovernmental payments charged to the level of government making final disbursement			
1902	230 (18.5)	1,013 (81.5)	1,243
1927	1,421 (16.5)	7,210 (83.5)	8,631
1938	5,045 (36.6)	8,757 (63.4)	13,802
1948	8,713 (33.0)	17,684 (67.0)	26,397
1958	15,165 (25.3)	44,851 (74.7)	60,016
1968	33,716 (24.8)	102,411 (75.2)	136,127
1978	103,911 (26.0)	295,510 (74.0)	399,421
1984	191,762 (28.8)	474,489 (71.2)	666,251
Intergovernmental payments charged to the originating level of government			
1902	237 (19.1)	1,006 (80.9)	1,243
1927	1,544 (17.9)	7,087 (82.1)	8,631
1938	5,807 (42.1)	7,995 (57.9)	13,802
1948	10,484 (39.7)	15,913 (60.3)	26,397
1958	20,000 (33.3)	40,016 (66.7)	60,016
1968	51,769 (38.0)	84,358 (62.0)	136,127
1978	183,083 (45.8)	216,338 (54.2)	399,421
1984	290,777 (43.6)	375,474 (56.4)	666,251

Sources: U.S. Census Bureau, *Historical Statistics of the United States: Colonial Times to 1957* (U.S. Government Printing Office, 1960), pp. 725, 727; Census Bureau, *Governmental Finances in 1983–84* (GPO, 1985), tables 10, 11, and earlier issues. In all tables years are fiscal unless otherwise noted and figures are rounded.

a. General expenditure excludes amounts expended in utilities, liquor stores, and insurance trusts, which are approximately offset by receipts; it includes intergovernmental transactions net of duplicative transactions between levels of government. Federal expenditure for civil purposes has been calculated by deducting from total federal general expenditure ($565 million in 1902 and $565 billion in 1984) the amount spent on national defense, international relations, veterans (not elsewhere classified), and interest on the federal debt ($335 million in 1902 and $109 billion in 1984). All state and local expenditures are regarded as civil. These assumptions are faulty. Reckoning what portion of interest on federal debt was incurred for civil purposes would be conjectural as would reckoning the portion of state-local expenditure made for war-related purposes.

Table A-2. *Tax Collections, by Type of Tax and Level of Government, Selected Years, 1902–84*

Millions of dollars and, in parentheses, percent of total

Level of government	Tax collections: Income	Consumption	Property	Other	Total
Federal					
1902	. . .(. . .)	487 (95)	0	26 (5)	513
1927	2,138 (64)	1,088 (32)	0	137 (4)	3,364
1938	2,610 (49)	2,021 (38)	0	713 (13)	5,344
1948	28,983 (77)	7,650 (20)	0	1,243 (3)	37,876
1957	56,787 (81)	11,127 (16)	0	1,902 (3)	69,815
1967	95,497 (83)	15,806 (14)	0	3,818 (3)	115,121
1978	240,940 (88)	25,453 (9)	0	8,126 (3)	274,519
1984	352,848 (85)	49,459 (12)	0	12,522 (3)	414,829
State					
1902	0 (0)	28 (18)	82 (53)	46 (29)	156
1927	162 (10)	445 (28)	370 (23)	631 (39)	1,608
1938	383 (12)	1,674 (53)	244 (8)	831 (27)	3,132
1948	1,084 (16)	4,042 (60)	276 (4)	1,340 (20)	6,743
1957	2,547 (18)	8,436 (58)	479 (3)	3,069 (21)	14,531
1967	7,136 (22)	18,575 (58)	862 (3)	5,353 (17)	31,926
1978	39,843 (35)	58,270 (51)	2,364 (2)	12,784 (11)	113,261
1984	74,453 (38)	95,801 (49)	3,862 (2)	22,679 (11)	196,795
Local					
1902	0 (0)	0 (0)	624 (89)	80 (11)	704
1927	0 (0)	25 (1)	4,360 (97)	94 (2)	4,479
1938	0 (0)	120 (3)	4,196 (94)	157 (4)	4,473
1948	51 (1)	400 (6)	5,850 (89)	298 (5)	6,599
1957	191 (1)	1,031 (7)	12,385 (87)	679 (5)	14,286
1967	917 (3)	1,956 (7)	25,186 (87)	1,015 (3)	29,074
1978	4,071 (5)	9,326 (12)	64,058 (78)	2,925 (4)	80,381
1984	7,215 (6)	18,296 (15)	92,595 (75)	5,291 (4)	123,397
All					
1902	0 (0)	515 (38)	706 (51)	152 (11)	1,373
1927	2,300 (24)	1,558 (16)	4,730 (50)	862 (9)	9,451
1938	2,993 (23)	3,815 (29)	4,440 (34)	1,701 (13)	12,949
1948	30,118 (59)	12,092 (24)	6,126 (12)	2,881 (6)	51,218
1957	59,525 (60)	20,594 (21)	12,864 (13)	5,650 (6)	98,632
1967	103,550 (59)	36,336 (20)	26,047 (15)	10,188 (6)	176,121
1978	284,854 (61)	93,049 (20)	66,422 (14)	23,835 (5)	468,160
1984	434,518 (59)	163,556 (22)	96,457 (13)	40,492 (6)	735,023

Sources: Census Bureau, *Historical Statistics*, pp. 722–24, 727–29; Census Bureau, *Governmental Finances in 1983–84*, table 4, and earlier issues.

Table A-3. *Direct General Expenditure for Civil Functions by All Levels of Government, Selected Years, 1902–84*

Millions of dollars

Function	*1902*	*1927*	*1938*	*1948*	*1958*	*1968*	*1978*	*1984*
Education	258	2,243	2,653	7,721	16,836	43,614	118,750	188,604
Highways	175	1,819	2,150	3,071	8,702	14,654	24,886	40,308
Public welfare	41	161	1,233	2,144	3,777	11,245	54,225	88,424
Health	18	84	182	536	806	2,778	10,249	18,138
Hospitals	45	347	496	1,398	3,849	7,801	22,837	41,247
General control	175	526	725	1,325	2,536	2,400	8,418	15,794
Police	50	290	378	724	1,769	3,700	12,877	21,354
Other	481	3,161	5,985	9,478	21,739	49,935	135,142	252,382
Total	1,243	8.631	13,802	26,397	60,014	136,127	387,384	666,251

Sources: Census Bureau, *Historical Statistics*. pp. 723, 727; Census Bureau, *Governmental Finances in 1983–84*, table 11, and earlier issues.

Table A-4. *General Expenditure for Civil Functions as a Percent of Gross National Product, by Level of Government, Selected Years, 1902–84*

Year	*Gross national product (billions of dollars)*	*Expenditure as a percent of GNP*		
		Federal	*State-local*	*Total*
1902	21.6	1.1	4.7	5.8
1927	96.3	1.5	7.5	9.0
1938	85.2	5.9	10.3	16.2
1948	261.6	3.4	6.8	10.2
1958	456.8	3.4	9.8	13.4
1968	892.7	3.9	11.5	15.8
1978	2,249.7	4.8	13.2	18.5
1984	3,774.7	5.2	13.4	18.9

Sources: Table A-1; Census Bureau, *Historical Statistics*, p. 139; *Economic Report of the President, February 1986*, pp. 252, 397, and earlier years.

Table A-5. *Annual Rates of Increase in State and Local Expenditures, by Function, 1958–73 and 1973–84*

Percent

Function	Annual rate of increase 1958–73	1973–84
Education	10.5	8.7
Highways	5.4	7.0
Public welfare	14.0	11.4
Health	12.9	12.4
Hospitals	8.8	10.6
General control	4.0	11.9
Police	9.9	10.2
Other	9.6	11.3
All functions	9.6	10.2
Consumer price index	2.9	8.0
Gross national product	7.5	9.7

Source: Table A-3; Census Bureau, *Governmental Finances in 1972–73*, table 7; *Economic Report of the President, February 1986*, pp. 252, 315.

Table A-6. *General Expenditure for Civil Functions by State and Local Governments, Selected Years, 1902–84*

Millions of dollars

Classification of payment and function	1902	1927	1938	1948	1958	1968	1978	1984
Intergovernmental payments charged to the level of government making final disbursement								
Education	255	2,235	2,491	5,379	15,919	41,158	110,758	176,108
Highways	175	1,809	1,650	3,036	8,567	14,481	24,609	39,516
Public welfare	37	151	1,069	2,099	3,729	9,857	37,679	64,709
Health	17	76	151	292	546	1,264	6,303	12,277
Hospitals	43	279	400	937	3,005	6,282	18,648	34,142
Other	486	2,660	2,996	5,941	13,085	29,369	97,513	176,532
Total	1,013	7,210	8,757	17,684	44,851	102,411	295,510	503,284
Intergovernmental payments charged to the originating level of government								
Education	254	2,225	2,379	4,961	15,226	36,431	99,156	162,500
Highways	175	1,726	1,386	2,718	7,089	10,190	18,412	29,312
Public welfare	36	150	851	1,375	1,930	4,450	17,628	24,655
Health	17	76	151	292	484[a]	701[a]	[b]	[b]
Hospitals	43	279	400	937	2,959[a]	6,128[a]	22,487	42,349
Other	481	2,631	2,828	5,630	12,288	26,458	58,655	145,453
Total	1,006	7,087	7,995	15,913	40,016	84,358	216,338	404,269

Sources: Census Bureau, *Historical Statistics*, pp. 725, 727; Census Bureau, *Governmental Finances in 1983–84*, tables 10, 11, and earlier issues.

a. In 1958 and 1968, hospitals are allocated $1 million and $2 million, respectively, designated as "other" under "health and hospitals" in the census classification.

b. Included in expenditure for hospitals.

Table A-7. *State and Local Expenditures as a Percent of Total Direct General Expenditure for Civil Functions, Selected Years, 1902–84*

Classification of payment and function	*1902*	*1927*	*1938*	*1948*	*1958*	*1968*	*1978*	*1984*
Intergovernmental payments charged to the level of government making final disbursement								
Education	98.8	99.6	93.9	69.7	94.6	94.4	93.3	93.4
Highways	100.0	99.5	76.7	98.9	98.4	98.8	98.9	98.0
Public welfare	90.2	93.8	86.7	97.9	98.7	87.7	69.5	73.2
Health	94.4	90.5	83.0	54.5	67.7	45.5	61.5	67.7
Hospitals	95.6	80.4	80.6	67.0	78.1	80.5	81.7	82.8
Intergovernmental payments charged to the originating level of government								
Education	98.4	99.2	89.7	64.3	90.7	83.5	83.5	86.2
Highways	100.0	94.9	64.5	88.5	81.5	69.5	74.0	72.7
Public welfare	87.8	93.2	69.0	64.1	51.1	39.6	32.5	27.9
Health	94.4	90.5	83.0	54.5	60.0	25.2	[a]	[a]
Hospitals	95.6	80.4	80.6	67.0	76.9	78.6	68.0	71.3

Source: Tables A-3, A-6.

a. Included in expenditure for hospitals.

Table A-8. *State-Local Per Capita General Expenditure Including and Excluding Federal Grants, by State, 1984*

State	Per capita state-local expenditure (dollars)			Rank (by net expenditure)	Expenditure index[a]
	Total	Funded by federal grants	Net		
United States	2,131.13	410.96	1,720.17	...	100
Alaska	8,729.32	985.83	7,743.49	1	450
Wyoming	3,903.81	919.21	2,984.60	2	174
New York	3,037.01	616.73	2,420.28	3	141
Minnesota	2,611.01	463.35	2,147.66	4	125
Nevada	2,394.23	327.52	2,066.71	5	120
New Mexico	2,465.02	458.82	2,006.20	6	117
Delaware	2,471.75	482.16	1,989.59	7	116
Wisconsin	2,363.25	423.91	1,939.34	8	113
Hawaii	2,428.89	491.15	1,937.74	9	113
New Jersey	2,290.13	371.25	1,918.88	10	112
North Dakota	2,464.52	548.20	1,916.32	11	111
Michigan	2,387.92	478.30	1,909.62	12	111
Oregon	2,382.88	474.23	1,908.65	13	111
Maryland	2,298.08	393.38	1,904.70	14	111
Washington	2,273.96	371.12	1,902.84	15	111
California	2,356.96	475.04	1,881.92	16	109
Rhode Island	2,355.19	507.21	1,847.98	17	107
Colorado	2,204.44	365.07	1,839.37	18	107
Louisiana	2,239.22	403.13	1,836.09	19	107
Montana	2,376.42	542.10	1,834.32	20	107
Arizona	2,079.95	281.35	1,798.60	21	105
Connecticut	2,156.39	360.82	1,795.57	22	104
Iowa	2,143.59	359.73	1,783.86	23	104
Kansas	2,079.53	329.34	1,750.19	24	102
Massachusetts	2,233.06	500.86	1,732.20	25	101
Nebraska	2,056.30	348.57	1,707.73	26	99
Vermont	2,220.95	573.97	1,646.98	27	96
Ohio	1,970.94	348.39	1,622.55	28	94
Illinois	2,030.14	416.70	1,613.44	29	94
Oklahoma	1,930.63	331.27	1,599.36	30	93
Utah	2,047.63	460.04	1,587.59	31	92
Texas	1,860.96	274.51	1,586.45	32	92
Florida	1,802.98	267.69	1,535.29	33	89
Virginia	1,805.81	313.27	1,492.54	34	87
South Dakota	1,995.05	510.06	1,484.99	35	86
Maine	1,945.91	461.57	1,484.34	36	86
Pennsylvania	1,835.61	390.65	1,444.96	37	84
West Virginia	1,815.10	404.93	1,410.17	38	82
Georgia	1,825.81	418.78	1,407.03	39	82
Indiana	1,718.59	322.97	1,395.62	40	81
New Hampshire	1,728.88	339.15	1,389.73	41	81
Alabama	1,739.38	386.13	1,353.25	42	79
Idaho	1,709.37	363.64	1,345.73	43	78
Kentucky	1,717.02	397.25	1,319.77	44	77
Missouri	1,621.89	325.62	1,296.27	45	75
Mississippi	1,686.57	407.93	1,278.64	46	74
North Carolina	1,602.38	345.58	1,256.80	47	73
South Carolina	1,569.16	336.18	1,232.98	48	72
Tennessee	1,590.95	391.27	1,199.68	49	70
Arkansas	1,477.74	373.25	1,104.49	50	64

Source: Census Bureau, *Governmental Finances in 1983–84*, table 24.

a. Net state-local expenditure divided by U.S. average net expenditure multiplied by 100.

Table A-9. *States' Ranks in Per Capita Income and Per Capita General Expenditure, Excluding Federal Grants, 1984*

State	Rank: Per capita income	Rank: Per capita expenditure	Difference between income and expenditure ranks
Alaska	1	1	0
Connecticut	2	22	20
New Jersey	3	10	7
Massachusetts	4	25	21
California	5	16	11
Maryland	6	14	8
New York	7	3	4
Colorado	8	18	10
Delaware	9	7	2
Nevada	10	5	5
Illinois	11	29	18
Kansas	12	24	12
Washington	13	15	2
Virginia	14	34	20
Hawaii	15	9	6
New Hampshire	16	41	25
Minnesota	17	4	13
Wyoming	18	2	16
Texas	19	32	13
Rhode Island	20	17	3
North Dakota	21	47	26
Florida	22	33	11
Michigan	23	12	11
Pennsylvania	24	37	13
Wisconsin	25	8	17
Ohio	26	28	2
Nebraska	27	26	1
Missouri	28	45	17
Oklahoma	29	30	1
Oregon	30	13	17
Iowa	31	23	8
Arizona	32	21	11
Indiana	33	40	7
Georgia	34	39	5
Louisiana	35	19	16
Vermont	36	27	9
Montana	37	20	17
Maine	38	36	2
South Dakota	39	35	4
North Carolina	40	11	29
New Mexico	41	6	35
Idaho	42	43	1
Tennessee	43	49	6
Kentucky	44	44	0
Alabama	45	42	3
South Carolina	46	48	2
West Virginia	47	38	9
Utah	48	31	17
Arkansas	49	50	1
Mississippi	50	46	4

Source: Table A-8; Census Bureau, *Governmental Finances in 1983–84,* table 27.

Table A-10. *Percent of State Tax Revenue Collected from Selected Taxes, by State, 1984*

State	Tax on: Total sales and gross receipts	General sales and gross receipts	Individual income
Nevada	85.0	47.8	[a]
South Dakota	81.0	49.9	[a]
Florida	78.2	54.3	[a]
Washington	76.2	60.0	[a]
Tennessee	75.6	54.0	[a]
Connecticut	68.6	43.4	[a]
West Virginia	65.0	45.9	23.0
Texas	64.9	38.7	[a]
Mississippi	63.6	49.8	14.9
Hawaii	62.6	51.2	32.3
Indiana	61.4	48.7	30.0
Arizona	59.3	45.2	20.9
New Mexico	56.8	42.0	5.4
Missouri	56.4	43.5	29.6
Utah	56.0	44.2	32.3
Alabama	55.9	27.2	23.0
Nebraska	55.8	35.0	28.5
Arkansas	55.0	36.5	28.2
Maine	54.8	34.3	28.5
South Carolina	53.6	33.5	33.4
Ohio	53.3	32.6	31.1
New Jersey	53.1	28.8	24.8
Idaho	52.6	35.2	33.1
Colorado	51.8	37.1	35.8
Rhode Island	51.4	30.6	35.2
Vermont	51.0	19.6	32.0
Georgia	50.7	34.4	37.1
Illinois	49.1	30.5	34.0
Pennsylvania	48.4	28.3	26.4
Iowa	47.4	32.8	32.2
New Hampshire	46.3	...	[a]
Maryland	45.2	25.0	40.7
Kentucky	45.0	27.0	25.4
Louisiana	44.9	28.3	13.0
Kansas	44.6	29.0	31.7
North Dakota	44.5	29.9	10.8
California	43.2	34.3	36.1
North Carolina	43.1	21.6	38.5
Virginia	41.7	20.3	43.3
Wisconsin	40.6	26.9	42.6
Minnesota	40.2	24.6	45.6
Michigan	37.2	26.5	39.5
New York	35.5	20.7	49.8
Massachusetts	34.1	21.4	47.8
Oklahoma	33.8	17.2	24.7
Wyoming	28.4	22.1	[a]
Montana	23.1	...	29.2
Delaware	13.1	...	48.2
Oregon	11.7	...	65.8
Alaska	4.5	...	[a]

Source: Census Bureau, *State Government Finances in 1984* (GPO, 1984), table 6.
a. State either has no individual income tax or taxes nonwage income only.

Table A-11. *Relative Per Capita Redistribution of Federal Income Attributed to Grant and Equalization Measures, by State, 1982*

State	Income redistribution (dollars)		
	Total	By grant formula	By tax incidence
Alaska	+346	+525	−179
Vermont	+228	+155	+73
Maine	+185	+96	+89
Mississippi	+182	+51	+131
South Dakota	+176	+96	+80
New York	+130	+157	−27
New Mexico	+129	+45	+84
Rhode Island	+124	+122	+2
Montana	+106	+68	+38
West Virginia	+104	+26	+78
Kentucky	+103	+16	+87
Arkansas	+99	−12	+111
Georgia	+87	+18	+69
Massachusetts	+80	106	−26
Alabama	+79	−15	+94
North Dakota	+73	+57	+16
South Carolina	+59	−45	+104
Utah	+59	−35	+94
Wisconsin	+58	+33	+25
Delaware	+57	+95	−38
Idaho	+56	−28	+84
Minnesota	+55	+58	−3
Hawaii	+37	+41	−4
Tennessee	+26	−46	+72
Louisiana	+26	−5	+31
Pennsylvania	+23	+21	+2
Michigan	+21	+29	−8
North Carolina	+18	−62	+80
Oregon	+12	−3	+15
Maryland	+9	+58	−49
Missouri	−7	−36	+29
Nebraska	−24	−38	+14
New Hampshire	−27	−36	+9
Oklahoma	−33	−58	+25
Ohio	−34	−35	+1
Nevada	−41	+4	−45
California	−48	−8	−40
Iowa	−55	−62	+7
Washington	−57	−4	−53
Arizona	−59	−97	+38
Wyoming	−60	+9	−69
Virginia	−64	−70	+6
Indiana	−65	−84	+19
Illinois	−77	−11	−66
Florida	−82	−95	+13
Colorado	−84	−66	−18
Kansas	−86	−77	−9
New Jersey	−94	−4	−90
Connecticut	−141	−14	−127
Texas	−142	−125	−17

Source: Tax Foundation, *Facts and Figures on Government Finance, 1983* (Washington: Tax Foundation, 1982), p. 160. Redistribution figured as difference between U.S. average grant per capita ($369) and state's grant receipt or tax contribution per capita. The methodology is explained on pp. 73–74, above.

Table A-12. *State Intergovernmental Expenditure, by Function, Selected Years, 1902–84*

Millions of dollars and, in parentheses, percent of total

Year	*Education*	*Highways*	*Public welfare*	*Other*	*Total*
1902	45 (86)	2 (4)	. . . (. . .)	5 (10)	52
1927	292 (49)	197 (33)	6 (1)	101 (17)	596
1938	656 (43)	317 (21)	346 (23)	197 (13)	1,516
1948	1,554 (47)	507 (15)	648 (20)	574 (18)	3,283
1957	4,212 (57)	1,082 (15)	1,136 (15)	1,009 (14)	7,440
1967	11,845 (62)	1,861 (10)	2,897 (15)	2,453 (13)	19,056
1978	40,125 (60)	3,821 (6)	10,047 (15)	13,294 (20)	67,287
1984	67,485 (62)	5,687 (5)	13,628 (13)	21,573 (20)	108,373

Sources: Census Bureau, *Census of Governments, 1957,* vol. 4, no. 2: *State Payments to Local Governments* (GPO, 1959), p. 100; Census Bureau, *Historical Statistics,* table 13; Census Bureau, *Governmental Finances in 1983–84,* table 10, and earlier issues.

Table A-13. *State Intergovernmental Expenditure as a Percent of Local General Expenditure, by Function, Selected Years, 1902–84*

Year	*Education*	*Highways*	*Public welfare*	*Other*	*All functions*
1902	18.9	1.2	. . .	1.0	5.4
1927	14.5	15.2	5.4	3.4	9.4
1938	30.6	38.0	56.2	5.9	22.0
1948	37.2	33.2	57.0	9.0	24.6
1957	35.7	36.8	68.5	7.0	24.2
1967	41.5	41.3	73.8	11.1	32.2
1978	49.4	38.4	84.1	16.6	36.8
1984	53.0	35.0	87.4	15.1	35.9

Sources: Table A-12; Census Bureau, *Census of Governments, 1957,* vol. 4, no. 3: *Historical Summary of Governmental Finances in the United States* (GPO, 1959), pp. 20–23, and no. 2, p. 100; Census Bureau, *Governmental Finances in 1983–84,* table 13, and earlier issues.

Table A-14. *State Individual Income Tax and General Sales Tax Collections Per Capita, Ranked by State, 1984*

	Individual income tax		*General sales tax*	
State	*Rank*	*Dollars*	*Rank*	*Dollars*
Delaware	1	560.28	...	...
Minnesota	2	556.55	14	300.54
New York	3	528.56	36	219.93
Massachusetts	4	481.21	37	215.25
Wisconsin	5	457.81	16	288.41
Oregon	6	455.44	...	...
Hawaii	7	387.70	2	615.25
Michigan	8	372.87	24	250.48
Maryland	9	369.63	35	227.24
California	10	360.57	11	342.95
Virginia	11	312.41	44	147.80
Rhode Island	12	296.40	21	257.57
North Carolina	13	289.54	42	162.55
Iowa	14	270.79	23	253.01
Illinois	15	257.24	33	230.31
Georgia	16	251.12	31	233.27
Vermont	17	249.35	43	153.01
South Carolina	18	241.05	26	242.09
Colorado	19	240.29	25	249.02
New Jersey	20	235.22	18	273.33
Utah	21	233.69	13	320.27
Kansas	22	232.76	38	212.84
Ohio	23	231.29	27	242.02
Idaho	24	227.54	28	241.58
Maine	25	226.61	19	272.81
Indiana	26	220.98	9	358.23
Pennsylvania	27	213.16	34	228.60
Montana	28	206.73	...	...
West Virginia	29	202.20	6	403.02
Oklahoma	30	199.46	45	138.47
Kentucky	31	190.83	39	202.61
Nebraska	32	189.49	32	233.21
Arkansas	33	184.77	29	239.54
Missouri	34	180.43	20	265.27
Arizona	35	173.03	7	373.64
Alabama	36	156.18	41	184.29
North Dakota	37	107.80	15	297.87
Mississippi	38	100.10	12	333.35
Louisiana	39	91.24	40	198.44
Connecticut	40	88.36	4	424.58
New Mexico	41	52.57	5	406.17

Source: Census Bureau, *State Government Finances in 1984*, table 26.

Table A-15. *Operating Revenue and Expenditure of Local Utilities, 1953, 1963, 1973, and 1984*

Utility and year	*Revenue (millions of dollars)*	*Expenditure (millions of dollars)*[a]	*Expenditure as a percent of revenue*
Water supply			
1953	939	631	67.2
1963	1,865	1,273	68.3
1973	3,463	2,650	76.5
1984	10,467	9,141	87.3
Electric power			
1953	713	453	63.5
1963	1,728	1,111	64.3
1973	3,355	2,513	74.9
1984	19,614	18,053	92.0
Transit			
1953	500	530	106.0
1963	639	723	113.1
1973	1,267	1,946	153.6
1984	3,792	9,318	245.7
Gas supply			
1953	85	56	65.9
1963	242	202	83.5
1973	536	439	81.9
1984	3,501	3,208	91.6

Sources: Census Bureau, *Census of Governments, 1962*, vol. 6, no. 4: *Historical Statistics on Governmental Finances and Employment* (GPO, 1964), pp. 45, 50; Census Bureau, *Governmental Finances in 1983–84*, table 19, and earlier issues.

a. Includes interest on utility debt.

Table A-16. *State Government User Charges, by Major Categories of Governmental Service, 1953, 1963, 1973, and 1984*

Governmental service	User charge 1953	1963	1973	1984
	Millions of dollars			
Education	410	1,260	4,891	14,593
Housing	. . .	8	19	204
Hospitals	111	333	1,306	5,731
Natural resources, parks, and recreation	81	118	275	1,152
Highways	103	461	975	1,683
Air transportation	2	13	73	263
Water transport and terminals	20	43	105	315
Other	77	226	965	1,797
Total	804	2,462	8,609	25,738
	As a percent of general revenue from own sources			
Total	6.8	9.6	10.7	10.3
	As a percent of direct expenditure for service			
Education	27.6	26.6	26.8	30.0
Housing	. . .	66.7	7.2	24.9
Hospitals	10.9	16.6	24.3	37.6
Natural resources, parks, and recreation	15.3	10.8	10.5	16.3
Highways	3.7	6.2	8.1	7.2
Air transportation	n.a.	41.9	29.9	68.1
Water transport and terminals	n.a.	52.4	62.5	78.4

Sources: Census Bureau, *Summary of Governmental Finances in 1954* (GPO, 1955); Census Bureau, *Governmental Finances in 1983–84,* table 11, and earlier issues; Census Bureau, *State Government Finances in 1984,* table 7, and earlier issues.

n.a. = not available.

Table A-17. *Per Capita Personal Income and Per Capita Long-Term State and Local Debt Outstanding, by State, 1984*

State	*Personal income*		*Long-term debt outstanding*	
	Rank	*Dollars*	*Rank*	*Dollars*
Alaska	1	17,194	1	18,898.26
Connecticut	2	14,895	20	2,297.78
New Jersey	3	14,122	18	2,389.07
Massachusetts	4	13,264	21	2,246.19
California	5	13,257	39	1,507.00
Maryland	6	12,994	15	2,585.45
New York	7	12,990	10	2,974.47
Colorado	8	12,770	19	2,333.53
Delaware	9	12,665	3	4,056.46
Nevada	10	12,451	17	2,536.98
Illinois	11	12,405	36	1,608.99
Kansas	12	12,247	22	2,238.42
Washington	13	12,177	4	4,031.70
Virginia	14	12,116	42	1,323.08
Hawaii	15	12,114	13	2,693.26
New Hampshire	16	12,021	24	2,195.80
Minnesota	17	11,913	12	2,779.02
Wyoming	18	11,911	5	3,886.77
Texas	19	11,685	23	2,237.50
Rhode Island	20	11,670	11	2,819.68
North Dakota	21	11,666	34	1,665.31
Florida	22	11,593	31	1,888.95
Michigan	23	11,466	37	1,576.52
Pennsylvania	24	11,448	29	1,973.47
Wisconsin	25	11,352	40	1,496.31
Ohio	26	11,216	43	1,273.54
Nebraska	27	11,212	7	3,355.15
Missouri	28	10,969	45	1,218.89
Oklahoma	29	10,963	28	2,014.64
Oregon	30	10,740	6	3,386.23
Iowa	31	10,705	50	1,043.18
Arizona	32	10,656	8	3,228.75
Indiana	33	10,476	48	1,108.37
Georgia	34	10,379	38	1,563.18
Louisiana	35	10,270	9	3,061.02
Vermont	36	9,979	25	2,098.97
Montana	37	9,949	26	2,096.71
Maine	38	9,847	35	1,631.98
South Dakota	39	9,847	30	1,955.90
North Carolina	40	9,787	46	1,188.31
New Mexico	41	9,640	14	2,636.42
Idaho	42	9,555	49	1,072.12
Tennessee	43	9,549	41	1,426.85
Kentucky	44	9,397	16	2,580.88
Alabama	45	9,242	32	1,747.99
South Carolina	46	9,187	33	1,696.05
West Virginia	47	9,159	27	2,088.40
Utah	48	8,993	2	4,127.27
Arkansas	49	8,967	44	1,265.34
Mississippi	50	8,098	47	1,177.35

Source: Census Bureau, *Governmental Finances in 1983–84,* tables 24, 27.

Table A-18. *Long-Term Debt of State and Local Governments Outstanding at End of Fiscal Year, 1949, 1957, 1968, 1978, and 1984*

Debt	*1949*	*1957*	*1968*	*1978*	*1984*
	Billions of dollars and, in parentheses, percent of total				
State and local	20.2 (100.0)	50.9 (100.0)	112.7 (100.0)	269.0 (100.0)	485.1 (100.0)
Full faith and credit	17.7 (87.6)	32.6 (64.1)	65.1 (57.8)	142.5 (53.0)	166.9 (34.4)
Nonguaranteed	2.5 (12.4)	18.3 (35.9)	47.7 (42.3)	126.5 (47.0)	318.2 (65.6)
State	4.0 (100.0)	13.5 (100.0)	33.6 (100.0)	99.7 (100.0)	183.2 (100.0)
Full faith and credit	3.4 (85.0)	6.5 (48.0)	14.7 (43.8)	46.3 (46.4)	57.3 (31.3)
Nonguaranteed	0.6 (15.0)	7.0 (52.0)	18.9 (56.3)	53.4 (53.6)	125.9 (68.7)
Local	16.2 (100.0)	37.3 (100.0)	79.1 (100.0)	169.3 (100.0)	301.9 (100.0)
Full faith and credit	14.3 (88.3)	26.1 (69.9)	50.4 (63.7)	96.2 (56.8)	109.5 (36.3)
Nonguaranteed	1.9 (11.7)	11.2 (30.1)	28.7 (36.3)	73.1 (43.2)	192.3 (63.7)
	Relative change in debt (base year 1949 = 100)				
State and local	100	251	558	1,332	2,401
Full faith and credit	100	184	368	805	943
Nonguaranteed	100	732	1,908	5,060	12,728
State	100	338	840	2,493	4,580
Full faith and credit	100	191	432	1,362	1,685
Nonguaranteed	100	1,166	3,150	8,900	20,983
Local	100	230	488	1,045	1,864
Full faith and credit	100	183	352	673	766
Nonguaranteed	100	589	1,511	3,847	10,121

Sources: U.S. Census Bureau, unpublished data for 1949; Census Bureau, *Historical Statistics*, p. 44; Census Bureau, *Governmental Finances in 1983–84*, table 18, and earlier issues.

Table A-19. *Distribution of States by Percent of State Government Net Long-Term Debt in Full Faith and Credit Form, 1941, 1949, 1966, 1973, and 1984*

Percent of debt in full faith and credit form	Number of states				
	1941	1949	1966	1973	1984
90 and over	18	21	4	2	1
80–89	7	2	3	6	7
70–79	4	1	4	5	6
60–69	2	2	4	7	5
50–59	3	1	5	2	3
40–49	2	0	2	4	4
30–39	1	3	3	3	3
20–29	4	3	5	5	4
10–19	0	3	2	3	2
Up to 10	1	6	9	1	6
None	6	6	9	12	9

Sources: Census Bureau, *Financial Statistics of States, 1941*, vol. 3: *Statistical Compendium* (GPO, 1943), pp. 63–65; Census Bureau, *State Government Finances in 1984*, p. 34.

Table A-20. *Net Long-Term Nonguaranteed State Government Debt, Per Capita, of States without Full Faith and Credit Debt, 1941, 1966, 1973, and 1984*

State	Debt (dollars)			
	1941	1966	1973	1984
Arizona	. . .	26.40	36.44	77.54
Arkansas	. . .	. . .	49.40	52.04
Colorado	. . .	47.63	43.50	41.26
Florida	a	105.50	142.01	224.37[b]
Georgia	. . .	123.67	145.16	66.75[b]
Indiana	2.40	. . .	93.26	139.64
Iowa	. . .	. . .	39.31	90.49
Kansas	. . .	. . .	80.75	110.29[b]
Kentucky	3.72	. . .	. . .	488.23[b]
Montana	. . .	. . .	103.59	67.61[b]
Nebraska	1.03	37.22	34.82	57.30
North Dakota	. . .	32.45	. . .	61.87
Ohio	1.82	. . .	. . .	266.49[b]
South Dakota	. . .	26.30	56.08	50.18
Wisconsin	1.74	63.55	. . .	98.10[b]
Wyoming	. . .	75.55	101.81	98.14

Sources: Census Bureau, *Financial Statistics of States, 1941*, vol. 3, pp. 63–65; Census Bureau, *State Government Finances in 1984*, tables 16, 36, and earlier issues.

a. No net long-term debt.

b. Long-term debt in full faith and credit form.

Table A-21. *State Expenditures and Revenues for Public Elementary and Secondary Schools, Ranked by Total Expenditure, 1984*

State	*Total current expenditures per pupil (dollars)*	*Source of revenue receipts (percent)*		
		Federal	*State*	*Local and other*
United States	3,001	6.6	48.3	45.0
Alaska	6,002	1.8	75.5	22.7
New York	4,364	3.8	41.4	54.9
New Jersey	4,337	3.4	40.0	56.6
Wyoming	4,243	3.3	28.7	67.9
District of Columbia	4,033	11.8	. . .	88.2
Connecticut	3,858	5.4	37.4	57.2
Delaware	3,578	8.6	68.2	23.3
Oregon	3,535	5.6	28.8	65.6
Montana	3,501	9.5	44.9	45.6
Rhode Island	3,484	4.6	35.9	59.5
Wisconsin	3,458	4.7	39.3	55.9
Pennsylvania	3,416	4.3	45.4	50.3
Maryland	3,401	5.6	39.6	54.8
Massachusetts	3,322	5.5	39.5	55.0
Vermont	3,264	5.9	34.7	59.3
Kansas	3,204	4.8	43.5	51.6
Hawaii	3,175	9.1	90.6	.3
Illinois	3,161	7.6	37.7	54.6
Minnesota	3,142	4.6	54.4	41.0
Iowa	3,097	5.5	42.5	52.0
Colorado	3,063	4.5	40.3	55.2
Oklahoma	2,970	7.5	62.4	30.0
Washington	2,934	5.6	75.1	19.2
Florida	2,913	7.8	53.7	38.5
North Dakota	2,833	7.1	59.9	33.0
Ohio	2,801	5.3	42.8	51.9
Nebraska	2,787	5.8	29.5	64.7
Texas	2,780	8.3	45.4	46.4
New Mexico	2,723	11.7	75.3	13.0
Nevada	2,718	4.1	39.9	56.0
Virginia	2,681	6.9	43.5	49.6
Maine	2,676	7.7	50.5	41.8
New Hampshire	2,601	3.6	8.1	88.2
Arizona	2,566	10.3	52.0	37.7
Louisiana	2,549	9.8	53.3	36.9
South Dakota	2,521	11.0	27.5	61.5
Indiana	2,452	4.2	53.4	42.4
Kentucky	2,407	10.5	70.2	19.4
North Carolina	2,314	10.4	61.3	28.3
Georgia	2,190	9.5	50.8	39.7
South Carolina	2,145	8.3	57.1	34.6
Arkansas	2,094	11.4	57.6	31.1
Tennessee	2,030	11.2	45.8	43.0
Mississippi	1,998	17.8	56.7	25.5
Alabama	1,978	12.7	70.7	16.6
Utah	1,937	5.8	53.2	41.0
California	n.a.	7.9	66.9	25.2
Idaho	n.a.	6.7	64.7	28.5
Michigan	n.a.	5.0	32.0	63.0
Missouri	n.a.	6.9	36.7	56.4
West Virginia	n.a.	8.1	62.8	29.1

Source: National Education Association, *Estimates of School Statistics, 1984–85* (Washington: NEA, 1985), pp. 37, 39. Includes the District of Columbia. Figures based on average daily membership.
n.a. = not available.

Bibliography

EXCELLENT SOURCES of statistical data on state and local public finance are prepared by the Bureau of the Census in the U.S. Department of Commerce. The important yearly publications are: *Governmental Finances; State Government Finances;* and *City Government Finances.* For historical material the most convenient sources are the Census Bureau's *Historical Statistics of the United States: Colonial Times to 1957,* published by the Government Printing Office in 1960, and later editions extending the data. The bureau's *Census of Governments,* taken in 1942 and every five years since 1952, is published in numerous volumes. Of special interest in the 1982 Census is volume 6, number 4: *Historical Statistics on Governmental Financing and Employment.*

Descriptions of state functional organization, as well as statistical material, are to be found in *The Book of the States,* issued biennially by the Council of State Governments, Lexington, Kentucky. The *Municipal Year Book,* issued by the International City Management Association, Washington, offers similar materials concerning local governments. *The Bond Buyer's Municipal Finance Statistics,* published annually by The Bond Buyer, New York, is a useful reference, and so also is *Facts and Figures on Government Finance,* issued annually by the Tax Foundation, Washington. The Commerce Clearing House of Chicago issues a looseleaf *State Tax Guide* showing rates and major state tax laws.

The Advisory Commission on Intergovernmental Relations, whose members are drawn from Congress, the executive branch of the federal government, governors, state legislatures, mayors, elected county officials, and private persons, has prepared and issued numerous and valuable reports dealing with specific intergovernmental problems. The commission's aim is to advance cooperation among levels of government to improve the effectiveness of the federal system.

Periodicals

Most useful for the general reader are:

Governmental Finance. Quarterly. Chicago: Municipal Finance Officers Association.

National Civic Review (formerly *National Municipal Review*). Monthly. New York: National Municipal League.

National Tax Journal. Quarterly. Columbus, Ohio: National Tax Association–Tax Institute of America.

Proceedings of the Annual Conference on Taxation. Columbus, Ohio: National Tax Association–Tax Institute of America.
Public Choice. Bimonthly. The Netherlands: Public Choice Society.
Public Finance Quarterly. Quarterly. Beverly Hills, Calif.: Sage Publications.

Special Studies

Aaron, Henry J. *Who Pays the Property Tax? A New View.* Washington: Brookings Institution, 1975.
Advisory Commission on Intergovernmental Relations. *Awakening the Slumbering Giant: Intergovernmental Relations and Federal Grant Law.* Washington: Government Printing Office, 1980.
——. *Bankruptcies, Defaults, and Other Local Government Financial Emergencies.* Washington: GPO, 1985.
——. *City Financial Emergencies: The Intergovernmental Dimension.* Washington: GPO, 1973.
——. *Financing Schools and Property Tax Relief—A State Responsibility.* Washington: ACIR, 1973.
——. *Fiscal Balance in the American Federal System.* 2 vols. Washington: GPO, 1967.
——. *Fiscal Disparities: Central Cities and Suburbs, 1981.* Washington: GPO, 1984.
——. *Local Revenue Diversification: Income, Sales Taxes and User Charges.* Washington: GPO, 1974.
——. *Measuring the Fiscal Capacity and Effort of State and Local Areas.* Washington: GPO, 1971.
——. *Regional Growth—Interstate Tax Competition.* Washington: GPO, 1981.
——. *The Role of Equalization in Federal Grants.* Washington: ACIR, 1964.
——. *The Role of the States in Strengthening the Property Tax.* 2 vols. Washington: GPO, 1963.
——. *Significant Features of Fiscal Federalism, 1984 Edition.* Washington: GPO, 1985.
——. *State Constitutional and Statutory Restrictions on Local Government Debt.* Washington: ACIR, 1961.
——. *Tax Capacity of the Fifty States.* Washington: GPO, 1985.
Aronson, J. Richard. *Municipal Fiscal Indicators.* U.S. Department of Housing and Urban Development, Office of Policy Development and Research, 1980.
Aronson, J. Richard, and Eli Schwartz, eds. *Management Policies in Local Government Finance.* 2d edition. Washington: International City Management Association, 1981.
Bahl, Roy W. *Financing State and Local Government in the 1980's.* New York: Oxford University Press, 1984.
Barfield, Claude E. *Rethinking Federalism: Block Grants and Federal, State, and Local Responsibilities.* Washington: American Enterprise Institute, 1981.

Bird, Frederick L. *The General Property Tax: Findings of the 1957 Census of Governments.* Chicago: Public Administration Service, 1960.

Break, George F. *Financing Government in a Federal System.* Washington: Brookings Institution, 1980.

Due, John F., and J. L. Mikesell, *Sales Taxation (State and Local Structure and Administration).* Baltimore: Johns Hopkins University Press, 1983.

Gold, Steven D. *Property Tax Relief.* Lexington: Lexington Books, 1979.

Heins, A. James. *Constitutional Restrictions Against State Debt.* Madison: University of Wisconsin Press, 1963.

Hillhouse, A. M., and S. K. Howard. *State Capital Budgeting.* Chicago: Council of State Governments, 1963.

Jensen, Jens P. *Property Taxation in the United States.* Chicago: University of Chicago Press, 1931.

Maxwell, James A. *The Fiscal Impact of Federalism in the United States.* Cambridge: Harvard University Press, 1946.

Moak, Lennox L., and Albert M. Hillhouse. *Concepts and Practices in Local Government Finance.* Chicago: Municipal Finance Officers Association of the United States and Canada, 1975.

Mushkin, Selma J., ed. *Public Prices for Public Products.* Washington: Urban Institute, 1972.

Mussa, Michael L., and Roger C. Kormendi. *The Taxation of Municipal Bonds.* Washington: American Enterprise Institute, 1979.

New York Legislature, Commission on State-Local Relations. *New York's Limits on Local Taxing and Borrowing Powers.* New York, 1983.

Nathan, Richard P., Allen D. Manvel, Susannah E. Calkins, and associates. *Monitoring Revenue Sharing.* Washington: Brookings Institution, 1975.

Oates, Wallace E. *Fiscal Federalism.* New York: Harcourt Brace Jovanovich, 1972.

Ott, David J., and Allan H. Meltzer. *Federal Tax Treatment of State and Local Securities.* Washington: Brookings Institution, 1963.

Ott, David J., Attiat F. Ott, James A. Maxwell, and J. Richard Aronson. *State-Local Finances in the Last Half of the 1970s.* Washington: American Enterprise Institute, 1975.

Pechman, Joseph A. *Federal Tax Policy.* Washington: Brookings Institution, 1983.

———. *Who Paid the Taxes, 1966–85?* Washington: Brookings Institution, 1985.

Penniman, Clara. *State Income Taxation.* Baltimore: Johns Hopkins University Press, 1980.

Ratchford, B. U. *American State Debts.* Durham, N.C.: Duke University Press, 1941.

Robinson, Roland I. *Postwar Market for State and Local Government Securities.* Princeton: Princeton University Press for the National Bureau of Economic Research, 1960.

Schwartz, E., V. Munley, and J.R. Aronson. "Reforming Public Pension Plans to Avoid Unfunded Liability," in International City Management Association, *Management Information Service Report.* Washington: ICMA, May 1983.

Sigafoos, Robert A. *The Municipal Income Tax: Its History and Problems.* Chicago: Public Administration Service, 1955.

Studenski, Paul, and Herman E. Krooss. *Financial History of the United States.* 2d edition. New York: McGraw-Hill, 1963.

Twentieth Century Fund, Task Force on Municipal Bond Credit Ratings. *The Rating Game.* New York: Twentieth Century Fund, 1974.

U.S. Commission on Intergovernmental Relations. *A Report to the President.* Washington: The Commission, 1955.

U.S. Congress. House. Committee on the Judiciary. Special Subcommittee on State Taxation of Interstate Commerce. *State Taxation of Interstate Commerce.* 4 vols. Washington: GPO, 1964 and 1965.

Index

Aaron, Henry J., 124n, 132n
Accelerated cost recovery system (ACRS), 104–05
ACIR. *See* Advisory Commission on Intergovernmental Relations
Adams, T. S., 86
Advisory Commission on Intergovernmental Relations (ACIR), 6, 29, 49n, 52n, 54, 78n, 83n, 86n, 87n, 88n, 91n, 92, 93n, 94n, 97n, 98n, 103, 104, 105, 132n, 135, 145n, 150n, 156n, 174n, 178n, 180–81, 186n, 197n, 202n; categorical grant study, 60–62; circuit breaker study, 138–39; creation of, 28; debt study, 164–65, 166–67, 175, 181–82, 231; interstate tax comparison, 45, 46; measure of fiscal capacity, 3, 37–40; sales tax study, 148–49
AFDC. *See* Aid to families with dependent children
Aid. *See* Intergovernmental transfers
Aid to families with dependent children (AFDC), 30, 67–68, 69, 71
Airports, grants for, 64–65
Alabama, 103n, 116, 117, 148n, 211
Alaska, 31, 43, 47, 74, 82, 86, 104, 145
Alcoholic beverage tax, 93, 226
Allen, Everett T., 195n
Anti-recession Jobs Appropriations Act, 66
Arizona, 118, 136n, 227, 228
Arkansas, 33, 148n, 162n
Aronson, J. Richard, 29n, 99n, 109n, 124n, 126n, 158n, 166n, 168n, 170n, 194n, 195n, 196n, 200n, 203n, 205n, 216n
Ashley, W. G., 152
Assessment, property tax, 5-6, 126–27, 128–35, 140

Bahl, Roy, 34–35n, 169n, 170n
Barfield, Claude E., 30n
Basic education opportunity grants (Pell grants), 215
Behrens, John O., 133n, 135n
Benker, Karen M., 226n
Benson, George C. S., 27n
Berne, Robert, 217n
Bird, Frederick L., 133
Bish, Robert L., 77n
Blinder, Alan S., 124n
Block grants, 3, 30, 54–56, 66, 73
Bloomfield, Mark A., 109n
Bollens, John C., 77n
Bonds: for industrial aid, 179–81; nonguaranteed, 7, 167, 176, 177–79, 181; tax-exempt, 170–75, 181; yield differential on tax-exempt, 172–74. *See also* Debt
Break, George F., 124n
Brown v. *Board of Education of Topeka,* 214
Browning, Edgar K., 99n
Bryce, James, 13
Buchanan, James M., 190n
Budget and Accounting Act of *1921,* 25
Budget Reconciliation Act. *See* Omnibus Budget Reconciliation Act
Budget: balanced, 184–85; capital, 7, 8, 203–07, 226; earmarked revenues, 188–94; form, 185; process, 7–8, 183–87; types, 186–87
Bullock, Charles J., 129
Burgess, John W., 12–13n
Burkhead, Jesse, 126n
Business cycle, 226
Butler, Pierce, 171

California: corporate income tax, 104, 115; death taxes, 117; home rule statutes, 143; individual income tax, 87–88; limitations on state government, 223, 225, 227, 228; property tax, 136n, 137; sales tax, 94, 148
Capital budgets, 7, 8, 203–07, 226
Carter administration, 73
Categorical grants, 3, 4, 30, 50, 53–56, 60–62, 66, 72, 73
CDBG. *See* Community Development Block Grant program
Central cities, 28–29, 75–76

CETA. *See* Comprehensive Employment and Training Act
Chicago, 64n, 75–76
Cigarette tax, 91–93, 226
Circuit breakers, 138–39
Cline, Robert, 156n
Clune, William H., III, 216n
Colorado, 104, 115, 118, 136n, 145, 216n, 225, 227
Committee for Economic Development, 27n
Community and economic development, 65–66
Community Development Block Grant program (CDBG), 66, 73
Comprehensive Employment and Training Act (CETA), 55, 73, 213
Congressional Budget Act of *1974,* 58n
Connecticut, 34, 36, 44n, 68, 74, 102, 104, 137n, 216n
Container Corporation of America v. *Franchise Tax Board,* 110, 113
Contraband Cigarette Act, 92–93
Coons, John E., 216n
Cooperative federalism, 22–24, 25, 29–30, 233
Corporate income tax: base, 104–05; dividends and, 113, 114–115; formulas, 105–08, 110–11, 112n, 114–15; incidence, 108–10; interstate allocation of income, 105–07; multinational corporations, 4–5, 110–15; need for uniformity, 233; overstating, 112–13; separate accounting, 105–06, 110–11, 112, 114–15; specific allocation, 106; state revenue, 47, 103–05; tax avoidance, 112; worldwide unitary combination and, 110–15
Cotton, John F., 35n, 187n

Death and gift taxes, 5, 43, 47, 115, 116–19, 233
DeBoer, Larry, 169n, 170n
Debt: bonds for industrial aid and nontraditional uses, 179–81; capital budgets and expenditures and, 7, 169–70, 204–07; defaults, 160, 161, 162; earmarked revenue and, 192; history, 160–67; life of, 169, 170, 178; limitations on, 7, 161, 175–76, 181–82, 228; nonguaranteed bonds, 7, 177–79; property tax and, 175–76; purposes, 168, 178–81; reform of borrowing limitations and, 181–82; tax exemptions and, 170–75; types, 167–70
Deductibility of state and local taxes, 46, 159, 223, 229–32
Deductions, income tax, 46, 88–89, 223, 229–32
Deficit Reduction Act, 181
Delaware, 87, 103, 127
Depression of the *1930*s, 17–19, 94
Dillon, John F., 10
District of Columbia: circuit breakers, 138; corporate income tax, 103; individual income tax, 86n, 87, 88–89; inheritance tax, 115; property tax, 137, 140n; sales tax, 91, 94, 96
Dividends, 113, 114–15
Dual federalism, 1, 19
Due, John F., 96n, 101n

Earmarked revenue, 8, 188–94, 224, 226
Economic Opportunity Act, 72, 213, 214
Economic Recovery Tax Act (ERTA), 4, 52, 105, 173–74
Education: earmarked revenue for, 192–93, 226; enrollments, 208, 210, 218; equity, 9, 213, 214–18; excellence, 9, 217–18; expenditures, 1, 9, 36, 37, 50, 208, 210–11, 212; federal role, 8–9, 48, 208, 210–11, 212–14, 217, 219–20; financing, 8–9, 157, 208–21; local role, 208, 210, 211; market-based approach, 220, 221; parental choice, 218–21; private, 218–21; property tax and, 125, 131; religion and, 220–21; as a service, 22, 23, 24; state government and, 4, 9, 81, 157, 168, 208, 210–11, 214, 216–17, 219–20, 221, 232–33
Education Amendments of *1974,* 215n
Education and Consolidation and Improvement Act, 213–14
Elementary and Secondary Education Act of *1965,* 72, 213, 214
Elementary and Secondary Education Assistance Programs, Extension, 215n
Employment Act of *1946,* 19n
Environmental and energy programs, 50, 65
Equity: deductibility of state and local taxes, 230–31; in education, 9, 213, 214–18; federal intergovernmental transfers and, 51–53, 74; horizontal, 53, 61, 98, 217n; intergenerational, 195–97, 204, 206; in public assistance, 66–68, 69; property tax, 5–6, 123, 129–31, 139–40; retirement systems and, 195–97; sales tax, 96, 97–100, 149; services and, 22; state grants and, 85; Tax Equity and Fiscal Responsibility Act, 71, 181; vertical, 98
ERTA. *See* Economic Recovery Tax Act
Estate tax. *See* Death and gift taxes

Excellence in education, 9, 217–18
Excise tax. *See* Sales tax
Exemptions from expenditure limitations, 8, 224–25, 227. *See also* Earmarked revenue
Exemptions, tax: homestead, 137–38; nonguaranteed bonds as, 181; personal income, 87–88; property, 126, 127, 132, 135–40; sales, 96, 97, 98; state and local bonds as, 170–75, 181; veterans', 137–38
Expenditure: cooperative federalism and, 29–30; for education, 1, 9, 36, 37, 50, 208, 210–11, 212; of federal government, 13–24, 33, 58; fiscal capacity and, 37–40; functional distribution, 21–24; interstate comparisons, 2–3, 31–47; local, 1, 14, 19–20, 24, 31, 46, 47, 79–80; patterns of aggregate, 32–37; per capita measure, 1, 31–34, 46–47; population density as measure, 34; public choice method of analysis, 36; state, 1, 14, 19–20, 24, 33, 80–81; tax effort and, 37–40; urbanization as measure, 34. *See also* Grants, federal; Grants, state; Intergovernmental transfers; Limitations on taxes and spending
Experimentation by states, 25, 27–28, 53

Federal-Aid Highway Act of *1956,* 62, 191
Federal government: education and, 8–9, 48, 208, 210–11, 212–14, 217, 219–20; expenditures by, 13–24, 33, 58; functions of, 1–2, 9; local government and, 222–23; state government and, 222–23; taxing power of, 12. *See also* Federalism; Federal taxes; Grants, federal; Intergovernmental transfers
Federalism: apologia for, 24–30; cooperative, 22–24, 25, 29–30, 233; dual, 19; first century of, 11–13, flexibility, 21; grants to local government and, 71–72; New, 9, 30; project grants and, 61
Federal taxes: corporate income, 104–05, 109; death, 116–18; estate, 116–18; incidence, 74; property tax and, 120; sales tax and, 91, 94; user fees and, 159. *See also* Exemptions, tax; Federal government
Feldstein, Martin, 211n
First Amendment, 220
Fiscal capacity, relative, 3, 37–40
Fisher, Glenn W., 35n
Florida, 5, 47, 104, 115, 116, 117, 136n
Food stamps, 30, 69
Ford administration, 72–73
Formula apportionment, 106–07
Formula grants, 4, 54, 62, 72. *See also* Categorical grants
Fourteenth Amendment, 27n, 215
Friedman, Milton, 220
Fulcher, Jack, 107n, 112n

Goetz, Charles J., 190n
Gold, Steven D., 135n, 139n, 224, 226n, 227n
Grants, federal: administration, 71–72; allocation of resources and, 4, 51–53, 73–74; design, 71–74; features, 58–60; federalism and, 61; forms, 3, 50, 53–58; functions aided by, 62–71; growth and decline, 3, 18, 24–25, 49–50, 72; implicit, 58, 229–30; local government and, 49–50, 51–52, 71–73; problems raised by, 60–62, 73–74; progressivity and, 4; rationale for, 50–53; state government and, 33, 49–50, 51–52; tax equalization and, 74. *See also* Intergovernmental transfers
Grants, state: for education, 4, 9, 81; for equity, 85; to local governments, 4, 78–85; for public assistance, 81; shared taxes as, 78–79, 83. *See also* Intergovernmental transfers
Graves, W. Brooke, 19n
Guaranteed debt, 167
Gulick, Luther, 18–19

Hansen, Reed R., 98n
Harberger, Arnold C., 109n
Harris, C. Lowell, 107
Hatch Act, 48
Hatry, Harry P., 187n
Hawaii, 44n; corporate income tax, 103n, 104; education, 211; expenditures, 31; individual income tax, 86; limitations on state government, 228; property tax, 127, 135, 136n; sales tax, 94
Hayden-Cartwright Act, 191
Head Start program, 214
Health. *See* Public health
Heins, A. James, 161n
Heller-Pechman plan, 56–57
Heller, Walter W., 56n, 86n
Higher Education Amendments of *1968,* 214–15
Highways, 2, 48, 62–64, 91, 157, 191–92
Highway Safety Act, 25
Highway Trust Fund, 91, 191
Hill-Burton Act, 70
Hillhouse, A. M., 161n, 162n, 203n
Hilton, George W., 14n

Holmes, Oliver Wendell, 171
Hospital Survey and Construction Act, 70
Housing Act of *1949*, 65
Housing and Community Development Act, 55
Housing assistance, 69–70, 157, 168
Howard, S. K., 203n

Illinois, 94, 127
Implicit grants, 58, 229–30
Income tax: business cycle and, 226; circuit breakers and, 139; compliance, 101–02; corporate, 47, 103–15, 233; deductions, 46, 88–89, 223, 229–32; definition, 149; earmarked revenue and, 192; individual, 86–90, 94, 100–02; limitations on, 227, 233; local, 142–43, 149–51, 227; origin of income and, 89–90; as progressive tax, 101, 102; residence and, 89–90; revenues, 87–89; state, 4, 43–45, 47, 86–90, 100–02, 139, 233; tax credits and, 87–88. *See also* Exemptions, tax
Incremental budgeting, 187
Indiana, 94n, 105n, 115, 136n, 137, 227
Industrial aid, bonds for, 179–81
Industrial property tax, 127–28, 136
Inheritance tax. *See* Death and gift taxes
Inman, Robert P., 227n
Intergenerational equity, 195–97, 204, 206
Intergovernmental Fiscal Cooperation, Task Force on, 56–57
Intergovernmental Relations, U.S. Commission on, 22, 27–28
Intergovernmental transfers: equity and, 51–53; federal, 48–74; to local governments, 77, 78–83; rationale, 50–53, 78; state, 75–85; trends, 48–50; types, 78–79. *See also* Expenditure; Grants, federal; Grants, state
Interstate tax competition, 45–46
Inventory. *See* Property tax
Iowa, 91, 105n, 136n, 149, 227

Jensen, Jens P., 140n
Johnson administration, 56, 72
Johnson, William R., 99n

Kansas, 136n, 148n, 216n
Kean, Stacey, 181n
Kent, Carolyn V., 172n
Kestnbaum, Meyer, 18n
Kestnbaum Report, 18n, 22, 27n, 28
King v. *Smith*, 67n
King, Arthur E., 166n, 170n
Krooss, Herman E., 120n

Leland, Simeon E., 18
Limitations on taxes and spending: business cycles and, 226; debt and, 7, 161, 175–76, 181–82, 228; earmarked revenues, 190–91, 193–94, 224; exemptions, 224–25, 227; future strength, 228; income tax, 227, 233; local governments, 77–78, 226–27; problems of designing, 225–26; property taxes, 6, 226, 227, 228, 233; Reagan proposal, 30; reform, 181–82; sales tax, 227, 233; state governments, 223–26; user fees and, 227, 233
Local debt. *See* Debt
Local government: education and, 208, 210, 211; expenditures, 1, 14, 19–20, 24, 31, 46, 47, 79–81; federal government and, 49–50, 51–52, 71–72, 81, 222–23; financing, 222–33; functions, 1–2, 9; limitations, 226–27; lotteries as revenue, 158; nontax revenue and, 151–59; problems, 75–78; public service enterprises and, 152–55; state government and, 4, 77, 78–85; structure, 75–78; surplus revenue, 52; user fees and, 155–56, 159, 227, 229. *See also* Debt; Federalism; Grants, federal; Grants, state; Intergovernmental transfers; Local taxes; Retirement systems
Local taxes: business, 227; deductibility, 223, 229–32; income and wage, 142–43, 149–51, 227; nonproperty, 6, 142–44; property, 5–6, 120–22, 126, 131–32, 134–35, 141, 142, 143, 144; sales, 91–94, 142–49, 227; use of, 40–46. *See also* Local government
Lotteries, 158–59
Louisiana, 47, 87, 103n, 128, 145, 228, 230
Lynch, Thomas D., 187n

McCulloch v. *Maryland*, 171
McEachern, William A., 36n
McGouldrick, Paul F., 169n
McLure, Charles E., Jr., 107n, 109
McMahon, Walter W., 190n
Maine, 36, 118, 136n, 137, 216
Manpower Development and Training Act, 213
Manvel, Allen D., 159n
Marshall, John, 171
Maryland, 135n, 136n, 149, 230
Massachusetts, 32, 44n, 104, 115, 136n, 223
Matching grants, 59–60
Maxwell, James A., 12n, 194n, 200n, 205n
Medicaid, 30, 70–71, 72
Melone, Joseph J., 195n

Metropolitan areas, 28–29, 75–76
Michigan, 104, 136n, 216n, 228
Mikesell, John L., 96n, 101n
Mill, John Stuart, 152
Minnesota, 88, 136n, 216
Mississippi, 32, 74, 68, 87, 94, 116
Missouri, 118, 148n, 216
Mitchell, William E., 176n
Model cities program, 65–66
Montana, 135n, 216
Morrill Acts, 48
Motor fuel tax, 90–91, 191–92, 226
Motor vehicle licenses, 43
Multinational corporations, 4–5, 110–15
Municipal Assistance Corporation, 166
Munley, V., 194n, 195n, 200n
Musgrave, Richard A., 204, 207n
Mushkin, Selma J., 35n, 187n

National Association of State Budget Officers, 175n
National Tax Association, 89
Nebraska, 105n, 116
Netzer, Dick, 126n
Nevada, 5, 117, 136n, 137n, 228
New Federalism, 9, 30
New Hampshire, 43, 102, 127, 158, 190, 211
New Jersey, 34, 102, 103n, 136n, 158, 216n, 223, 227, 230
New Mexico, 34, 87, 116, 136n, 137n, 148n
New Orleans, Louisiana, 94, 142
New York, 230; budget process, 185, 186; education, 211; expenditures, 33; income tax, 88; lotteries, 158; property tax, 127, 136n, 137n; sales tax, 102; transfer taxes, 47
New York City: debt, 7, 166, 170n; earmarked revenue, 190; federal grants, 64n; income and wage taxes, 149; sales tax, 6, 94, 142
Nixon administration, 54–55, 56–57, 72–73
Nonguaranteed bonds, 7, 167, 176, 177–79, 181
North Dakota, 115, 118, 127

Odden, Allan, 218n
Ohio, 48, 103n, 136n, 143, 149
Oklahoma, 25, 47, 88, 94, 137n, 145, 148n
Okner, Benjamin A., 99n
Old-age assistance, 66–67
Omnibus Budget Reconciliation Act, 3, 55–56, 68, 69, 70, 71, 73
Omnibus Crime Control and Safe Streets Act, 54
Ostrom, Vincent, 77n
Ott, Attiat F., 166n, 194n, 200n
Ott, David J., 194n, 200n

Palmer, John L., 30n
Payroll tax. *See* Corporate income tax
Pechman, Joseph A., 30n, 56n, 99, 123–24, 231n
Penniman, Clara, 86n, 90n, 101n
Pennsylvania, 103n, 123–24, 127, 143, 149, 202
Petersen, John E., 169n
Philadelphia, Pennsylvania, 6, 94, 64n, 142–43, 149
Pick-up tax, 118–19
Planning-programming-budgeting (PPB) system, 186–87
Power, distribution of governmental, 11–20, 53
Private education, 218–21
Progressivity: federal grants and, 4; federal and state taxation, 99–100; income taxes and, 101, 102, 150; inheritance taxes and, 116; property tax and, 124, 141; of tax structure, 230–31; total tax on individuals and, 99–100; yield differential on tax-exempt bonds and, 173–74
Project grants, 54, 61. *See also* Categorical grants
Property tax: administration, 121, 128, 134, 135; assessment, 5–6, 126–27, 128–35, 133–34n, 135n, 140; base, 123, 126–28, 135–40; debt limitations and, 175–76; economic effects, 123–25; education and, 125, 131; equity and, 5–6, 123, 129–31, 139–40; exemptions, 126, 127, 132, 135–40; federal government and, 120; incidence, 123, 125–26; intangible, 47, 127–28, 136; limitations on, 6, 226, 227, 228, 233; local, 5–6, 120–22, 126, 131–32, 134–35, 141, 142, 143, 144; personal, 126–28, 136; as a progressive tax, 124, 141; real, 126–28; reform, 6, 134–35; as a regressive tax, 123–24, 141; services and, 124–25; shared taxes and, 78–79; state government and, 40, 43, 120–22, 126, 131–32, 134–35, 139–41
Public assistance, 1, 18, 50, 66–68, 69, 81, 193, 233
Public health, 1, 50, 70–71, 233
Public service enterprises, 6, 152–55
Public transportation, 63–64

Ratchford, B. U., 160n, 161n, 162n
Reagan administration: federal grants, 3–4, 50, 55–56, 73; New Federalism, 9, 30;

revenue sharing, 3–4; role in educational financing, 213–14; tax reform, 223, 229; Worldwide Unitary Taxation Task Force, 113–15
Regressive tax, 5, 97–100, 123–24, 141, 154
Religion and education, 220–21
Resources, allocation of, 51–53, 73–74, 78
Retirement systems: cost projections, 199; features, 194–95; financial volatility, 8, 199–202; funding, 195–97; intergenerational equity and, 195–97; monitoring, 202; outlook, 197–99
Revenue. *See* Earmarked revenue; Grants, federal; Grants, state; Intergovernmental transfers; Local taxes; State taxes
Revenue bond. *See* Nonguaranteed bonds
Revenue sharing, 3–4, 50, 56–58
Rhode Island, 136n, 137
Robinson, Roland I., 168n, 169n
Rolph, Earl R., 205n
Romer, Thomas, 36n
Rosen, Sam, 158n
Rosenthal, Howard, 36n

Sales tax: administration, 92, 93–94, 96–97, 101–02; alcoholic beverages, 93; business cycle and, 226; credits, 98; defeats, 149; Depression of *1930*s, 94; earmarked revenue and, 192; equity, 96, 97–100, 149; exemptions, 96, 97, 98; federal government and, 91, 94; general retail, 93–97; incidence, 145–47; in interstate transactions, 93–94, 96; limitations on, 227, 233; local, 91, 94, 142–49, 227; motor fuel, 90–91; as percent of family income, 97–98; rationale, 90, 95; as a regressive tax, 5, 97–100; selective, 90–93; services, 96; state government and, 5, 43–45, 90–102, 233; sumptuary, 90, 91–93; supplementary use, 96; tobacco, 91–93, 226; total tax burden and, 98–100; user charges and, 156n. *See also* Corporate income tax
San Antonio Independent School District v. *Rodriguez*, 215
San Diego, California, 94
Sanford, Terry, 27n
Sawhill, Isabell V., 30n
Schick, Allen, 187n
Schwartz, Eli, 126n, 168n, 194n, 195n, 196n, 200n, 203n
Selective sales tax, 90–93
Seligman, E. R. A., 134
Separate accounting, 105–06, 110–11, 112, 114–15
Services, 6–7, 22–24, 41, 85, 124–25, 156, 231
Severance taxes, 47
Shahen, Timothy G., 98n
Shapiro v. *Thompson*, 67n
Shared taxes, 4, 78–79, 83
Sheffrin, Steven M., 107n, 112n
Sinking funds, 167
Sixteenth Amendment, 86, 171
Smith, Adam, 128
Social Security Act of *1935*, 18, 25, 66
Social Security Amendments of *1960* (Kerr-Mills Act), 70, 71
Social Security Amendments of *1972*, 68
South Carolina, 116, 228
South Dakota, 127, 230
Sprenkle, Case M., 190n
SSI. *See* Supplemental security income
State and Local Fiscal Assistance Act of *1972*, 57
State debt. *See* Debt
State government: education and, 208, 210–11, 214, 216–17, 219–20, 221, 232–33; expenditures, 1, 14, 19–20, 24, 33, 80–81; experimentation, 25, 27–28; financing, 222–33; functions, 1–2, 9; highways aid, 62–63; intergovernmental transfers, 75–85; limitations on, 223–26; revenue from lotteries, 158–59; service revenue, 157; surpluses, 52, 223–24. *See also* Debt; Federal government; Federalism; Grants, federal; Intergovernmental transfers; Retirement systems; State taxes; User fees
State taxes: composition, 17, 20; corporate income, 4–5, 103–15, 233; death and gift, 5, 115–19, 233; deductibility, 223, 229–32; federal tax credit and, 116–18; income, 4, 86–90, 94, 100–02, 139, 233; property, 40, 43, 120–22, 126, 131–32, 134–35, 139–41; sales, 5, 90–102, 233; use of, 40–46. *See also* State government
Stiefel, Leanna, 217n
Studenski, Paul, 120n
Subsidies for public service enterprises, 154–55
Sugarman, Stephen D., 216n
Sumptuary sales tax, 90, 91–93, 189n
Supplemental security income (SSI), 68, 69, 71
Supplementary use sales tax, 96
Supreme Court, U.S., 93–94, 96, 117n
Surface Transportation Assistance Act, 63, 64, 191

Tax avoidance, 112
Tax burden, 98–100

Tax credits, 5, 87–88, 98, 116–18
Tax deductibility, 46, 223, 229–32
Tax effort, 37–40
Tax equalization. *See* Equity
Tax Equity and Fiscal Responsibility Act (TEFRA), 71, 181
Taxes. *See* Local taxes; State taxes
Tax Foundation, 74
Tax relief. *See* Circuit breakers; Exemptions, tax; Tax credits
Tennessee, 44n, 103n
Tenth Amendment, 10
Texas, 47, 74, 94, 103n, 118, 137n, 215, 216
Tilove, Robert, 194n
Tobacco tax, 91–93, 226
Tuition tax credits, 214, 219–20, 221
Twenty-first Amendment, 93

Uniform Division of Income for Tax Purposes Act (UDITPA), 106, 109
User fees, 6–7, 155–56, 157, 159, 227, 229, 231, 233
Utah, 34, 115, 118, 137n, 148, 216

Vermont, 118, 129
Vertical fiscal imbalance, 51–52
Veterans' exemptions, 137–38
Virginia, 118

Wage tax. *See* Income tax
Walker, Charls E., 109n
Walsh, Cornelius, 158n
Washington, 94, 118, 148
Washington, D.C. *See* District of Columbia
Water Pollution Control Act, 65
Water's edge approach. *See* Separate accounting
Weeks Act, 48–49
Weintraub, Andrew, 158n
Weist, Dana, 169n, 170n
Welfare. *See* Public assistance
West Virginia, 136n
Wilson, Woodrow, 27
Wisconsin, 25, 86, 89, 103, 105n, 216n
Worldwide unitary combination method, 110–15
Worldwide Unitary Taxation Task Force, 113–15
Wyoming, 82, 118, 137n, 230

Yoo, Jang H., 166n

Zero-based budgeting (ZBB), 187
Zimmerman, Dennis, 35n